WILLIAM SHEPPARD
CONGO'S AFRICAN AMERICAN LIVINGSTONE

WILLIAM SHEPPARD

CONGO'S AFRICAN AMERICAN LIVINGSTONE

William E. Phipps

Geneva Press
Louisville, Kentucky

Quotations on pages 55, 119, 125, 127, 139, 176, and 207 are courtesy of Hampton University Archives.

Book design by Sharon Adams
Cover design by Lisa Buckley
Cover illustration: Courtesy of Mary Blakely. Portrait of William Sheppard, which hangs in the entrance of the William Sheppard Library at Stillman College, Tuscaloosa, Alabama.

First edition
Published by Geneva Press
Louisville, Kentucky

This book is printed on acid-free paper that meets the American National Standards Institute Z39.48 standard. ∞

PRINTED IN THE UNITED STATES OF AMERICA

05 06 07 08 09 10 11 — 10 9 8 7 6 5 4 3 2

Library of Congress Cataloging-in-Publication Data

Phipps, William E., 1930–
   William Sheppard : Congo's African American Livingstone / William E. Phipps.— 1st ed.
      p. cm.
   Includes bibliographical references (p.).
   ISBN 0-664-50203-2 (pbk.)
   1. Sheppard, William H. (William Henry), 1865–1927. 2. African American missionaries—Congo (Democratic Republic)—Biography. 3. Missionaries—Congo (Democratic Republic)—Biography. 4. African American Presbyterians—Congo (Democratic Republic)—Biography. 5. Presbyterians—Congo (Democratic Republic)—Biography. 6. African American missionaries—Biography. 7. Missionaries—United States—Biography. 8. African American Presbyterians—Biography. 9. Presbyterians—United States—Biography. 10. Presbyterian Church in the U.S.—Missions—Congo (Democratic Republic)—History. I. Title.

BV3625.C63 S546 2002
266'.51'092—dc21
[B]   2001040945

*In honor of my sister Kamuanya Ruth;
her husband Mupindula Bill Metzel;
their children, Kapinga Sarah, Tshimanga John, and Kasonga Daniel;
and in memory of their son Kasai Jeffrey.
Their devotion to Africans has been phenomenal.*

Contents

Significant Dates for William Sheppard

1865	Born in Waynesboro, Virginia
1880–83	Studies at Hampton Institute in Virginia
1886	Graduates from Tuscaloosa Theological Institute
1888	Ordained in Atlanta as pastor of Zion Presbyterian Church
1890	Commissioned as missionary to Central Africa
1891	Co-founds, with Samuel Lapsley, the American Presbyterian Congo Mission at Luebo
1892	Bonds with Kuba king in Mushenge
1893	Elected Fellow of the Royal Geographical Society
1894	Marries Lucy Gantt, educator and musician
1899	Documents atrocities of Leopold's agents
1905	Meets with President Roosevelt about Congolese plight
1908	Charged with libel by the Belgian Kasai Company
1909	Vindicated by court in Kinshasa
1910	Resigns as missionary
1911	Arranges for Hampton Museum to receive Kuba artifacts
1912–26	Pastors Grace Church in Louisville
1927	Dies in Louisville

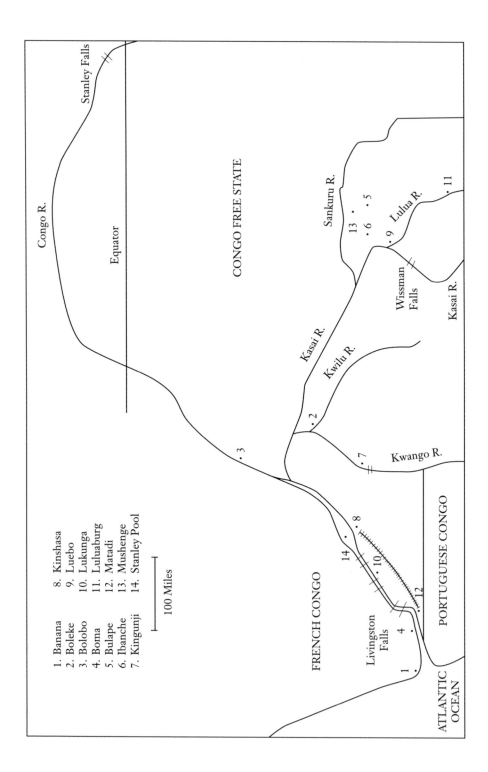

Foreword

"The Dark Continent" has long been a common designation for Africa, but the darkest thing about it has been outsiders' ignorance of its people. In 1991, I attempted to shed some light on a critical period in Congolese history in my book *The Sheppards and Lapsley*. Information from the sketch I gave of the African American missionary William Sheppard was featured in Adam Hochschild's best-selling *King Leopold's Ghost*, published in 1998. Fresh international interest in the person who was working effectively at the epicenter of one of the most significant human rights campaigns in modern history has motivated me to delve much more deeply into his life story. My research has also been stimulated by the appreciation that is surging for Sheppard's collection of Kuba art and artifacts, increasingly acclaimed as among the finest anywhere. Although first recognized as a pioneer missionary to the Congo, Sheppard has been acknowledged as a pioneer activist for African rights and as a pioneer collector of African art. Any one of these roles should suffice to give him an important place in history.

There is also a personal reason for my interest in writing this biography. Sheppard and I were born in the same town in Virginia. Growing up during the Great Depression, I can identify with his account of spending summers "bare-headed, bare-footed, and bare-backed" in Waynesboro.[1] But ironically, racial segregation was less a part of his youthful experiences than mine. Because he lived closer to the time of emancipation, he had some close interracial ties and belonged to the same church that I attended as a boy sixty years later. In Presbyterian congregations of Virginia during the late nineteenth century, blacks sometimes made up a significant portion of the total membership.[2]

Had Sheppard been my contemporary, we would have had little opportunity to know one another as we grew up. Because our pigmentation differed, attending church together would not have been permitted. Unlike the old Presbyterian Cemetery in Waynesboro, where both races were buried, there was in the twentieth century a separate cemetery for "colored folks" because segregation extended even to life after death in the imagination of white people. Due to the 1896 *Plessy v. Ferguson* Supreme Court ruling requiring "equal but separate accommodations," I would not have been allowed to sit with Sheppard on our municipal buses and railroads. Jim Crow laws would also have resulted in his being invisible at the schools, physician offices, movie theaters, and hotels, all of which had, in fact, separate but unequal accommodations. I was not well acquainted with a single black person because my parents could not afford to employ a servant. One of the few places I encountered black men indoors was as shoeshine "boys" in barber shops, where only whites cut the hair of the exclusively white patrons. In the segregation era, black was more than a color; whites treated it like a disease that required quarantining of those infected. Sheppard's Christian and democratic education would have been truncated, as was mine, by that pervasive caste system.

Comments made about Sheppard in Waynesboro when I was a boy reveal much about our culture. An old lady who lived on the block where I was born said, "He was such a good darky; when he returned from Africa he remembered his place and came to the back door." Her education and accomplishments were negligible compared to Dr. Sheppard's, but she was a carrier of the social disease that made race the primary mark of status. Sheppard's humility and sense of humor enabled him to tolerate graciously such belittlements.

My mother told me of a time when Sheppard returned to his childhood church where she was a member. Since she had supported his work even as a child by contributing pennies to purchase a steamboat for the Congo mission, she was thrilled to hear what he had to say. In the American South, segregation applied less to a person standing in a pulpit than sitting in a home. After leaving the church he was invited by Lou Withrow, who had first encouraged him to become educated, to her home for dinner. She lived in one of the oldest and finest houses in Waynesboro. Those who gathered there wanted to ask him questions, but it was taboo for blacks and whites to sit around the same table. A window separating the dining room from the back porch provided a creative solution to the problem. On the porch a small table was set for Sheppard next to the raised window, and all sat around what appeared to be an extended table. Conversation, along with the food, then passed back and forth between Sheppard and members of one of his supporting congregations.

Liberation from childhood ethnocentrism has been slow and painful. When a college professor assigned a report on Jane Austen's novel *Pride and Prejudice*, I had to consult a dictionary to find how to pronounce and define "prejudice." Whites growing up in the South did not even use the term. It was not until after graduating from a North Carolina Presbyterian college for whites only that I became fully aware of the injustice of the white supremacy dogma. I attended seminary in the city where the Confederacy was last seated and where there are monuments galore to slaveholders who fought to preserve their culture. While in Richmond I worked with a penitentiary chaplain and encountered on death row seven blacks who allegedly had raped a white woman. It caused me consternation to realize that no white man had ever been executed in Virginia for raping a black woman. One Virginia leader explained that this was because no white male ever had an impulse to demean himself in that way. Subsequently, I attended a Scottish graduate school and learned much from bright and friendly students from black Africa.

In 1956 several members of my family, with missionary Bill Metzel as guide, toured through much of the Congo River basin on unpaved roads and navigable rivers. There being no bridges for hundreds of miles, our Volkswagen van was ferried across rivers on logs lashed together. Such overland travel would be even more difficult now because the roads have greatly deteriorated. On a cargo boat we viewed the same vistas that the Sheppards encountered on their way to and from the Kasai region. Subsequently, I have tried to integrate these experiences into my teaching in America and in Africa.

My research task has been made easier by collections of Sheppard material at several institutions. Thanks largely to the diligence of Hampton University's former archivist, Fritz Malval, many boxes pertaining to Sheppard have been awaiting the organizational skills of a biographer. The art and artifacts collected by Sheppard that are on display in Hampton's Museum have provided inspiration as well as information. Also, William Bynum of the Presbyterian Historical Society in Montreat, North Carolina, and Robert Heath, director of the Sheppard Library at Stillman College in Tuscaloosa, Alabama, assisted me when I visited their institutions to examine relevant documents. In addition, there is an excellent store of documents on Congo missions in Richmond at the library of Union Theological Seminary/Presbyterian School of Christian Education. I am indebted to John Trotti and his library staff for all the help they have given me there.*

---

*Abbreviations used in this book include APCM, American Presbyterian Congo Mission, and PCUS, Presbyterian Church in the United States (for former southern Presbyterian Church [1861–1983]).

1

Preparation

SOUTHERN EDUCATION

William Henry Sheppard Jr. was born in March 1865, a month before slavery was eradicated in the United States by the Confederate surrender at Appomattox. His family lived in a rented house near the railway station in Waynesboro, Virginia, a village in Augusta County.[1] His mother's maiden name was Sarah Frances Martin, and she came from neighboring Nelson County in the hill country of Virginia. She was registered there as a "dark mulatto" who was born free in 1837.[2] According to the 1705 Virginia Code, "All children shall be bond or free, according to the condition of their mother."[3] Thus, William was not born into slavery even though Jefferson Davis was his president. Following an unspoken custom of Virginia "gentlemen," Sarah Martin's mother may have been her master's black concubine, although a few mulattos in Virginia had white mothers.

Martin probably married a freed black, although there seems to be no record to confirm this. In antebellum rural Virginia there were considerably more freed black males than females, but the number of all freed blacks was a small proportion of the total black population.[4] According to the 1860 census, there were 486 free blacks in Augusta County, about one-tenth of the total black population.

In the 1860s, there were about half a million blacks living in Virginia. The state always surpassed other states in slave population, and Richmond had become a principal port of entry for Africans in the eighteenth century. In 1808, after federal law prohibited the importation of slaves into the United States, Virginia developed slave-breeding farms. Richmond then became the largest slave market for the export of surplus young slaves to cotton and sugar plantations in the deep South. A freed status before the end of the Civil War would have placed the Sheppards among the elite of the black community and brought them more respect from white folks.

The Sheppards might have been among the historically first families of Virginia. A year before the Mayflower arrived in New England, a Dutch warship brought to the Virginia colony twenty Africans who had been taken as prisoners of war from a Portuguese caravel sailing for the Caribbean. When exchanged for supplies at Jamestown, they were given the same seven-year indenture contracts as many of the English who came to the colony. They had probably been captured from the Kingdom of Kongo, which included the delta of the Congo River as well as land to the south and east for some two hundred miles.

Most of the several hundred Africans brought to Virginia during the colony's first half century belonged to Bantu tribes from the Congo delta. Some of them earned their freedom and obtained an acreage to farm.[5] After 1640, blacks in Virginia of African origin were regarded as chattel and sold in perpetuity. An early ancestor of Sheppard, like the great-grandfather of Supreme Court Justice Thurgood Marshall, might have been among the several million who were taken to the New World from the Congo in chains.[6] The Africans brought with them from their villages stories of the "Uncle Remus" type that are similar to those still told in the Congo.

Slaves were usually listed in census records under the names of their owners, but information is lacking for William Sheppard Sr., who was presumably born a slave. Several months before the junior William was born, his father was probably forced to engage in labor for the Union army. From their winter encampment a few miles from Waynesboro, the Yankees sent a cavalry unit to Waynesboro to cut off the Confederate supply route through the Blue Ridge mountains. They attempted to sabotage the Virginia Central Railway's tunnel, then the longest in the world. Augusta County historian Joseph Waddell tells of the raid, "They impressed all the negro men into their service, and took them down the railroad to destroy the track and bridges."[7] That skirmish resulted in the plundering of homes by the invaders and increased hardships for all living in the area.

The last "battle" of the Shenandoah Valley Campaign was fought at Waynesboro during the month of William's birth. Union General George Custer's cavalry division, along with other units, marched on the town. The encounter turned out to be a rout, and the few Confederate soldiers who escaped retreated eastward to join General Lee in his final resistance against General Grant.[8]

At that time Waynesboro was a community of about 500 inhabitants in the Shenandoah Valley at the foot of the Blue Ridge mountains. A century earlier the area had been settled by the Scotch-Irish, who built many churches for the expression of their Calvinist faith. Compared to the eastern part of Virginia, where slaves often outnumbered non-slaves, there were few slaves in the Valley. According to the 1860 census, Augusta County's slave population was 21 percent, while Albemarle, the county of Thomas Jefferson that bordered Augusta to the east, had more than twice that percentage. "The institution of slavery never had a stronghold on the people of Augusta County," Waddell states; "The Scotch-Irish had no love of it."[9] In 1860 only one out of twenty-five whites in Augusta County was a slaveholder.

William Sheppard Sr. was the village barber and the sexton for the brick Presbyterian Church. The Sheppard family were devout members of that church, the oldest one in the community. His wife expressed her faith by praying with her son as well as by her generosity. Her son later gave this tribute: "Mother never turned anyone from her door who came begging, whether white or colored, without offering them such as she had."[10]

It is notable that race relations were more amicable in that day than after the Jim Crow laws were established at the turn of the twentieth century.[11] Most Caucasians living in the region quietly assumed the superiority of their race but did not require public accommodations to be segregated. They showed some civility toward blacks without concerning themselves with their civil rights. Charles Wynes shows that interracial public associations, which were unthinkable in Virginia in the first half of the past century, were accepted before 1900; for example, blacks could then sit among whites when traveling.[12] In the 1880s, Waynesboro had a racially inclusive inn: "The proprietor of the Jefferson House was black, but the inn was used by both black and white patrons."[13] In Sheppard's barbershop, white men were given shaves and haircuts. But in the early twentieth century the marginalization of African Americans in Virginia became more intense. It is especially notable that their voting rolls dropped from about 147,000 to less than 10,000.

Frequent interracial contact in the postbellum American South is significant in understanding the Sheppard family. The preeminent black sociologist William Du Bois, a contemporary of Sheppard, has this to say about racial associations then:

> Before and directly after the [Civil] war, when all the best of the
> Negroes were domestic servants in the best of the white families, there
> were bonds of intimacy, affection, and sometimes blood relationship,
> between the races. They lived in the same home, shared in the family
> life, often attended the same church, and talked and conversed with
> each other.[14]

Sheppard frequently recalled an experience he had as a small boy: "A
beautiful Christian lady, Mrs. Ann Bruce, said to me one day, 'William,
I pray for you, and hope some day you may go to Africa as a missionary.' I had never heard of Africa, and those words made a lasting
impression."[15] Playing with his favorite toy also had overtones for his
future; he was enchanted by the elephants, lions, and other exotic animals in his model of Noah's ark.

The establishment of schools for African Americans was one of the
most important outcomes of the Confederate defeat. Literacy among
blacks had been generally prohibited in the era of slavery because masters found it difficult to make obedient servants out of those who knew
how to read and write. In 1874 Waynesboro's "public colored school"
did more than teach literacy. An inspection of its teachers and students
displayed that "in arithmetic, geography, grammar, [and] penmanship
few schools in the land would make a better show."[16] One of the school's
textbooks has been preserved; personal possession is indicated by the
name "Willie Sheppard" written in a child's script. Entitled *Union
Primer* because it was published by the Sunday School Union, it contains stories and poems as well as biblical quotations and Isaac Watts's
catechism for children.[17] By becoming literate at an early age, Sheppard
distinguished himself from most other African Americans at that time.
After school he spent much time on the nearby South River, swimming
as well as catching "eels by night and water snakes by day."[18]

Sheppard's education was informally continued in Staunton, the
county seat of Augusta County. When he was around ten years old, Dr.
S. H. Henkel, an officer in the First Presbyterian Church of that city,
invited him to live in the Henkel home. The Henkels provided him
instruction and lodging in exchange for his cleaning the dental office,
caring for the horse, bringing in the coal, and answering the doorbell.
Regarding this period of life, Sheppard told of theological concerns and
of pleasant interactions with the white couple:

> In a back room of the doctor's office was a box filled with teeth. It puz-
> zled me much to think how in the world the people on resurrection
> day were to get their own teeth back. I loved my new home, for Dr.

> Henkel and his wife were so kind to me. They spent much time in
> instructing me in my books at night.[19]

The friendship between Sheppard and the Henkels continued for life.

During his early teen years, Sheppard continued to work closely with whites. He became a McCurdy House waiter in towns west of Staunton, advancing to become the headwaiter at Covington. In 1880 he took the money he had saved and enrolled at Hampton Normal and Industrial Institute on the Virginia coast.[20] The school was one of many for emancipated blacks funded by the American Missionary Society, a Calvinist group.

General Samuel Armstrong had founded Hampton as a place where blacks could receive mental, manual, and religious training. A son of Calvinist missionaries, Armstrong had been born in Hawaii and was well prepared for the educational task. After teaching in the manual skills school established for the Hawaiians by his father, he completed a degree at Williams College where Mark Hopkins, the famous educator, was president. During the Civil War, Armstrong commanded a black regiment of Union troops, and after the war he headed the Hampton branch of the Freedmen's Bureau. Then he opened the first school for male and female blacks in Virginia that offered instruction beyond the elementary level. Armstrong envisioned the school as having a mission that extended beyond the local region. His aim was to "educate the whole black race by creating the people who would be its teachers and leaders."[21]

When fifteen-year-old Sheppard arrived at Hampton he likely was impressed with a particular oak tree that was then, and continues to be today, a campus landmark. Under that tree Lincoln's Emancipation Proclamation was read without fear because the headquarters for the Union Army of the Potomac was in Hampton. From his first contact onward, Sheppard had only positive associations with Hampton:

> General Armstrong, President of the Institute, received me kindly. The first year I worked on the farm, and later worked in the bakery, going to school at night. I loved to swim and fish, and every advantage was afforded me. The Hampton creek was filled with fish, oysters and crabs, and the broad ocean beyond was at my disposal. General Armstrong was my ideal of manhood: his erect carriage, deep, penetrating eyes, pleasant smiles and kindly disposition drew all students to him. He was a great, tender-hearted father to us all, and the teachers were also deeply interested in the welfare of the students.[22]

Armstrong recruited Native Americans as well as African Americans to study at his high school. Sheppard told of being inspired for life by his vision:

> There were scores of young men and women who were without a dollar, without even a change of clothing. But in spite of their poverty and their nakedness General Armstrong saw in them the image of God. . . . He saw, not what they had been, not what they were, but what they could be.[23]

Sheppard was strongly affected by the "Curiosity Room" in which Armstrong exhibited visual art from Hawaiians and Native Americans. The Virginia native learned to appreciate the way in which craftspeople from nonindustrialized cultures could make objects that were both beautiful and useful. A Hampton publication explains how the special room fit in with Armstrong's philosophy of education:

> Hampton developed a program of study that sought to train "the head, the hand, and the heart." Instruction in world geography, cultures, and history was solidified through close examination of museum objects while students learned the dignity of labor by practical, hands-on training in the school's many workshops and on the school's farms. In addition, the museum collection served as a vehicle to teach students a pride in their heritage, to reinforce self-esteem, and to encourage cross-cultural understanding.[24]

The Presbyterian minister who succeeded Armstrong as president of Hampton had an abiding impact on Sheppard as well:

> Dr. H. B. Frissell, who was chaplain of the Institute, was also a loving, congenial friend to us all. One Sabbath afternoon he asked me to accompany him and some of the teachers to establish a mission Sunday-school at Slabtown, a small village of poor colored people about a mile from the school. I went with him gladly and carried some of the Bibles and hymn books. I felt from that afternoon that my future work was to carry the gospel to the poor, destitute, and forgotten people.[25]

Prior to going to Alabama in 1881 to establish Tuskegee Institute, Booker T. Washington taught at Hampton, where he had graduated in 1875. He had organized a night school during his last year at Hampton, and Sheppard was among his few students. The routine was rigorous: excepting Sunday, ten hours of manual work preceded two hours of evening instruction. Washington told of a student—possibly Sheppard—who prepared for class by writing on a piece of slate whenever he could steal a spare minute from the hard toil.[26] While he was night school principal, Washington pursued further studies at Hampton, and he later remembered Sheppard as a fellow student.[27] Armstrong's educational enterprise transformed these young men into two of the most outstanding Americans of the next generation. Washington would heed one of Armstrong's lessons better than Sheppard; namely, that blacks should avoid interfering with the dominance of government by whites.[28]

While at Hampton, Sheppard was also probably influenced by another outstanding black leader. Dr. Edward Blyden, a brilliant Presbyterian minister who served as president and classics professor of Liberia College in West Africa, spoke to the student body in 1882.[29] He affirmed that the races "are distinct but equal" and hoped that blacks now being educated at Hampton and other American institutions "will accomplish wonders" by "returning from exile" to the land of their forefathers. While being aware of the commercial development of Africa that King Leopold of Belgium was promoting, Blyden pointed to the greater need for "holy pioneer" African American missionaries to establish schools and churches.[30]

Rev. Frank McCutcheon, minister of the Presbyterian Church in Waynesboro, was mindful of Sheppard's abilities and vocational interest. The church now had a prominent sanctuary on Main Street with the largest seating capacity in town. That hometown pastor led his session, the congregation's governing body, to certify Sheppard's "physical, mental, and spiritual fitness" for the clerical calling.[31] On October 28, 1883, he was formally received as a candidate for the ministry by Lexington Presbytery, the regional governing church body.

Virginian Presbyterians belonged to the southern sector of American Calvinists. After the Civil War began, that denomination split over the question of slavery and the rebel portion named themselves "The Presbyterian Church in the Confederate States of America." The commissioners to its first General Assembly in 1861 signed a document containing this affirmation:

> The only rule of judgment is the written word of God. The Church ... has no right to utter a single syllable upon any subject except as the Lord puts words in her mouth. . . . As we contemplate their [the slaves] condition in the Southern States, and contrast it with that . . . of their land, we cannot but accept it as a gracious Providence that they have been brought in such numbers to our shores, and redeemed from the bondage of barbarism and sin. . . . Without it [slavery] we are profoundly persuaded that the African race in the midst of us can never be elevated in the scale of being. As long as that race, in its

comparative degradation, coexists, side by side, with the white, bondage is its normal condition.[32]

When the Civil War ended, southern Presbyterians changed their official name to "The Presbyterian Church in the United States" (PCUS), and continued as a separate Presbyterian body for more than a century. The chastened PCUS displayed little of the bigotry of four years earlier when its General Assembly met. It now claimed to recognize "the Christian equality and brotherhood" of "the colored people within our bounds" and "rejoiced to have their association in Christian union and communion in the public services and precious sacraments of the sanctuary."[33]

In the year of its inception, the PCUS General Assembly of 1861 expressed its aim "to make our beloved church an eminently missionary church" and singled out Africa as a potential place of labor.[34] A year after General Sherman's devastating sweep through Georgia, the General Assembly met in that state. The denomination resolved to give "attention to Africa as a field of missionary labor peculiarly appropriate to this Church; and with this in view to secure as soon as practicable missionaries from among the African race on this continent who may bear the gospel of the grace of God to the homes of their ancestors."[35]

John Leighton Wilson, the first Secretary of the PCUS Foreign Missions Committee, joined with visionary Isaiah in being fascinated with the terra incognita "beyond the rivers of Ethiopia."[36] He was eager to send missionaries to Africa, but not to the West African region where he had labored as a missionary for nearly twenty years before the Civil War. While there he supervised in the 1840s the printing of some of the earliest books in sub-Saharan Africa.[37] Wilson recognized that the coastal areas where he had worked were known as a "white man's grave." Subsequently, of the six hundred Europeans contracted to serve near the mouth of the Congo River, only five remained in good health to complete their three-year contracts.[38] In an excellent history of the Atlantic coast area of Africa that Wilson had written during his years there, he expressed the need for African American colleagues who have disease-resistant bodies that whites lack, and who also have mental and spiritual qualifications. He hoped that "colored men of education, intelligence, and of humble and undoubted piety could be found willing to engage in the work." At such time white missionaries "who are now in the field would not only give them a hearty welcome as fellow-laborers, but if they were sufficiently numerous, would cheerfully commit the whole work into their hands."[39]

Wilson was subsequently stimulated by reading that David Livingstone, when working for the London Missionary Society, considered the Congo region to be a "fine missionary field." When that Scotsman traveled from Angola to Mozambique in 1856, he discovered the headwaters of the Kasai and some of its tributaries. Providing the first accurate geographical information about the Congo basin, he noted that the Kasai flowed northwest and "after the confluence of the Kasai with the Kwango, an immense body of water . . . finds its way out of the country by means of the river Congo or Zaire on the west coast."[40] Wilson advocated locating mission stations on healthier plateau land along navigable rivers in the upper Congo where economic exchange, intercommunication between peoples, and diffusion of the gospel could be facilitated.[41] He may also have had special interest in the Congo because he believed that many descendants of the Kongo people could still be identified in the United States.[42]

Pastor McCutcheon recommended Sheppard to Dr. Charles Stillman, the president of the Tuscaloosa Theological Institute in Alabama, which would be renamed Stillman College after his death in 1895. He founded the seminary in 1877, primarily to enable blacks to carry out the PCUS concern to send black missionaries to Africa. Stillman hoped that this effort "would soften prejudice against blacks in the home church."[43] The seminary was housed in a small building containing two rooms for classes and one for a library. A photograph shows a dapper Sheppard standing outside the building (now restored and called Stillman House) amid all the students and faculty. There were no residential facilities there, so Sheppard arranged to stay with a family nearby. Pertaining to his work in Tuscaloosa, he said, "I studied theology, homiletics, moral and mental philosophy, and other things." The "other things" in the Institute's curriculum were literature, physiology, and mathematics.[44]

Since Stillman's time was largely filled with duties at the Presbyterian Church in Tuscaloosa where he was pastor, most of the instruction for the fifteen students was done by Dr. David Sanderson, a white man who had completed his undergraduate and theological degrees in Princeton, New Jersey. On Mondays each student preached a sermon at the Institute, which was followed by a criticism from the professor and the fellow students. After Sheppard preached on "Service" on one occasion, Sanderson rose to say they would only engage in prayer that day and not in criticism.

One time while attending class in the Stillman House, Sheppard heard someone screaming "Fire" at a distance. He leapt through the open window, ran up the stairs of a burning house, and rescued an invalid. When he returned to bring out some household goods, the blaze forced him to leap for his life from a second-story window. In Tuscaloosa he also stopped a runaway horse pulling a carriage containing a woman and her grandson. The grateful woman employed him as caretaker of her house as long as he lived in the city.[45]

During his three years at Tuscaloosa, Sheppard continued the pattern of home mission work begun in Hampton by visiting and praying with the sick in Alabama communities. During that time one concern was much on his mind:

> A question asked me in my examination by both the Presbytery in Waynesboro, Va., and by the faculty of Tuscaloosa Institute was: "If you are called upon to go to Africa as a missionary, would you be willing to go?" I promptly answered, "I would go, and with pleasure."[46]

While in seminary, and for a year after graduating in 1886, Sheppard served the Calvary Presbyterian Church in Montgomery. He preached a trial sermon at the First Presbyterian Church in Tuscaloosa when being licensed to preach. After his ministry in what had been the first capital of the Confederacy, he was ordained in 1888 by Atlanta Presbytery to be pastor of Zion Church. That Presbyterian congregation had been organized for blacks in 1879 and was located on Harris Street in Atlanta.[47] Du Bois, another well-educated black in Atlanta at this time, gave this description of the city, "She has religion, earnest, bigoted; . . . how pressing here the need of broad ideals and true culture."[48] Sheppard's work was in the same city where Martin Luther King Jr. several generations later had similar responsibilities. While pastoring churches there, both men were stimulated by the needs of a more global parish.

During his years in Atlanta, Sheppard became convinced that God had destined him to serve his ancestral people in their homeland. The environmental situation of a black living in the Deep South contributed to that divine call. Walter Williams sheds light on the frustrations that Sheppard was encountering:

> He did not adapt well to the strict segregation of the urban South, and in 1887 he petitioned the mission board to send him to Africa. . . . By becoming a missionary Sheppard could gain the respect of both blacks and whites that he so dearly valued. . . . Since mission work was highly

regarded by both white and black Americans, a missionary held a relatively prestigious position, and was able to work without much of the
interference commonly caused by racial prejudice. . . . As refined Victo-
rians, the [black] missionaries strongly identified as "civilized" people.
Such a characterization was not only a result of their family background
and education, it was also a reaction to racist stereotypes of black "savagery." Anxiety over their status caused educated African-American elit-
ists to do everything within their power to separate themselves from that
categorization, and African mission work helped to fulfill this need.[49]

Year after year Sheppard applied to the PCUS for missionary work
in Africa and traveled to Baltimore to talk with the Foreign Missions
Committee, but the PCUS was slow to put into practice the policy
statement made in 1865 to establish a mission in Africa by African
Americans. In an 1888 report to the PCUS General Assembly about
missionary applicants, Committee Secretary Matthew Houston was
especially pleased to tell of one who came from the Waynesboro church
that had earlier sent him and his wife Evelyn to serve in China. Dr.
Houston borrowed autobiographical words from Isaiah to tell of Sheppard's calling: "One of the sons of Africa is even now saying 'Here am
I, send me!'"[50] Houston recommended that the Assembly heed the
"Captain of our salvation as he looks down upon that great continent"
and establish a mission there "as speedily as practicable."[51]

Funding was recognized as the main obstacle to establishing a mission in Africa by African Americans, and an attempt to get the Northern Presbyterians to cooperate in a joint Congo operation was not
successful.[52] Sheppard had declined appointment by the Baptists to
their Congo Bolobo Mission and by the Northern Presbyterians to
their work elsewhere in Africa because he preferred to represent his
own denomination. E. T. Thompson states that "no action had been
taken because it was felt that he should not be sent out alone and there
was no other applicant for that field."[53] The church leaders, guided by
the apostolic pattern, were unwilling to consider sending out one person by himself to a high-risk field.

In 1889, PCUS leaders were spurred to implement a mission aim that
had fallen dormant on learning of someone else who was also eager and
well-qualified to be sent to Africa. That person was Samuel Lapsley,
who, along with Sheppard, had been one of the two licentiates of
Tuscaloosa Presbytery. Lapsley was twenty-three, one year younger
than Sheppard. He was the son of former slaveholders who continued
to be prosperous after the Civil War.

Judge James Lapsley, Samuel's father, was so widely recognized as a church leader that in 1893 he became the first layman to be elected to the highest office of his denomination, Moderator of the General Assembly. The Judge's conscience was burdened by the failure of whites in his region to provide schools for those whom it had previously been illegal to teach. During his term as moderator he urged PCUS members to overcome their prejudices against Northern Presbyterians, who had been associated with earlier abolitionist efforts, and work with them to educate southern African Americans.[54] "Sam" began to teach blacks in his church near Selma at the age of twelve. He especially enjoyed discussing biblical doctrines with William Clark, a blacksmith and preacher.[55]

The brilliance of young Lapsley was displayed in various ways. He composed music as well as played the organ at his church. On entering the University of Alabama in Tuscaloosa at the age of fifteen, he was advanced to the sophomore class. For each of his three years there he ranked at the top of his class in scholarship. Even before graduating, and for a year afterward, Lapsley held the rank of assistant professor. University president B. B. Lewis evaluated his performance as the most outstanding of any student since the Civil War. He was also captain of the military corps, and helped his brother James organize an interdenominational Young Men's Christian Association on campus.[56] Lapsley graduated in 1884 during the time when Sheppard was enrolled at Stillman, a few blocks down the street.

Addressing Lapsley's graduating class at the University of Alabama was George Cable, a Presbyterian elder and Confederate veteran as well as a noted novelist. His speech, "The Freedman's Case in Equity," was later published in the prominent *Century Magazine* and was widely recognized then as one of the strongest defenses of civil rights for African Americans. The exposure of racial discrimination by a fellow son of slaveholders must have resonated loudly in Lapsley's soul. Cable discussed the outrageous racial tyranny practiced by many Americans who only verbally acknowledged that the Creator has bestowed on all people the inalienable right of human equality. He insisted "that the freedman be free to become in all things, as far as his own personal gifts will lift and sustain him, the same sort of American citizen he would be if, with the same intellectual and moral calibre, he were white." He claimed that thousands of Southerners were against segregation and told approvingly of some racial integration in his home city of New Orleans, "I have seen the two races sitting in the same public high-school and grammar-schools reciting in the same classes."[57]

Lapsley began his preparation for the Presbyterian ministry at Union Theological Seminary, located then on the campus of Hampden-Sydney College in Virginia. After one year's work, he returned to Alabama to teach again in his home church school for a year. He may have left Virginia because his idealism on human equality clashed with the racism of Robert Dabney, whose decades of teaching had left an indelible mark on the seminary. Lapsley then separated himself from the heavily traditional orientation of the South, and went to Chicago, where the pioneer spirit was bubbling. He enrolled at McCormick Seminary to finish his formal theological studies.

This was the period when Dwight Moody was the world's leading evangelist, with headquarters in Chicago. As a layman he taught in a simple and nonsectarian manner the "three R's" of the gospel: "Ruin by sin, Redemption by Christ, and Regeneration by the Holy Ghost." Moody held enthusiastic revival meetings that featured his remarkable gospel song associate, Ira Sankey. Lapsley involved himself in Moody's city missions[58] and finished his theological degree in 1889.

Upon graduation, Lapsley applied to the PCUS for mission service in Africa. The General Assembly of that year, recognizing an increase of funding for causes it deemed important, surprised its own Mission Committee by deciding to launch an African mission immediately. Sheppard and Lapsley met with the Foreign Missions Committee and received their approval. The two "brethren" were told that they were to work as "coequals."[59] In January 1890 a commissioning service was held at the First Presbyterian Church in Nashville. The fledgling missionaries took the opportunity to address the congregation about the joint work they anticipated doing.

William Morrison's authoritative history of the Congo mission asserted that the appointment of Lapsley and Sheppard "inaugurated the unique principle of sending out together, with equal ecclesiastical rights and, as far as possible, in equal numbers, white and colored workers."[60] The PCUS interracial policy established at the beginning of the African mission continued in subsequent years. Thompson notes that "every member had an equal voice in mission affairs, and each of them received the same salary."[61] The initial annual compensation for Sheppard and Lapsley was $500 each (about $12,000 in year 2000 dollars), plus their large costs for supplies and travel.[62] For a church that originated at the beginning of the Civil War out of a determination to preserve slavery and white supremacy, the status it gave Sheppard is amazing! (Without primary source authority, some secondary sources err in stating that Lapsley was designed as Sheppard's superior). *The*

Encyclopaedia of Missions published in 1891 gave more attention to Sheppard than to Lapsley, and stated:

> The appointment of Mr. Sheppard (who has already proved to be a most valuable worker) was of special interest, since he was the first fruits of a long cherished desire on the part of many in the Southern Church to see some of this race bearing the gospel to the land of their forefathers.[63]

The Missions Committee informed its controlling body, the General Assembly, what was expected from this missionary team:

> They are instructed to ascertain the most eligible site for a new mission station in West Central Africa. The station selected should be sufficiently separated from other missions to give it a thoroughly independent work. It should, as far as possible, be in a healthful locality, probably on the highlands removed from the coast, and yet not too distant from the base of supplies. It should be among a population large enough to constitute a good mission field, and using a language which is widely current. In selecting the station the preference should be given to the Congo Free State.[64]

Before embarking, Lapsley and Sheppard began to establish a support network by visiting churches and cities in several states. Senator John Morgan, a former partner of Judge Lapsley in a leading Alabama law firm, assisted them in Washington by making political connections that could help their mission. An appointment was made for the judge and his son to visit President Benjamin Harrison in the White House. Harrison expressed his sympathy for the undertaking and attempted to offer comfort. He said that electricity had made foreign places closer than they had been previously, a remark that would prove facetious a year later. Harrison had Secretary of State James Blaine send letters of introduction to ambassadors who could be of assistance to the missionaries.[65]

Morgan's advocacy of American blacks was ambivalent. Although he had been a Confederate general, his first vote in the federal government was to confirm Frederick Douglass as marshall for the District of Columbia. On the other hand, his interest in Sheppard's going to the Congo was primarily related to the senator's desire to export American blacks and manufactured goods. An unreconstructed Southerner, Morgan rejected the notion of a biracial American citizenry. He hoped black leaders would lead their freed people on an "exodus" from their western Diaspora to their fatherland. "By emigrating to Africa," he thought, "blacks could prosper personally while advancing American commercial interests and African civilization."[66]

JOURNEY TO THE CONGO

"Brother Sheppard and I sailed from New York for Liverpool by the steamer Adriatic," Lapsley wrote to inform fellow Presbyterians.[67] Mother Sara Lapsley called out as she waved goodbye, "Sheppard, take care of Sam."[68] On leaving the harbor, Sam thought of lines from a hymn written for sailors by a New York City pastor:[69]

> Unknown waves before me roll,
> Hiding rock and treacherous shoal;
> Chart and compass come from Thee;
> Jesus, Savior, pilot me.

Those words would take on more meaning as the small ocean craft encountered raw weather in the iceberg-infested North Atlantic, and later when Congo riverboats were tempest tossed.

Some of Lapsley's letters home tell of social relations with his bachelor companion. The ship purser, who treated Sheppard "very politely," shared with Lapsley his disdain of a white supremacist passenger who complained about the racial integration on board. Lapsley liked what that officer said, "If a man acts the gentleman we make him have a good time, white or black." Alluding to his partner's color, Lapsley wrote a southern friend: "As to Sheppard, the English don't notice what seems very odd to us. He is very modest, and easy to get along with; also quite an aid in sight-seeing, and in anything else where I need help."[70]

The missionaries completed their ocean travel in the Irish Sea, where they disembarked at Liverpool on December 7, 1890. Sheppard probably became aware of how the slave trade had enabled that port to become, a century earlier, the largest and most prosperous in Europe. Some of the public buildings still revealed what once had been a lively business in black cargo.

The two Americans were excited to visit London, the seat of a burgeoning global empire, and they saw the elderly Queen Victoria sallying forth from Buckingham Palace for her afternoon drive. That city was the place to gain much practical knowledge about staying alive in tropical Africa and to obtain the necessary equipment, clothing, and

Rev. Samuel N. Lapsley (1866–1892)

food staples. On their Atlantic voyage, Sheppard and Lapsley had learned about Robert Whyte, a devout Presbyterian and leading London wholesale exporter. He was persuaded to supply them with most of their needs, and he continued his help for many years as the London representative for the American Presbyterian Congo Mission (APCM). Sheppard told of exchanging dollars for their future currency: cowrie shells, beads, salt, and brass wire.[71] Lapsley saw a notice about a lecture by explorer Henry Stanley, who had recently left Central Africa for the last time after four trips over two decades, and he tried to work it into his schedule.[72]

Sheppard wrote about the interesting people he got to know at the place where he and Lapsley stayed in London:

> We received the greatest hospitality possible at "Harley House" from Dr. Henry Grattan Guinness and family. They spared no pains in helping us in every way they could. We hadn't words to express our gratitude to them. This whole family was imbued with the missionary spirit.[73]

Harley House was another way of referring to the East London Institute, a mission school headed by Dr. Guinness where "ambassadors for Christ" were trained for African service. The Guinnesses had been missionaries in the Congo, where Dr. Guinness had established the Livingstone Inland Mission. That oldest Protestant mission in the Congo had been transferred in 1885 to the American Baptists. In addition, Guinness was the director of the new Congo Bolobo Mission in the equatorial district. He told of the vast challenge for Protestant missionaries because there was only one of them for every several hundred thousand non-Christians in the world population of 1,400 million.[74] Fanny Guinness had just written a book about the Baptist work there. She gave the Americans a woman's perspective on the Congolese. Lapsley remembered Mrs. Guinness saying that men at church make their wives and children sit separately not because of a gender segregation custom but because they want to avoid being troubled by their babies.[75]

In March, Lapsley was invited to Brussels by Henry Sanford to visit with Belgians who had Congo interests. Sanford made these arrangements after receiving a letter from Senator Morgan on behalf of the American missionaries. Sanford had served as ambassador to Belgium during the Lincoln administration, and afterward he assisted King Leopold II in his business ventures. By way of promoting the Congo to Americans, he wrote President Harrison: "We are destined to be large traders there, and to be one, if not the greatest source of supply of manufactured goods in that region."[76] Lapsley, like others, gave Sanford the title "General," earned not through military service but rather for his purchase of artillery for the Union army. Lapsley described him in this way: "He is a zealous Congo man, not a visionary, for he has large interests there. He treats me as if I were on his business; directs all my movements, takes me to see everybody of importance to me." Sanford also supplied Lapsley with letters of introduction to his Congo friends and to the Governor-General there.[77] Like Morgan in Washington, Sanford gave no attention to Sheppard; both white politicians shared the usual secular outlook on blacks.

Sanford was able to obtain for Lapsley an audience with King Leopold, and following Sanford's advice, Lapsley wore a silk top hat. A letter to Mrs. Lapsley shows how her naive son was convinced that the charming king had Christian concerns:

> He warned me of the entire rudeness of the country, commended our plan of beginning on a small scale, until the tide comes in on the completion of the railways. . . . "The Congo has a future," he said. "I cannot believe that God made that great river with its many branches all through the land, for any lower purpose." He explained that if American negroes came, they must not hope to remain a separate colony, distinct from the State, but become citizens of the country and obey its laws. He also warned me of the danger of wine drinking in Africa. About my location, he recommended the Kassai. . . . "I would ask you not to go to the Ubangi yet; we cannot protect you, if you go so far from our stations." He said he admired the Americans, and wished his people to learn from our amazing progress. "Our people are slow," he said. The king asked my age, and said he was glad I had begun the work of Christ so soon. I quite forgot he was a Catholic or a king, when he spoke with so much apparent sympathy of my mission. . . . His expression is very kind, and his voice matches it. . . . His English is full, ready and expressive. . . . I wonder now how God has so changed the times that a Catholic king, successor to Philip II, should talk Foreign Missions to an American boy and a Presbyterian. I treated him just as I

would any man I thought good and great. I asked nothing of him but his protection.[78]

Pertaining to the "rudeness" of the Congolese, Lapsley elsewhere wrote that Leopold had this to say about those "wild and barbarous" Africans: "The people can only be civilized very gradually. Domestic slavery, for example, is forbidden, but it would be most unwise to suppress it by force at once."[79] Leopold's comment on the repatriation of American blacks pertained to Morgan's determination to return them to their continent of origin. Sanford had earlier accepted the senator's resettlement scheme and had obtained his Belgian client's endorsement of it. They had approved it in order to obtain Morgan's support in the Foreign Relations Committee for American recognition of the Congo Free State.[80] The King may have recommended the Kasai district to Lapsley because the Americans could then be under the surveillance of Leopold's agents from posts that had recently been located along the Kasai River.

Leopold was at this time interested in encouraging any missionaries who could dilute the influence of the Portuguese and French priests in the Congo. The King was disturbed by the Holy Ghost Fathers, a French order that had established the first Congo Catholic mission in 1880.[81] The king perceived that they might encourage powerful France to claim some of what he considered his personal possession. At Leopold's urging, Pope Leo XIII arranged for the Scheut order in Belgium to send priests to the Congo, and they arrived there in 1888. Leopold also secured Belgian priests for his tropical estate from several other orders: the Jesuits, the Trappists, and the Sacred Heart of Jesus.[82] As their numbers increased, Leopold was less interested in having Protestants there. Ruth Slade Reardon writes:

> In his anxiety to attract Belgian missionaries to the Congo, King Leopold facilitated their settlement in every possible way. They were freely given large concessions of land. . . . The Protestants continually felt themselves at a disadvantage due to the fact that they were treated as "foreign" missionaries, unwanted intruders, while the Catholic Belgians always seemed to have the support of the administration.[83]

After his brief trip to Brussels, Lapsley returned to London. Sheppard reported to Lapsley's mother, "We spent a month in England, being together always."[84] Joined by seven Swedish and four British missionaries also headed for Africa, Sheppard left London for Rotterdam a day before Lapsley in order to make advance preparations for the

African voyage. Through his various speaking and visiting activities in London he had acquired a number of friends who gathered at the rail station to bid him farewell. Subsequently, travel in another continent at a mile an hour caused him to long remember that he went "speeding along the ringing rails at a mile a minute" until reaching Harwich. On a ferry across the heavy sea to Holland, Sheppard estimated that he lost from vomiting all the weight he had gained in England!

Passage had been booked on the *Afrikaan,* a small Dutch vessel, because the Belgians had no merchant marine. For much of the three-week trip from England to the Congo, nausea was the principal concern. "We had a good supply of a cure for sea-sickness," Sheppard reported, "but when we were well out where the wind blew we found that meals and medicine forsook us."[85]

Any homesickness Sheppard might have felt on leaving the United States was quickly dispelled after he set foot on the continent of his ancestors. On sailing from New York, he had lamented: "It is sad to leave home, friends, and native land and seek a home among strangers."[86] But he affirmed in a letter written from the Congo three months later, "I am certainly happy in the country of my forefathers."[87] He was proud to be the first African American to become a missionary to central Africa and thereby fulfill the policy established a quarter century earlier by the southern Presbyterians. Although Africa is the ultimate place of origin of all human foreparents, Sheppard had been separated by only several generations rather than by several thousand generations. His ancestors may actually have come to America from the area where he disembarked, as the mouth of the Congo was the point of embarkation for thousands of slaves to the Western hemisphere. It is even possible that one of his forefathers or foremothers came from the Kasai area because some Congolese had been captured there and led down a long trail to the Atlantic coast.[88]

LEOPOLD AND THE CONGO

The confrontation between Western civilization and the Congolese culture began in 1482 when Diogo Cão was the first European to discover the mouth of the Congo River. The river was named for the Kongo people who lived along its lower portion. To acknowledge Portugal's alleged sovereignty in the region, Cão placed a stone pillar on the south bank of the Congo bearing the royal coat of arms with a cross on top. He seized four Kongo tribesmen and took them to Lisbon, not as slaves but as exotic tropical curiosities to show King John II. The monarch's excitement over Cão's progress toward a sea route to India probably contributed to his decision to concentrate exclusively on sailing around Africa. At that time Christopher Columbus, who was living in Lisbon, proposed to King John a voyage westward to India, but that radical idea was rejected.

The four Congolese were taught the Portuguese language and became converted to Christianity. Catholic missionaries accompanied them when they were returned to Africa three years later. Baptized in 1491 were the King of Kongo, his eldest son—who took the name Afonso—and many subjects who followed the royal example. After Afonso became king, the first church south of the Sahara was built in his capital, renamed São Salvador. In 1518 his son Henrique became bishop after receiving theological training in Rome.

After the discovery of the Western hemisphere, the interest of the Portuguese shifted from the Congo to the Amazon region, and they looked to Africa as a source of labor for plantations in Brazil. During Afonso's reign in the first half of the sixteenth century, he wrote the king of Portugal about his intense Christian devotion while pleading for an end to slave exportation. Afonso informed him that "each day the traders are kidnapping our people" and pleaded that "we need in this kingdom only priests and schoolteachers." As Kongo's population was being ravaged, even boys from Afonso's own family were being shipped out as slaves.[89] Much of the earliest Atlantic slave trade in the Congo was by Portuguese monks. Robert Rotberg writes, "They sold the household servants that had been given to them by Afonso; they possessed private residences, mistresses, and illegitimate children."[90] The initial Congolese interest in Christianity was removed by its endorsement of the Portuguese slave trade, which continued legally and illegally until 1878.[91]

The gun was the hallmark of the Western influence in Africa. The slave trade could not have operated without the guns that outsiders used against the Africans and supplied for Africans to use against other Africans. The power wielded by firearms caused the users to presume their civilization was superior. After both sides had guns, power was determined by the rapidity of gunfire from the more sophisticated weapons.

Anglo-American interest in central Africa began with Stanley's reports from that region. He had emigrated from Wales to America and had fought on both sides in the Civil War. He then returned to the other side of the Atlantic to search for even more daring adventures. While serving as a journalist for the New York *Herald*, he was sent to Africa to find Livingstone. That Scottish explorer had been so intent on discovering the source of the Nile and the extensiveness of slave trading that he had dropped out of contact with his British sponsors for two years. Stanley finally attained his goal in 1871 at a remote village in East Africa, and the world was charmed to learn of his alleged greeting, "Dr. Livingstone, I presume?"

While still a journalist, Stanley returned to equatorial Africa in 1874 to cross the continent from east to west and carry on Livingstone's river exploration. He started out with a large party overland from Zanzibar to the Lualaba River, which Livingstone had begun to explore. Being of pugnacious temperament and equipped with superior weapons, Stanley led his men as they massacred many Africans who tried to resist the intruders. Finding that the Lualaba was a tributary of the Congo, Stanley's party followed that river on its great arc around the equator. The grueling trek down uncharted waters cost the lives of most of Stanley's men, but a ragged remnant finally succeeded in reaching the Atlantic Ocean. He memorialized his own exploration by naming the termini of internal river navigation Stanley Falls and Stanley Pool. He detailed the difficulties and accomplishments of his trip in the book *In Darkest Africa*. A PCUS journal carried this comment, "On the return of Stanley from his wonderful journey of three years across the Dark Continent, the whole civilized world became intensely interested in this new region."[92]

In 1876, Leopold called an international conference of geographers in Brussels to discuss ways of "opening to civilization the only part of the globe where it has not yet penetrated." He assured the representatives of six nations gathered there that he and his nation had no vested colonizing interests. Then he offered to provide leadership for scientific and humanitarian efforts in equatorial Africa. He asserted:

> The slave trade, which still exists over a large part of the African continent, is a plague spot that every friend of civilization would desire to see disappear. The horror of that traffic, the thousands of victims massacred each year, . . . the still greater number of perfectly innocent beings who, brutally reduced to captivity, are condemned en masse to forced labour . . . makes our epoch blush.[93]

Leopold was welcomed to preside over "The International Association for the Exploration and Civilization of Africa." This organization proved to be a subterfuge, because Leopold's interests were neither international nor philanthropic. Although it met only once, it achieved the king's aim of establishing himself as someone with highminded interests. In Leopold's early move regarding Africa, he masked a cunningness that was to become a lifelong characteristic. Because of the relative insignificance of his country, he was able to pursue his colonial ambitions for years without suspicion from the larger powers.

Belgium had split off from the Netherlands in the 1830s and was no older than Leopold. The kingdom was not only one of the youngest in Europe but also one of the smallest. On ascending the throne in 1865, Leopold was disturbed by his confinement to such a tiny area of the globe. Envious of the wealth of his cousin, Queen Victoria, he was determined to move from the minor to the major league of European monarchs. He realized that the small Portuguese, English, and Dutch nations had gained global prominence by having colonies to supply raw materials and to provide an overseas market for finished European goods. However, he could not convince the Belgians that colonizing in the tropics would be worth the risks involved, and as a constitutional monarch he did not control government policy. Consequently, Leopold decided to obtain valuable property for himself anywhere he could grab it on the globe, separated from the oversight of any nation. In his search of several continents he found that there was the vast Congo basin that no major power had claimed. Using stealth to get ahead of other Europeans, he ended up with the only colony in the world owned by one person. Leopold I had well described his son as subtle and sly as a fox.[94] The father had also been obsessed to possess a colony somewhere.

In 1877, after following the Congo from its headwaters to its mouth, Stanley returned to Europe eager to interest Britain in planting her flag in the region. But that empire on which the sun never set already had more colonial lands on several continents than could easily be managed. Also, Stanley's account of the long series of impassable rapids on the way into the Congo basin confirmed for the British its inaccessibility for commerce. English Captain James Tuckey had led an expedition to the Congo that had failed in 1816. He and his sixteen men were struck down by fever after penetrating only fifty miles beyond the lower rapids.

In 1878 Sanford was made an officer in the Order of Leopold and for the next seven years he was Leopold's prime spokesperson for his African campaign. Sanford's first assignment was the recruitment of Stanley, who reluctantly responded to an opportunity to be employed by Leopold on finding that his native country was preoccupied with colonial rule elsewhere. At this time Leopold made an honest disclosure to his ambassador in Britain:

> I'm sure if I quite openly charged Stanley with the task of taking possession in my name of some part of Africa, the English will stop me ... So I think I'll just give Stanley some job of exploration which would offend no one, and will give us the bases and headquarters which we can take over later on. . . . I do not want to risk . . . losing a fine chance to secure for ourselves a slice of this magnificent African cake.[95]

Before Stanley returned to the Congo, Leopold took another step in his grand scheme for obtaining possession of territory equal in size to all of western Europe. He called another meeting in Brussels for the purpose of obtaining international endorsement of Stanley's further explorations. The king set up the Committee for the Survey of the Upper Congo and became its chairman. The Committee obtained funding from a banking consortium for an expedition by Stanley, allegedly to obtain accurate information about the region.

Back in the Congo, Stanley established a central station at Vivi, near Boma, and eventually claimed that he negotiated some 450 treaties with tribal chiefs. He did not know the local languages, so the bamboozled chiefs did not understand the documents upon which they placed their signature marks. They allegedly surrendered political power to a foreign sovereign in exchange for a little gin and cloth. By way of subduing potential rivals, Stanley made the powerful slaver Tippo Tib governor of the eastern region of the Congo.[96]

Stanley visited a camp where Tippo Tib's henchmen were holding 2,300 captives who had been taken in raids on 118 villages. He observed: "There are rows upon rows of dark nakedness. . . . The children over ten are secured by three copper rings [around neck and legs]. . . . My nerves are offended with the rancid effuvium of the unwashed herds . . . bound and riveted together by twenties." Stanley reckoned that six natives had died for every one enslaved.[97]

In 1884, at the end of Stanley's five-year contract with Leopold, a two-hundred-mile road had been constructed around the raging rapids below Stanley Pool, five steamers had been built at the lakelike Pool, and forty "hospitable and scientific" stations had been started along a thousand miles of the upper Congo. Leopold was furious that Stanley had not killed explorer Pierre de Brazza when he met with him and that he had not wiped out his French settlement among the Teke on the north bank of Stanley Pool.[98]

Competing interests for African land was now raging in Europe. Appropriately, the *Times* of London wrote of "the scramble for Africa." The European "powers" assumed that Africans were too primitive to govern themselves, but no assignment of caregivers had been agreed upon. A game of monopoly was being played on an African map that was accurate only along the well-explored continental coast. When one European power placed a flag, fort, or gun on one area, the others agreed to respect the claim. Culturally arrogant and racist, the white colonialists had convinced themselves of their "manifest destiny" to steal lands and resources from the blacks.

Leopold realized that he, as a minor king, needed the support of a major nation before the colonial powers would recognize any private fiefdom that he staked out. To achieve that end, he called upon his American agent to lobby at the highest levels. In 1883, Sanford entertained President Chester Arthur, a fellow Republican, at the hotel on his citrus plantation on St. John's River in the new town of Sanford, Florida. Sanford delivered to Arthur copies of Stanley's treaties, omitting the limitation on free trade proviso, to show that the Congo Free State should receive diplomatic recognition. The next week, Arthur included in his annual message to Congress most of what Sanford had drafted about Leopold's desire to open the Congo to freedom of trade.

Sanford next convinced American legislative leaders that Leopold was eager for European and American merchants to engage in free trade in Central Africa. They were led to believe that the United States Constitution would serve as a model for the government of the Congo. Sanford beguiled Congress through Morgan, a ranking member of the Senate Foreign Relations Committee. The senator stated: "The enlightened King of the Belgians has supplied the means from his private purse to inaugurate civilization in the Congo country under the authority of its native rulers. He has no thought of extending the power of his realm over that country." Morgan was convinced that the golden star on the flag of the Congo Free State "represents hospitality to the people and commerce of all nations." Little did Morgan realize that "Free" in the title was a part of Leopold's deception, for free international trade was heavily restricted and the Congolese had much less personal freedom after his guns penetrated the heart of Africa. Nor did "Free" have any reference to local self-government, for no provision was made for a Congolese parliament or court system with even limited power.

On February 25, 1884, a joint resolution of Congress recommended that the president recognize the Congo Free State.[99] Accordingly, Pres-

ident Arthur gave Leopold a huge boost by becoming the first head of
state to recognize the Congo Free State. European governments soon
followed America's first venture into African land matters and also
granted recognition.

Portugal was a problem to other European nations because of its his-
toric claim to land on both sides of the lower Congo River. To settle
this and other disputes over land rights, and to decide how territories
should be developed in tropical Africa, Otto Bismarck convened the
Berlin Conference for representatives of fifteen nations during the
winter of 1884–85. Sanford, working as a double agent, promoted
Leopold's interests at the Conference while running the affairs of the
American delegation. The German chancellor was mainly interested in
obtaining assurances of open trade and thereby lowering the possibility of more war among the Europeans. Having somehow become aware
of unscrupulous Leopold's "pretentious egoism," Bismarck wanted to
establish international agreements for keeping him in check.[100] Accordingly, the first article ratified was that no nation could have an economic
monopoly in the Congo basin.

Article VI of the Berlin accord was also of special importance:

> All the Powers exercising sovereign rights or influence in the afore-
> said territories bind themselves to watch over the preservation of the
> native tribes, and to care for the improvement of the conditions of
> their moral and material well-being, and to help in suppressing slav-
> ery, and especially the slave trade. They shall, without distinction of
> creed or nation, protect and favor all religious, scientific, or charitable
> institutions and undertakings created and organized for the above
> ends, or which aim at instructing the natives and bringing home to
> them the blessings of civilization. Christian missionaries, scientists,
> and explorers, with their followers, property, and collections, shall
> likewise be the objects of especial protection. Freedom of conscience
> and religious toleration are expressly guaranteed to the natives no less
> than to the subjects (of the sovereign states) and to foreigners. The
> free and public exercise of all forms of divine worship, and the right to
> build churches, temples, and chapels, and to organize religious mis-
> sions belonging to all creeds, shall not be limited or fettered in any way
> whatsoever.

The European governments who were represented in Berlin
accepted Leopold's assurance that Stanley obtained territory legiti-
mately. Stanley was the only one at the Conference with firsthand
knowledge of at least some of central Africa. Although he was a delegate from the United States, he enhanced Leopold's interests by drawing boundaries that made his Belgian employer the big winner. There

being no African delegates at the Conference, the continent was represented by the Mercator projection. That map had long been popular in Europe because it reinforced the biases of those who belonged to Gerard Mercator's continent. The equator is two-thirds the way down the map, suggesting the relative greater importance of the northern hemisphere. The southern hemisphere is beneath the northern, in token of its subordination. Like the distorting mirrors at a carnival, land areas of Europe appear much larger than the same square mileage in the continent divided by the equator.[101] With a lust for territory and an arrogance toward its inhabitants, the delegates at Berlin resolved conflicting claims among themselves as they drew arbitrary lines on the map with no regard for tribal groupings. Knowing that their weapons were more destructive than those of the Africans, no one worried over having the power to confiscate the appropriated areas. Like predators of a huge tropical mammal, fourteen European hunters each tore off satisfying portions for themselves.

At the Berlin Conference, "Leopold goaded the goliaths—France, Germany and Britain—and the lesser players—Portugal, the Netherlands, Spain and Italy—into formal declarations of their imperial intentions which, by mischievous design, also allocated a large section of central Africa to Leopold himself."[102] As a result, about one million square miles and fifteen million people in the Congo basin were handed over to the machinations of Leopold. A land area one-third that size was assigned to Portugal, located south of the mouth of the Congo River, and one-quarter of that amount, located along the north bank of the Congo, was given to France. By means of the Berlin Conference banditry, Leopold became the absolute ruler of a territory more than seventy times the size of Belgium. The Belgian Parliament agreed in 1885 that the Congo State would be an "exclusively personal" possession of their king.[103] "I am the state," could more accurately have been claimed by Leopold than by Louis XIV of France. His sovereignty in the Congo was unchecked by the Belgian legislature or judiciary.

The agents of European nations who met in Berlin dismissed the thought that Africans should continue to have sovereignty over their kingdoms. The unspoken assumption was that the Europeans had a sacred duty to rule primitive people who could not govern themselves. Africans in the Congo basin had no idea that their economic and political fate had been sealed by European agreements. Its reality began to be felt in 1886 when the Congolese were conscripted into the Force Publique. Leopold's officers found that some African slavers and cannibals were willing to become State agents for personal gain. This army terrorized the countryside, searching for porters, foods, and exportable goods. Leopold decreed that he owned all the *terres vacantes* [unoccupied land], that is, all except what was being used for houses and gardens. Thus, a Congolese could be charged with the crime of trespassing if he hunted in the forests of his region. As for the traditional custom of moving from exhausted agricultural land to fresh tracts, Leopold was unaware and unconcerned. Traders who were not his agents could not deal in ivory and rubber because forests had become exclusively his personal property.

In 1890, about the time that Lapsley was in Brussels, Sanford was participating in an Anti-Slavery Conference there. Leopold, the chairman, persuaded the European representatives to curtail free trade in the Congo by imposing a 10 percent import tax. He justified this by nobly claiming that the elimination of slavery required such financing. Actually, the traditional slave trade there was rapidly declining and Leopold had begun to impose a terror on the Congolese worse than enslavement. Eager to appear philanthropic, Leopold joined with the others in proclaiming that European powers had this duty:

> To support and, if necessary, to serve as a refuge for the native populations; to place those under their sovereignty in a position to cooperate for their own defence; to diminish intertribal wars by means of arbitration; to initiate the natives in agricultural pursuits and industrial arts, so as to increase their welfare; to raise them by civilization and bring about the extinction of barbarous customs, such as cannibalism and human sacrifices; and, in giving aid to commercial enterprises, to watch over their legality, controlling especially the contracts for service entered into with natives.[104]

At the beginning of the last decade of the nineteenth century, three men confronted one another. Two were young idealists with a religious and educational agenda; the other was a cynical materialist and sleazy manipulator. A clash between the missionaries and the monarch was bound to happen, but it would take many years for Leopold's hypocrisy to be widely exposed.

2

Beginnings in Africa

UP THE RIVER

After noticing many miles of the "tea-colored" ocean resulting from the enormous outflow of a muddy river, Sheppard sighted land. On May 9, 1890, the *Afrikaan* anchored in the fifteen-mile-wide river mouth, where the peninsulas on either side protrude like shark's jaws. Here the Americans had their initial exposure to African culture. Lapsley's diary describes the antiphonal cadences of the canoe paddlers who ferried them to shore:

> It was pleasant to hear them sing. . . . The "stroke," a fine-looking fellow, took the verse and the rest joined heartily in the refrain. The words were simple sounding and musical; the syllables are so many and quick that the rhythm is marked and carries you along. The tones are weird and strange.[1]

The dominating river of west central Africa, which is longer and wider than the Mississippi, has had several names. It has been most commonly known as the Congo, in honor of the largest tribe who live around the lower portion of the river. The Portuguese called the river "Zaire," from the Bantu words *zai*, "river," and *dia*, "eat." The Congolese picturesquely thought of it as the serpentine river that swallows up other streams. Stanley attempted to give the name of his hero Livingstone to the river, but only his Livingstone Falls designation for the cataracts on the lower river continued to be used. Livingstone mistakenly believed the Lualaba River was a source of the Nile when it is actually the name for the segment of the Congo that flows northward, thousands of miles from the Atlantic.

The missionaries stopped over at a trading post named Banana, near Sharks' Point. Sheppard noted that those place names were appropriate because thousands of banana trees were growing in the delta area, and "the river swarmed with man-eating sharks." After eating many bananas at their first dinner on shore, they informed the waiter that they came from a country where they were scarce and would enjoy a few more. He returned with as many as he could carry and they stuffed themselves until they were embarrassed. Their first crisis in Africa came just before Lapsley rushed shouting from the surf where he was bathing. Overcome by fright, he uttered, "I was nearly taken by a shark."[2]

While at Banana, Lapsley and Sheppard went in a canoe, with rowers standing in the prow and stern, up a small river to visit a woman missionary. Without other staff at her station, she was working with the struggling self-support mission operation of Bishop William Taylor, a Methodist from California.[3] They also stopped at a village where they encountered their first member of African royalty. Sheppard wrote:

> We were escorted by a native brother to visit his majesty King Dom-golia. . . . The king has not learned to wear pants, hat, or shoes yet. He had a piece of cloth around his shoulders and waist, and a staff in his hand. . . . On leaving . . . we gave him (as is the custom) a dash (twelve pence). In return, he gave us three eggs and an invitation to come again.[4]

For a month the Americans lived along the lower Congo, six degrees south of the equator. They learned about the predicament of the Congolese there while making preparation for going overland to the upper Congo. They became aware that Stanley and other agents of Leopold were viewed quite differently by the Congolese than by Westerners. Lapsley observed the two ways by which foreigners were classified:

> The State officials, and even the white settlement here, is called Bula Matari. (Stanley's native name [also spelled Bula Matadi]; it means breaker-of-rocks, from his road-making achievements!) White man is mundila; the missionary is mundila-nzambi, "God's white man"; or, sometimes, nganga-nzambi, "God's medicine man." If a party of white men approaches a lower Congo village the cry goes round: "Who is coming?" Answer, "Mundila." "What mundila?" Answer, "Mundila-nzambi"; then out they all come to talk to and welcome the traveller. But if "Weh! Bula Matari!" then "Sh-sh!" And whiz they all go to hide in the long grass![5]

The "State officials" (meaning agents for Leopold's private enterprise) seemed to like being feared. When Stanley died in Britain, "Bula Matari" was inscribed on his tomb. He once wrote that his title was given by chiefs who watched him demonstrate the proper use of a sledge-hammer.[6] The Congolese, however, associated Stone Smasher more with his strong-armed tactics toward humans. Heavily armed during his tours of the Congo, he seemed to relish shooting any "savages" who appeared inhospitable. His journal states, "Natives extremely insolent, had a brush, two natives killed"; and "We have attacked and destroyed 28 large towns."[7]

Leopold's agents were mainly from Belgium, but mercenaries were also employed from other European countries. Ludwig Bauer charac-terizes them in this way:

> They were uprooted men, malcontents, malicious-minded, with impulses previously repressed and now given free rein. They grew irri-table under the burning equatorial sun, were petty tyrants with no one to control them. . . . They were rarely prosecuted, received light sen-tences and were then pardoned.[8]

After a short stay along the river estuary, Sheppard and Lapsley took a river steamer fifty miles upstream to Boma, a name that means "python." That large snake, along with crocodiles, lived in the marshes surrounding the town. The main business of the Europeans living there had long been slave trading. Human cargo, numbering more than a million units, had been shipped from ports of central Africa to the New World. Stanley, who was guilty of using a veiled type of slavery himself, hypocritically denounced what had only recently ended:

> Boma has a history, a cruel blood-curdling history, fraught with hor-ror, and woe, and suffering. Inhumanity of man to man has been exem-plified here for over two centuries by the pitiless persecution of black men, by sordid whites. The natives formerly were purchased by thou-sands, forcibly expatriated, enchained by dozens, packed closely in the holds of slave-ships, and shipped to the Brazils, West Indies, and North America.[9]

Boma, capital of the Congo Free State, was the most European town in the Congo. There were fewer than a thousand Westerners in the Congo at that time, and a sizeable portion of them lived on the lower Congo. Lapsley met with the governor-general, the official in charge of carrying out Leopold's orders there, and obtained valuable geo-graphic information from him.

Sheppard told about learning the finer points of effete society at a Portuguese hotel in Boma:

Being very hungry, we had soup twice, a good helping of fish followed, then came beef and vegetables. Thinking this was all, we ate like wild men. Our plates were taken away and soon a new course was brought in. We refused. (Had to.) Pretty soon another course. Others at the table who had eaten more moderately and knew there were six more courses smiled at us every time fresh plates were brought. And there we sat, certainly an hour, and very uncomfortable, until dessert was served.[10]

Near Matadi, across the river and upstream from Boma, hospitality was extended to Lapsley and Sheppard by the English Baptists at Tunduwa (also called Underhill in honor of an English missionary). While there the neophytes were eager to learn from the experiences of the seasoned staff about what to expect as they began evangelistic work. They also visited the "mounds of triumphant martyrs,"[11] a missionary cemetery near the river bank. Sheppard reflected on how those buried there had, like himself, been sent off from their home countries on "their mission of love" by friends with "a kiss upon the cheek, a mingling of tears, a wave of the handkerchief." But their lives soon ended, "Emaciated by deadly fevers, pelted by tropical storms, stung by the tsetse flies fresh from the lazarette of misery, fatigued and foot sore from many a tramp, they have laid themselves down in this pleasant dale."[12]

The mortality rate at that time was much higher in Africa than for any other area of missionary activity. By the time one lower Congo mission had twenty-five converts, more than that number were buried in their Tunduwa missionary cemetery. More poignantly, most of those who were buried there were in their twenties.[13] An 1891 mission publication sounded this warning: "The lower Congo . . . is not a region in which a precious human life ought to be risked for forty-eight hours. Fifty-five missionaries, nearly all of them on this lower Congo, have died within ten years."[14] At that time and in that region only one out of four survived the first term of service. Wags quipped, "If you want to go to heaven soon, become a Congo missionary." Sheppard noticed that the Europeans at Matadi "were very yellow from the effects of the sun and fever."[15]

At Tunduwa both Lapsley and Sheppard experienced what they called "blackwater fever," meaning that their urine became like black ink. It was accompanied by intense chills and temperatures as high as 105 degrees. Sheppard wrote about the torturous treatment for killing the fever: "Hot tea, cup after cup, followed in quick succession, and soon we were like two ducks in a puddle of water. We had never perspired so in all our days. . . . On a day when it was 99 in the shade . . .

we were under six blankets."[16] Lapsley reflected on this illness, "Whenever I am in the oven stage of a fever, I think of the dreadful fire to
which these poor people are exposed."[17] Hellfire for non-Christians
was more a part of the theology held by him than by Sheppard.

Educated Westerners then knew that quinine and other drugs were
effective in the treatment of what is now called malaria, but they did
not understand its cause. Once Lapsley guessed that it was caused by a
draft coming through a hole in his undershirt. Lapsley and Sheppard
did use mosquito nets at night, but this was intended to prevent dis-
comfort rather than disease. Mosquitoes and other insects were sometimes so thick on the net that they interfered with the air circulation. It
was not until 1899 that Ronald Ross, a British physician, proved that
the blood disease was caused by the anopheles mosquito, which transmitted a parasite from animals. Sheppard recorded twenty-two bouts
with malaria during his first two years in Congo.[18] Those with African
ancestry are not immune to tropical diseases; malaria is especially likely
to be fatal to African children.

Sheppard went out to gain experience in handling the African canoe,
which was dug out of the trunk of a large hardwood tree. He was insuf-
ficiently aware of the tumultuous whirlpool at the navigational head of
the lower Congo, where the river makes an acute turn and is only a half-
mile wide. A million cubic feet of water per second squeezes through
the canyon there. In a poetic manner, Sheppard wrote about "Hell's
Cauldron":

> The moaning of the seething sea-serpent can be heard a mile away.
> Being ignorant of its great drawing power, we tried to cross the river,
> three hundred yards above. In spite of our desperate efforts to reach
> the north bank we were drawn in as a floating stick. We spun round
> and round like a top, the boat all the time at an angle of about forty
> degrees, till we were dizzy. Natives on shore informed the other mis-
> sionaries of our perilous predicament. We thought of our watery
> graves and all of our past life flashed before us. "Oh! save us Master,
> or we perish," we prayed. In a moment, as if miraculously, the seething
> cauldron ceased for a second, and by an awful struggle for life, we
> rowed out and landed, to the delight of the excited crowd.[19]

While in the Matadi area, the Presbyterians hiked up a 1,700-foot
hill to visit Palabala, where the American Baptists' first Congo station
was started in 1884. They were continuing the work that Henry Craven
of the Livingstone Inland Mission began there in 1878. Lapsley noted
that these Baptists included abstaining from alcohol as a requirement
for becoming a Christian. They told of a king in their area who was

much interested in their religion "but would not give up the white man's drink, with which the traders were too ready to supply him, and he died unsaved, clinging to his bottle."[20] There is little in the record of the pioneer Presbyterian missionaries about abstinence from alcohol. With some reservations they imbibed palm wine when served by an African host.[21]

The lack of penetration of Euro-Americans beyond the coastal region was typical of their presence in other areas of tropical Africa; the earliest ones there found the hinterland inaccessible due to thick jungles and difficult topography. A sharp rise in elevation from the narrow coastal plain caused a number of African rivers to plunge down over rapids, prohibiting ocean navigation to the interior. Lapsley and Sheppard found that some Catholic and Protestant missions were already located at sites along the lower Congo where transportation to Europe was easier. The Presbyterian team knew that they should, in compliance with the directives of their sponsoring church, search for a site on the healthier vast upland plateau that was not saturated with mission stations. So after brief visits in communities along the lower Congo, Sheppard and Lapsley were ready to begin the difficult journey away from the coast.

Eight years earlier a rough and narrow road had been cut through forests and over the Crystal Mountains—so named for the masses of quartz they contained. The road began at Matadi, which was located as far upstream on the turbulent Congo as an Atlantic ship could ply [see map]. The road ended where river navigation resumed 800 feet higher on the continental shelf above the thirty-two cataracts of Livingstone Falls. Leopold and Stanley had realized that the Congo River could never become a grand commercial highway until the cataract obstacle was overcome. From its terminus in Matadi, several miles of rail line to Stanley Pool had been completed near the caravan road. During the next two years, about half of the seven thousand Africans recruited for railway construction would die or desert. The high mortality rate would continue until the rail reached its upland destination in 1898.[22]

Many rail workers had been brought to Matadi from Liberia and British colonies in West Africa. Those foreign laborers were preferred for the industrial skills that some possessed and because they could not easily run away from the deadly construction work. If an overseer became too demanding, Congolese workers could flee into the bush and take refuge among fellows with whom they could communicate. Some West Africans spoke freely to Sheppard in pidgin English about the harsh treatment they had received from white overseers. One of the workers said: "No good here for Sierra Leone man; plenty sick, too much flog."[23] Sheppard's rapport with those expatriates was remembered years later by a missionary in the Congo who remarked, "Rev. Mr. Sheppard is said to have moved to tears a large congregation of the hardest African natives known [Guinea coast railroad laborers], because of the intense emotional power of his manner in speaking to them, and many of them began better lives."[24]

Sheppard claimed that there were 40,000 Congolese porters along the caravan route. The disease-carrying tsetse fly made it impossible for the usual horse or donkey burden bearers to live long in tropical Africa. "There is not so much as an ox or mule in all this Congo region," Lapsley observed.[25] Consequently, Lapsley and Sheppard hired two dozen porters for their caravan, recognizing a porter's capacity to be about sixty pounds. Five were needed to carry their bedding and tent; others were needed for what Sheppard called their "European food," which consisted of "corned beef, sugar, tea, coffee, and butter."[26] Lapsley noted that it took seven to carry their "pocket-book," which consisted of nine hundred red bandanas and a bale containing several dozen twelve-yard pieces of cheap cloth. Their "cash" in the money-less economy also included coils of brass wire, beads, bells, and cowrie shells. Those goods used for bartering had been brought from England because their cost would have been several times higher if purchased from European stores in the Congo.

Since malaria had sapped some of their strength, Sheppard and Lapsley hired eight "hammock men." The trek inland was begun by alternating between walking and being carried in what they called their "Pullman palace coaches," consisting of canvas suspended on thick bamboo poles.[27] The speed with which these men moved was due, Sheppard was told, to the heat of the rocks under their bare feet. Another user of this common Congo conveyance gave this description:

> Each end of the pole rests on the shoulder of a lithe, powerful young native and one's weight swings just a few inches above the trail as they glide swiftly along. The carriers are stripped to a scant loin cloth; bodies, glistening with perspiration, shine like polished bronze; beneath a silky skin every movement displays a wonderful play of rippling muscles. Four to six others trot swiftly behind, waiting for their turn at the pole.[28]

The missionaries were traveling during the month of June, which was in the drier and cooler part of the year. Lapsley noted: "We would have had a very different trip six months later on. Then it would be both dis-

agreeable and dangerous, very hot, . . . rains drenching everything on
short notice, and making great torrents of the little branches that cross
the road every half mile."[29] Sheppard told of the daily routine:

> We would walk in the cool of the morning from five o'clock to ten. In
> the middle of the day the mercury goes up to 108 in the shade. . . . We
> would stop in camp till four, then walk till six and then pitch our tents
> for the night. We always sleep under blankets; the change in temper-
> ature at night is tremendous. . . . We walked from ten to twenty miles
> a day, according to the condition of the road.[30]

The caravan moved in single file, Sheppard wrote, "on a trail about
twelve inches broad and running as crooked as a snake down and up
hills, over rough stones, and through high grass." On the first day they
encountered the swift Mpozo River and were ferried across in a native
canoe. Sheppard described their first and typical campout:

> By the help of the natives we soon had our tent stretched, the ground
> sheet spread inside, and the couches made up. One of the natives
> brought us an armful of wood and the camp fire was started. . . . We
> had for our first supper crackers, jam, tea and river water. We were up
> at five o'clock, had breakfast, an exact duplicate of our supper, and
> began to climb over stones, around cliffs, following the narrow trail
> for three hours till we reached to top, footsore and hungry.[31]

Sheppard learned the need to haggle when making purchases, and
the wisdom of *caveat emptor*:

> I saw a woman with a basket of eggs; I . . . asked, "How much?" So
> many brass rods. I paid her and took the eggs. One of my carriers came
> up and said, "You must be fresh in this country." "Yes," I said, "I came
> in the last steamer." "I thought so! to buy eggs without examining
> them, and to pay whatever is asked." He looked over the eggs and
> found some good ones.[32]

Lapsley and Sheppard stopped over at the American Baptist mission
in Banza Manteke where they were surprised to find an iron church
capable of seating six hundred. Weighing six tons, it had been shipped
from Boston and carried the fifty-five miles from Matadi by porters in
hundreds of loads. The sanctuary's structure was welcomed because
metal is impervious to the termite, the most destructive tropical pest.
Sheppard noted that two boys rang the church's bell for two hours
before the daily service. At its entrances were large offering baskets that
worshipers filled with strings of beads. Sheppard also observed:

A woman would go to service with two children tied on her back, a pot of water balanced on her head, a basket in one hand and a large child held by the other; . . . sometimes they would cry, but nothing would interrupt the service unless [there was] a dog fight. Then the congregation will rush out to see whose dog is getting whipped.[33]

Sheppard and Lapsley had probably learned from Guinness about a Mr. Richards, an outstanding missionary stationed at Banza Manteke, who was on furlough when they arrived there.[34] Pertaining to the Congolese Christians, he taught:

They are exactly like us inside; the difference is only skin deep! They are intensely sincere. What is in comes out! There are no restraints of any kind—no delicacy or consideration or deference to public opinion or conventionalities. . . . My dear wife was very ill one night; I was up with her and anxious, and I suppose I looked pale next day. Lydia, a woman who kindly came in to help, observed it, and I overheard her saying to a neighbour, "What do you think? These white people actually love each other like we do!

When Richards was asked why natives often dislike white people, he explained:

Remember that they knew white men before they knew missionaries! It is not long since slavery was done away. Traders and officers are not always so kind as they should be. Any way, the African idea of a white man is that he is a devil; and it takes a good deal of intimate association with one who obeys the law of love, and treats him as a brother and an equal, before he begins to feel that a white man can be a human brother![35]

Along the path the Americans "met numerous ivory caravans with loads amounting to at least five tons . . . [and] a few caravans with rubber."[36] On returning upcountry from Matadi the Congolese carried imported goods, such as trading trinkets and machine parts. The upper Congo had been opened to foreign traders for thirteen years, and thousands of loads of commercial goods moved along that trail monthly. Sheppard was disturbed by the "sun-bleached skeletons of native carriers here and there who by sickness, hunger or fatigue, had laid themselves down to die, without fellow or friend." He and Lapsley were especially chagrined that they could not help one of them who was suffering with a disease brought in by Europeans. Sheppard wrote, "In passing a cluster of bushes we heard groans of a native, and on making our way into the thicket found a man dying of smallpox."[37]

Lukunga, another American Baptist station along the trail, served as a transfer point for porters and as a resting place for weary trekkers. The missionaries were able to dispense with their tents for one night and stay in cool mud-walled houses. Their host came to the room that Lapsley and Sheppard shared in hopes of assuring them that the numerous spiders, half the size of a hand, were harmless. "But," he said as he pointed to a hole over the door, "there is a nest of scorpions; you must be careful in moving in and out, for they will spring upon you." Sheppard said they spent much of the evening using their shoes to decorate the walls with smashed spiders. The next morning he saw a twenty-five foot long python—which he called a boa—that had squeezed a donkey into a pulp for swallowing.[38] The way to kill a python, a Kongo man claimed, is to thrust out one's fist, which the snake obligingly swallows; then its head can be severed with a knife in the free hand.[39]

The pleasure of the stopover at Lukunga was diminished by the sand there that was "a hotbed for miniature fleas [chigoes], or 'jiggers.'" While there, Sheppard and Lapsley had swollen and itchy feet from a common ailment of all who lived in tropical Africa. The female flea burrows into tender flesh and lays her eggs. The spot swells to the size of a pea as the next generation matures, causing considerable pain. Sheppard greased his toes with palm oil to ward off jiggers and frequently he pried them out from under his toe and finger nails to prevent losing those nails.[40]

The Americans visited a native market near the caravan path, taking in ever more sights. Sheppard wrote:

> A number of women had their faces, hair and loin cloths smeared over with a black preparation which trickled all down their legs. On inquiry we were told that it was a tar made from burned peanuts, palm oil and palm nuts. It was their mode of mourning for the deceased. . . . [For food sale] there were hogs, dogs, ducks, goats, sheep, rats, bats, chickens and caterpillars in numbers and abundance. . . . We saw piles of native bread made from the roots of manioc. This bread was round like a man's head, wrapped in greased banana leaves, weighing about five pounds. In appearance and eating it is like putty.[41]

The last escapade on this trek came when another tributary of the Congo River was reached. All were ferried across in canoes except Sheppard and Lapsley, who decided to swim. Their survival surprised the porters who had observed that the river was filled with crocodiles disguised as floating logs![42]

After two weeks of exhausting travel, Lapsley and Sheppard were relieved to arrive on the south side of Stanley Pool at Kinshasa—soon to be renamed Leopoldville. There the Congo River widens to about ten miles for a length of twenty miles and becomes the heart of a vast circulatory system of commerce. From that terminus, more than eight thousand miles of navigable mainstream and tributary waters could be reached by paddle-wheel steamers. Those found there had been manufactured in Europe, disassembled and carried in small portions over the trail from the lower Congo. Missionary societies were among the first to build steamers on the upper Congo, and Stanley seized the one owned by the Livingstone Inland Mission to use on his military expedition upriver.[43] Kinshasa grew rapidly as the main supply and communications center for government and mission stations on the second largest river system in the world.

Coincidentally, Joseph Conrad, who would become one of the greatest writers of English literature, went up the same path from Matadi the same month as the American missionaries. He had also been disturbed by the sight of unburied two-legged beasts of burden along the way. Conrad had been employed as a steamer captain but remained in Africa for only a few months. Lapsley encountered this "gentlemanly fellow" in Kinshasa while both were receiving medical attention from Dr. Aaron Sims, the first missionary doctor in the Congo.[44] Since there were only a few English-speaking Euro-Americans in the area, they probably enjoyed one another's company. Conrad left the Congo with similar perceptions to those of Sheppard and Lapsley about the harsh treatment of Africans by the State.[45]

Sims was a brilliant missionary, his skills extending far beyond providing medical services for the entire missionary and trading community of Kinshasa. He was also a versatile linguist, an accomplished botanist, and a home builder. Moreover, as Stanley stated, "Dr. Sims was the first to navigate any portion of the waters of the Upper Congo."[46]

When Lapsley and Sheppard were in Kinshasa, another African American Protestant clergyman, and eminent historian, was also visiting there. George Williams wrote an open letter at that time to Leopold about his six-month tour of upper Congo, boldly informing the king that the "King of Kings" was not pleased with what was happening in the Congo. Sheppard may have met him, or at least had read his soon-to-be-published letter. He characterized Leopold's agents as uninterested in learning Congolese languages or in providing educational or medical assistance. Worse yet, they kidnapped women for use as concubines and murdered men who would not submit to slave labor.

Pertaining to the State stations, Williams wrote, "These piratical, buccaneering posts compel the natives to furnish them with fish, goats, fowls, and vegetables at the mouths of their muskets; and whenever the natives refuse . . . white officers come with an expeditionary force and burn away the homes of the natives."[47] A year later Williams died, which left the publicizing of human rights abuses in the Congo mainly to Sheppard and Lapsley.

Sheppard then went back to Lukunga to recruit assistants for an upstream exploration while Lapsley embarked on a voyage to a location near where the Congo crosses the equator in order to consult with George Grenfell. That outstanding English Baptist missionary was living among the Bolobos, the largest tribe north of the Kasai on the Congo. In 1886 Grenfell had ventured in his little steamer, *Peace*, up the Kasai River and was especially impressed with the energetic Luba people. Lapsley obtained from him expert advice on virgin missionary areas and his recommendation of the Kasai region as a promising field of labor. Also he made copies of Grenfell's high-quality maps, for which he had been awarded membership in the Royal Geographical Society of England.

In a letter written at Bolobo, Lapsley commented: "Sheppard is still away getting men for our trip of exploration. . . . The Bateka think there is nobody like 'Mundele Ndom,' the black white man." Lapsley elsewhere provided this clarification, "Mundele means 'man with clothes,' but it is the usual word for white men, as none but white men wear clothes."[48] So, "Black Man with Clothes" was the literal meaning of one of Sheppard's Congo names. Lapsley also offered this assessment: "Sheppard is a most handy fellow and is now a thorough river-man. . . . His temper is bright and even—really a man of unusual graces and strong points of character. I am thankful to God for Sheppard."[49]

While Lapsley waited many weeks for a steamer on which he could return to Kinshasa, Sheppard relieved an acute food shortage there. After being informed by a Kete chief that his people were starving, Dr. Sims requested that Sheppard use his powerful Martini-Henri rifle to kill some of the abundant hippopotami in Stanley Pool. Assisted by a native guide, Sheppard killed two when they exposed their heads above the water. Dozens of men then went out and retrieved carcasses that weighed more than four tons. On the bank, the flesh was stripped off, some to be eaten fresh, but much to be dried and stored. In appreciation of Sheppard, Sims told Lapsley, "You have a treasure in him; the very best companion you could have on your trip."[50]

While in the Stanley Pool area, Sheppard killed many more hippopotami and sold the dried meat to defray expenses. These huge animals were dangerous, but by quick and accurate use of his rifle he saved the life of a missionary whose canoe was being crushed by one. After shooting another one, Sheppard teased the Africans with him for being too timid to swim out and tie a rope around its nose. They refused because the area was infested with crocodiles. Sheppard admitted that this episode taught him the hard way to accept African savvy:

> Taking the rope and putting the loop on my arm, I jumped in and swam to the hippo. As I began to tie the rope around her nose, up came a monster crocodile and made a terrible lunge at her neck. Not a moment did I tarry to see what effect his sharp teeth had on the hippo, but turned the rope loose and under the water I went, and was half way to the shore when I came up. The natives were very much excited and assisted me in landing. I begged their pardon and was ashamed of my bravery. Many times in Central Africa foreigners get into serious difficulties from which they cannot extricate themselves, by disregarding the advice of natives.[51]

On another occasion "a very large bull hippo bowed his neck, grunted in a deep bass voice, and came rushing toward the bank" a few yards from Sheppard. The Congolese urged him to put his rifle down because the spirit of Banqua, their chief, dwelt in that particular hippo and if it died Banqua would also die. Sheppard "gave attention to their superstition" and did not shoot it.[52]

While on one hippo hunt, Sheppard encountered an elephant nearby. The accompanying Congolese urged him to kill it, but he realized that they could not use its meat. "I told them it was not right to kill simply to be killing," Sheppard said, "and as we have no steamboat to carry the meat away, it would lie here in the sun and decay."[53]

When Lapsley returned to the American Baptist station in Kinshasa, he wrote his home headquarters:

> Brother Sheppard has, in every way, justified the predictions of his friends. He has won the esteem of all the missionaries as a true man and a gentleman, while with the natives he is, according to Dr. Sims, the most popular man that ever came to this station. He has the constitution needed, and the gift of getting on in Africa. While I was away he devoted much time to hunting on the river, and has actually brought home twelve "hippos," to the great delight of the blacks and admiration of Europeans.[54]

In searching for a mission site, the Presbyterians did not accept without further exploration the advice of Leopold and Grenfell, to look for a place along the Kasai. They recalled that their mission board had instructed them to settle within a reasonable range of a supply base. If a site along the upper Kwango River could be found, it would be accessible by several days' travel to Kinshasa [see map]. That main supply center for upper Congo could be reached overland from Kinkunji, located at the head of Kwango navigation, faster than by boat should immediate supplies or a physician be needed. In October of 1890 the Americans intended to head eastward by a new road to the state trading post at Kinkunji. To return, they would descend in canoes due north down the Kwango, west down the Kasai, and then south down the Congo.[55]

As the Americans were about to set out from Kinshasa, they were confronted with the desertion of the porters whom Sheppard had hired for 190 foot-long brass rods each. They all vanished the night after learning that they were expected to go into the territory of their dreaded enemies. Lapsley then took a month to go back westward and recruit seventeen brave men from another tribe for the trip.

Anticipating the hostilities they might encounter in the region between Kinshasa and Kinkunji, as well as the difficulty of obtaining canoes once they arrived, Lapsley and Sheppard decided after further consideration to use waterways for the entire trip. In December 1890 they and the men they had hired boarded the *Henry Reed*, the same Baptist steamer Lapsley had traveled on before, and headed up the mile-wide Congo. It towed a canoe for use on the Kwango that Sheppard had rented in exchange for a large quantity of hippo meat.

Steamboating was only a daytime activity on the Congo. Each evening the crew would gather dry wood, chop it into two-foot lengths, and store it on deck for the next day's run. Sheppard quickly learned that knowing how to communicate with natives along the river could prolong life. He was told about a captain who started down a path to a village in search of a food market. A native asked, "What do you want here?" Not understanding the common question used to discern friend or foe, the captain did not reply; whereupon he was shot through the head with an arrow.[56]

The steamer's destination was north of the Kasai, so the mission explorers disembarked at its mouth. They were left to paddle on their own up the largest tributary of the Congo, which had sources far to the southeast near the Zambezi River. Before starting out, they were able to purchase a large four-by-forty-foot second dugout canoe. With eagerness to find an appropriate environment for staking out a station, they headed up the Kasai on Christmas day. For a feast that evening, an eagle and a large red monkey were killed.[57]

The lower Kasai was especially dangerous at that time of year because it was the height of the rainy season, and paddling against the swift current was difficult. Lapsley wrote that he could feel the boat spring forward when the "Bishop" (Sheppard) assisted with the oars.[58] Later Sheppard took over as pilot of one canoe after a boatman continually steered it off course.[59]

For one day's relief they were permitted to lash their canoes alongside a passing steamer by bartering with food that Sheppard had taken from the river. On seeing the *Stanley* approaching, puffing like a train engine, they exchanged a ton of dried hippo meat for the privilege of hitching a ride to its next port. Sheppard relished his role as hunter, but he refused to kill game if it obviously destroyed family bonding. When he saw parent ducks with six ducklings paddling near him he lowered his gun because he could not bear to think of mother and offspring mutually bereft of one another.[60]

At Musyi, they waited for Lapsley to recover from one of his frequent bouts with malaria. While there, Queen Gankabi stepped into the canoe where he lay in an attempt to be of help. Sheppard later provided this description, "Her Majesty being nearly six feet high, having a stout form and an earnest look, constituted a good specimen of an African woman." Years earlier, Stanley had provided this word portrait:

> Without the slightest sign of timidity she steered her forty-five foot canoe alongside. . . . She brought her paddle inboard, and with her right arm to her waist, she examined us keenly. . . . Her attentive survey of "Bula Matadi" was with interest reciprocated. Excepting her hair and color she had nothing negroid about her. Draw a figure with . . . sturdy, square shoulder, substantial form, with an ample grass cloth about her; bare bust, bare feet and bare head, with no ornaments about her except a heavy copper wristlet, and you have a life-like picture of Gankabi.[61]

When Sheppard was shown the Queen's royal houses, he was alarmed by the human skulls that decorated them. Yet she warned the Americans that the people who lived further upriver were the fierce ones, and she invited them to stop and erect "God's house" in her town. Sheppard also came upon a witch doctor in the area who ground roots in his "laboratory." He and his patients drank their fill of palm wine while "he rang bells, played the banjo, sang, and talked loud like a preacher."[62]

Intense hostility was encountered from riverside villages as they went further up the Kasai. The oarsmen explained that the villagers feared that any white man was a devil who might kidnap them at night.

Since Leopold's agents had stolen men from the district for servitude in the Matadi area, the Congolese apprehensions over outsiders were well founded. Sheppard told of an anxious occasion when they attempted to set up camp:

> Villagers were up and under arms in a moment's notice. The war drum beat, the women screamed, and the whole town was in a terrible state of excitement. Guns, spears, bows and arrows were in the hands of the men, who were rushing in our direction. I stepped forward quickly and, picking up some beads and calico cloth, held them aloft and pleaded with the men not to shoot but let us land for the night. They brandished their spears, pointed their guns and called to us to leave at once or we would be killed. With all my pleading and offering of presents they would have nothing to do with us.[63]

To escape from the perilous situation, Sheppard had the oarsmen row across the wide Kasai to the other side. They ended up that evening on an island infested with hippos, and even campfires did not keep the snorting water horses far away. But those animals were not the main terror that night. Lapsley, who until midnight was very ill with a temperature of 106 degrees, wrote the next day:

> A big storm came last night, but Sheppard was equal to it. He ran here and there, always in the nick of time, and saved the canoes from being swept down to Banana. . . . Then he swung on to the guy rope just as its peg gave way and the tent was getting ready to fly over land to Kintamo.[64]

The dozens of hippos in their midst caused several of their crew to cry like babies from sheer fright. But the next day Sheppard frightened the beasts with the noise of his rifle and finished one off with a shot to the center of his forehead. As usual, beef was carved off the carcass and part of it was dehydrated over a slow fire. Villagers from across the river who had been so belligerent the day before, gathered like scavenger birds around a kill and became friendly when given cuts of meat.

At Boleke, near the confluence of the Kwango with the Kasai rivers, Lapsley observed other villagers:

> They were a little timid, but not ill disposed, afraid to invite us ashore, yet not at all desirous that we should leave. So we landed quietly and stood about, as unconcerned as could be. They crowded around us in a few minutes, but if we happened to look straight at any fellow, he would dodge behind somebody like a flash. Finally Sheppard, born trader, started buying wood and fish, and the ice was broken. Women crowded around with enough wood to build a small shanty, and fish for two meals, fresh, sweet and large, for a trifle.[65]

To help establish rapport, Sheppard brought on the trip a pet monkey that a friend had given him at Stanley Pool. He named it Tippo Tib, to mock the detested ruler of the region from which it came. The usual Congolese wariness of foreigners was dissipated by Sheppard's possession. Lapsley noted: "Tippo Tib was the object of unbounded amusement and delighted admiration. Every wise wink, and every time he stuffed another goober into the little pocket in his jaw . . . called down shouts and screams of laughter."[66] Sheppard added to this account:

> After an hour's pulling [rowing] we came to a very large village. The people were timid and had their spears, bows and arrows. As we pulled slowly to the landing the people rushed back from the beach, some of them running behind their houses; but with our many smiles and the tricks of our monkey, "Tippotib," who was playing at the bow of the first canoe, the villagers were attracted and came nearer.[67]

Lapsley modestly acknowledged that Sheppard's charm and color resulted in at least one of them being accepted: "The canoes begin to stream across and a great crowd surround our camp, showing much fondness for Sheppard, but rather afraid of the other 'mundele.'"[68] Lapsley called Sheppard "the arch-trader," and preferred that he do most of the buying.[69] When traders surrounded him, he bantered with them while effectively haggling to obtain some calabashes and strips of buffalo hide.[70] Lapsley also relied on his partner's resourcefulness and handiness in times of danger. There may have been a double reference when Lapsley sang Anna Laetitia Waring's "In Heavenly Love Abiding," which he learned in England:

> Wherever He may guide me, no want shall turn me back;
> My Shepherd is beside me, and nothing can I lack.
> His wisdom ever waketh, His eyes are never dim;
> He knows the way He taketh, and I will walk with Him.[71]

Sheppard's caution sometimes took priority over his boldness. One evening they found a place to camp by following an elephant path from the river to a clearing. Lapsley made this diary entry about what followed:

> A loud noise startled us and I heard the cook exclaim, "Nyau!" (elephant) Sheppard went to see about him, and presently we heard the crack of his rifle, and I hurried through the tangle of brush and broken trees to share the hunt. Heard Sheppard say in a queer voice (meant for me to hear and not the elephant), "Don't come; they are right here!" Lo and behold, he and Nkala were safe up a tree! an example which I followed quite promptly. He had a close shot, and had put

the Martini-Henri bullet into the elephant's ear. But when the brute seemed unconcerned about it, he did not try another until he had made sure his retreat. And the elephants went a little way off for awhile. . . . We heard the nyau before day, breaking down a tree in the woods not far from the tent. The woods here look as if a cyclone has been throwing the trees about.[72]

On a later occasion Sheppard found himself in the midst of a herd of elephants in a ravine. "They made a terrible noise which sounded like a thunderstorm," he said. Convinced that they were chasing him, he ran back to get his rifle from the man who was carrying it. Sheppard said:

> My man saw me coming, so he put out [in retreat] at full speed. . . . But when they were out of the ravine and on the plain, and could hear the cracking limbs and falling trees in the distance, we felt better, at least safer. After a good laugh and teasing each other about running away, we started down . . . to the village.[73]

Sheppard realized that he needed to be vigilant with respect to the hippos that were frequently nearby. He said, "We met many herds of hippos which would open their great jaws like barn doors, and follow our canoes, anxious to spill us out." One behemoth, he had been told, raised up under a canoe, tossed it like a toy, and then crushed the bones of one of the men who was thrown out.[74]

This six-week trip up the Kasai and its tributaries taught Lapsley and Sheppard much about Congo topography and the products of field, forest, and river. Sheppard found that shots from his rifle could continually supply meat, not only from hippos but from buffalos, monkeys, ducks, and other game. After exploring the lower Kwango, and then up the Kwilu River, they decided that there was no place along those waterways suitable for a mission station. Sheppard gave these reasons for their decision: "The country was too low and swampy, the villages small and far apart. They had no king, but were governed by small chiefs."[75]

On returning to Boleke at the mouth of the Kwango, Lapsley and Sheppard were dismayed. Earlier hundreds of the villagers had expressed friendliness and the tribal chief had offered them free land on which they could build. They had made a tentative arrangement with that chief for establishing a mission there if a more suitable site was not found upstream. But they found the people now resentful toward all white people because villages in the area had been burned by the "Van Kerckhoven Expedition."[76] In 1890, Leopold had sent out

Captain Guillaume Van Kerckhoven with fourteen officers from Belgium to raid for ivory. Commanding five hundred native soldiers who were armed with rifles, they succeeded in capturing great quantities of tusks. They also left a trail of devastation at settlements along the main rivers of the Congo Free State.[77]

Lapsley quickly made clear that he did not work for Leopold. He recorded how he dealt with the Boleke villagers:

> I took this chance to explain that our business was not to trade, but to teach the will of their King and ours, the God who made us both; that we teach that God forbids men to kill, steal, and commit adultery; and that our teaching is the best pledge that we will be good neighbors.[78]

Lapsley told how Leopold's agents were making it difficult for a white man with a different purpose to function, "I found many of them afraid that I was a State man, come to tie somebody up; but I managed to scatter the news that missionaries had come to teach them about God and heaven." Again: "There had been a fight between the town . . . and some State people in a small steamer. . . . The quarrel was because the steamer took the people's wood without buying it. . . . We assured them that we were not Bula Matadi, that we would not hurt them." Lapsley told of another clash precipitated by State officers who carried off from Musyi even Queen Gankabi's two sons for forced labor on the lower Congo.[79] Disappointed but wiser, the missionaries rowed speedily down the Congo to Kinshasa.

The Americans now boldly resolved to head for an even remoter area, more than twice the distance of their previous steamboat trip. The Belgian Trading Company had recently established several new stations on the upper Kasai that would guarantee, by means of their steamer, some connection with the outside world. They prepared for their "momentous departure" with a biblical precedent in mind: "We go like Abraham, 'Not knowing whither we go.'. . . It seems to have been ordered by Providence that we should come at the very instant the Kassai is being opened."[80] Identifying with all of Africa a psalmist's prophecy pertaining to a country on that continent, Sheppard hoped that "Ethiopia shall soon stretch out her hands unto God."[81]

Sheppard and Lapsley arranged to travel aboard the *Florida*, a flat-bottomed sternwheeler that operated between trading posts in the Congo basin. Henry Sanford had named the boat for his previous business venture in Florida. He put it into service in 1887 when he established the Sanford Exploring Expedition, the first trading company on the vast upper Congo. English reformer Henry Fox Bourne singled out Sanford as "the pioneer of the direct trade with the natives of the interior in ivory and rubber which has been attended by such appalling mischief."[82] Before his Congo company was absorbed by the Belgian Trading Company in 1888, 35,000 pounds of ivory and 61,000 pounds of rubber had been exported. Conrad had been assigned to command the Florida, beginning in late 1890, and would have taken Sheppard and Lapsley to the Kasai had he not returned to Europe after being debilitated by dysentery.[83]

The Belgian captain of the *Florida* was willing to take only half the missionaries' baggage because of limited cargo space. Moreover, the small steamer lacked the power to tow the canoe that had been purchased for the Kwango expedition. They had hoped to have it for use after reaching Luebo, the head of steamer navigation on the Lulua River tributary of the Kasai. Their tentative judgment was that the best mission site would be near the junction of the Sankuru and the Kasai rivers, which they would pass on the way to Luebo. That was the nearest river point to the great Kuba kingdom, which was centered on high ground far inland between the large rivers. Also, one of Leopold's stations was located at the confluence of those rivers. Taking their large canoe to Luebo would have made it easier to go downstream with their supplies and settle at the most promising site they had found on the way upstream.[84]

Frustration over having to be at the mercy of steamers that were primarily for their owners' transportation needs caused the Presbyterians to hope for possessing someday a steamboat similar to the Baptists'. The fourteen-ton *Henry Reed* had been their lifeline to the upper Congo since 1884. Its 160 plates were riveted together at Stanley Pool after porters carried the parts up from Matadi.[85] On March 10, 1891, the eve of embarking from Kinshasa, Lapsley wrote his father, "I think we shall suffer from delays, etc., until we do our own transport with a Presbyterian Mission steamer."[86] That communication was eventually to bear fruit because the letters and other reports of missionaries were published in a monthly journal called *The Missionary*, which kept southern Presbyterians well informed about its global work.

Judge Lapsley shared the letter containing his son's transportation dream. The idea of financing a steamer for the APCM caught the imagination of a Mrs. Sampson in Selma, Alabama. After she conveyed her enthusiasm for the project to her Sunday school class, one pupil sent a letter to the editor of the *Christian Observer* containing this appeal: "Our teacher says the missionary was once a little barefooted boy like we are and played in the very playground we play in. . . . He writes home that he does not see how his work can succeed without a boat. . . . We ask every . . . Christian in the United States to give at least one cent to God to help get this boat." There was a widespread response when the letter was published in December 1891.[87] Many American children first learned of the Congo as they gave their pennies to support this effort. Someone thought up this promotional device, "Every child, or every class in the Sunday School that sends $1.00 for the Congo Boat will receive a certificate and hold a share in the steamboat."[88] In a year, children succeeded in raising the $10,000 that would cover the estimated cost of the vessel, but a decade was to pass before the Presbyterian steamer was launched.

The *Florida* was so crowded that Sheppard and Lapsley had to sleep on the benches beside the dining room table. Above them, on the only other deck, was a small pilot house and a chicken coop.[89] At a State post where the *Florida* stopped for supplies, Sheppard took a canoe to investigate a large town where Van Kerckhoven's raiders had been. He found its buildings destroyed and the place deserted, similar to the devastation by that Belgian unit that he had heard about on his earlier canoe trip.[90]

The natural vistas seen by the Americans along the Congo must have resembled those that Conrad wrote about in his novel:

> Going up that river was like travelling back to the earliest beginnings of the world, when vegetation rioted on the earth and the big trees were kings. An empty stream, a great silence, an impenetrable forest. The air was warm, thick, heavy, sluggish. . . . The broadening waters flowed through a mob of wooded islands; you lost your way on that river as you would in a desert, and butted all day long against shoals, trying to find the channel.[91]

One perilous happening on the voyage was occasioned by a storm that caused big waves to break over the deck. "Lightning licked out red tongues, like a mad snake," Lapsley recorded; "then the waves began to pitch the boat from side to side and up and down, and I fully expected her to go down."[92] Sheppard also wrote about what happened to the little craft:

> The captain called to me and asked if he should stop, but I answered quickly, "No, captain, never; run her full speed on the shallow bank." By so doing she stuck fast in the sand while the men quickly (and I assisted them) made the chain fast around a near tree. . . . When the storm had passed all hands, with the engines going full speed astern, pushed her off and we continued our journey.[93]

The next day they reached the Kasai mouth, where there was a relentless rush of water. Sheppard described the danger that followed:

> At its mouth the Kasai is only about 150 yards across, with a great wall of rocks on either side. The fire bars of the boiler had been complained of by the engineer, who was unable to get up sufficient steam. The captain called me to the wheel house and asked that I take the wheel while he directed the course. I did so with pleasure. We steamed off, turned the nose of the steamer around the sharp point and into the strong current of the Kasai. . . . The Florida did her best, but the current was too strong. She quivered under the strain and was forced backward to the point from which she had started. Again we tried, but with the same result. The whirlpools and strong current seemed too much for the *Florida*'s strength. . . . The engineer was doing his best at firing. The captain again rang for full speed; we steamed for five hours, making only a half mile. While the steamer was under such an awful strain, the rudder chain snapped and there we were in that awful current between a hill of stones and no rudder chain. I called out to the captain to keep her going, and then ran back to the stern of the boat, got hold of the iron bar that governs the rudder, and as the captain signalled to me with his hand, guided her safely to a sand spot just between two enormous boulders.[94]

At another time Sheppard went down the chain to where the anchor had snagged a tree root fifteen feet below the surface in order to release the tangled anchor.[95]

Due to delays caused by repairs, the food provisions aboard were nearly exhausted. When Sheppard went out in a canoe to hunt, he returned with ducks given him by a native to whom he had given a strip of hippo meat on his earlier trip up the river. Another day a large reptile was killed on the bank, which provided "crocodile cutlets."[96] At some villages where the missionaries had previously been able to trade for supplies, fear that all white men were out to steal provisions and capture Africans for slave labor caused the inhabitants to vanish into the woods.

On the ninth day into the Kasai, they encountered the treacherous Swinburne rapids. Sheppard's diary contains this entry:

> We struck the swiftly running current. The ship staggered, careened to one side, and tried it again. The many whirlpools shifted her from side to side. A number of times the water ran over the deck. The whole pass is a succession of stony reefs. There was a death-like quietness with both crew and passengers. Only the heart throbs of the engine under her great strain and struggle could be heard. We breathed a sigh of relief when we looked back and saw the rapids running wild in the distance.[97]

The perils, challenges, and hardships that Lapsley and Sheppard encountered even before their mission work began parallel those recounted by the apostle Paul from his experiences: "Frequently near death, . . . in danger from rivers, . . . in peril in the wilderness, . . . often exhausted without food."[98] Sheppard was grateful to God for being delivered from "a watery grave" when "the steamer came near capsizing, caused by strong currents and whirlpools" on four different occasions.[99] His role on board the *Florida* was somewhat like that of Paul on his voyage to Italy. Although Paul was a passenger, his previous perils at sea enabled him to offer sound advice for saving the ship and lives aboard.[100] However, the apostle's counsel was mostly rejected and a shipwreck followed.

Toward the end of the voyage, Sheppard recorded these observations about the fauna:

> We saw scores of large black monkeys leaping from tree to tree, and droves of parrots flying in the air as thick as blackbirds. . . . On both banks of the river there is a dense forest of mahogany, ebony, iron wood, evergreens and palms. The natives came alongside our steamer today and sold to the captain and crew about fifty pounds of fresh fish and eels. We have seen their seines a hundred feet long. They drag for the fish between the sand banks. These fish are dried for future use. The streams all abound with splendid fish. . . . There are plenty of elephant, buffalo and antelope; their tracks and trails are all along the river bank. In this dense and impenetrable forest there must be everything imaginable.[101]

Sheppard's journal shows that the people and their culture fascinated him even more than the wild life:

> The steamer tied up early near a village where houses are different from others we have seen. They are made of bamboo about nine feet high. The door is reached by a ladder, which at night is pulled inside and the door shut so they are safe from leopards. . . . The people here wear copper rings on their wrists and necks, so we believe there must be a copper mine somewhere back in the hills. Speaking of engagement rings, we have seen them weighing thirty pounds on the necks of the women. . . . We went to the village a half mile away into the jungle and found it to be large and walled in. The only entrance was by a small trap-door. . . . The people crowded around Mr. Lapsley and asked to see his hands. . . . They laughed heartily. . . . They had never seen a white man before.[102]

After a month of misadventures, the battered *Florida* entered the Lulua River and continued eastward when the Kasai turned southward (see map). The next day they arrived at Luebo in the heart of the Congo Free State. The Belgian trading post there had been established in 1885 by physician Ludwig Wolf, a member of Major Hermann Wissmann's party of Germans who explored the Kasai basin.[103] Wolf discovered the cataracts at the head of navigation on the Kasai River and named them Wissmann Falls. The post at Luebo, near the mouth of the small Luebo River and on the south bank of the Lulua, became the site of the State-operated Belgian Trading Company. It was placed there mainly for collecting tusks of ivory and balls of rubber from tribes in the area. Before the Americans arrived, the foreign population consisted of four Europeans—two traders and two government officers. Mr. Engeringh, the Belgian commissioner of the Kasai district with headquarters in Lulua-aburg (now Kananga), was in Luebo at the time the *Florida* arrived. He encouraged the Presbyterians to settle on the north bank of the Lulua, across from the State station. This advice was accepted because the center of the Kuba confederation of tribes was on that same side. Also, at a native village a short distance away regional languages could be learned and supplies could be purchased. Engeringh immediately gave his approval to an application for land on which the APCM would be located. Later, in 1891, the Scheut Fathers from Belgium began a Catholic mission further upstream on the Lulua at Luluaburg.

SETTLING AT LUEBO

Sheppard and Lapsley were relieved to find a promising place to establish the APCM mission soon after arriving in the Lulua area of Kasai. That province was one of the least explored of the twelve districts of the Congo Free State. The Kuba people in the region especially interested them because of "their apparent superiority in physique, manners, dress, and dialect."[104] Agreeing with their selection, the Nashville-based Foreign Missions Committee reported to the PCUS: "There are no finer people in the whole Congo Valley than those found between the Sankura and Lulua rivers. Their cloth, vessels, and weapons are said to be simply wonderful for beauty of design and finish."[105]

Lapsley clearly recognized the pivotal importance of the Luebo site: "It is the centre of influence from which the lines of trade radiate."[106] The missionaries realized that several major tribes could be contacted at Luebo. The Kubas were continually passing through because they ruled over the tribes surrounding Luebo. In addition to the Kete people that lived in the Luebo area, the Bena Lulua and the Luba were centered upstream on the Lulua River. Sheppard estimated that nearly two million people lived in the Kasai,[107] making it a comparatively well populated region. It was about the size of Virginia, his home state.

This region of the Kasai also fulfilled the Committee's instruction to seek out an area less susceptible to disease. It was about fifteen hundred feet above sea level and had an average daily temperature of seventy-five degrees Fahrenheit year-round. Sheppard gave this explanation of the weather: "A year was divided into two general seasons, the rainy (eight moons), the dry (four moons); though even in the rainy season it doesn't rain every day and very seldom all day at any time; and in the dry season there is an occasional refreshing shower."[108] The coolness at night in unheated housing was actually more uncomfortable than the daytime heat. Sheppard found only a few mosquitos there and no tsetse flies, the carrier of the deadly sleeping sickness.[109] Robert Bedinger, writing in 1920, claimed that "typhoid fever, yellow fever, scarlet fever, bubonic plague, and pellagra have not reached Kasai."[110] Other positive factors were abundant food and great expanses of savanna grassland in a region that receives about sixty inches of rainfall annually.

Lapsley and Sheppard did find a danger near their landing place on the river, where they went to bathe as well as to play leap frog and run races on the sand. On one occasion a good native swimmer who was with them disappeared under the water and a thorough search did not discover his body. "Could a crocodile have taken him off so quickly?" Sheppard wondered.[111]

Shortly after arriving, the Americans went to the nearby Kete village of Bena Kasenga and spoke to the elders through an interpreter. As it was the first time these Congolese had seen missionaries, this exchange followed: "They asked, 'Will you trade in ivory or rubber?' We said, 'No, we do not wish to trade; our work is to teach about God.' They laughed and thought that was a strange business."[112]

When the *Florida* left Luebo, the missionaries realized that many months would pass before the boat would call again with supplies and mail. On returning to Stanley Pool it carried tusks, some weighing about a hundred pounds each, and more than ten tons of rubber. With no electrical telegraph system or through roads in the Congo, steamers were the only link with the outside world. They operated irregularly and only from October to May when the water level was high enough for navigation in the shallow Lulua tributary of the Kasai. Pondering this isolation, Sheppard expressed trepidation and courage, "At this point we are 1,200 miles from the coast and 800 miles from the nearest doctor or drug store, but we were comforted by these words, 'Lo, I am with you always.'"[113]

In spite of Jesus' assurance to evangelists, forlornness was conveyed in Sheppard's record of the first day at the APCM:

> We pitched our tent in an open space between the forest on the north side of the Lulua River. The natives from a nearby town came swarming around to see the faces of the newcomers. They were well armed with bows, arrows, and spears, but we put on our broadest and best smiles. . . . The darkness of the night added fresh fears. We could hear the howling of the jackals in the jungle and the hooting of the owls. Mr. Lapsley on his couch was sobbing audibly and so was I. So far from home, with thousands of people and yet alone, for not a word of their dialect could we speak. About five o'clock in the morning how our hearts were cheered when we heard the chickens in the town crowing. We laughed heartily and said, "Well, there is one language we understand, for the roosters crow in the same language as our American roosters."[114]

Even so, Sheppard discovered that some of the other domestic animals did not speak the same "language" as their American cousins. The dogs, raised for human food, howled but did not bark and the cows did not low.[115] In the Sheppard archives at Montreat is a bell for tying on a dog. The distinctive sound of each bell identified the location of each dog.[116]

Sheppard indicated that much of their early months was spent in learning the local culture:

> We made daily visits to the village, mingling with the people, learning their language and curious customs. They all wore their native cloth ranging from the waist to their knees. They were given to hearty laughter, joking, playing games, and running races. Many of them cultivated the ground, raising manioc, peas, beans and tobacco, and others spent their time hunting and fishing. Every night there was a dance held in the big square in the center of the town. The noise from their tom-toms, ivory horns, and singing filled the air until midnight.[117]

Writing with considerable anthropological discernment, Sheppard often transcended his Christian perspective. For example, his descriptions of the Teke rest day does not include his personal view of ancestral spirits:

> Every fourth day no one on account of the spirits went a long journey, hunted, fished or worked in his fields. The day was spent sweeping around their houses, mending their nets, making mats, weaving cloth,

and holding court. Court was held in the square of the town under a large shed. The people had their judges, jurors, lawyers and officers of the town, but no written laws, and all evildoers were punished by fines. A man that was found guilty of murder was forced to hang himself.[118]

Sheppard's comment on an alleged weather controller was also more descriptive than judgmental: "We saw a rain-maker . . . dressed up in leopard skins and his hair filled with hawk feathers, and in his hand were a buffalo tail and a sprig of a tree. This wild man claimed that he could bring rain, stop rain, quiet storms, and protect the people from lightning."[119]

Some of the Kete had never seen a white man before and were highly amused at Lapsley's appearance. They wondered if the same strange color extended from head to feet. Often he satisfied their curiosity by pulling off his socks, which they called bags. When the Africans handled the pink and tender exhibition, ticklish Lapsley joined with his admirers in the hilarity.[120] Sheppard told how Lapsley's mysterious pocket watch also drew a crowd:

> The back was opened and they saw a little wheel, a forward and backward movement. They then asked us to show them the little men down inside who do the pushing. Mr. Lapsley tried to explain, but it was useless. . . . With the Bakete [the prefix "Ba," a plural, meaning "people of," is usually omitted by contemporary scholars] even the sun didn't go of itself, but there were great big strong men who caught it as it descended, put it into a great canoe, and pulled it across the deep waters, and early every morning with their combined strength started it again on its journey.[121]

The Congolese regarded matches as another bit of foreign magic. Sheppard stated: "Matches were a wonderful fire producer. I have many times bought a chicken for a box of matches. It takes about two minutes to get fire out of two dried sticks in the native way, but with one stroke of a match on the box you have fire. They were a great novelty to the people."[122]

Lapsley and Sheppard used their bargaining skills to purchase nine acres from the Kete in exchange for twelve yards of cloth, one-sixth of what was asked. They also bought palm oil and a mortar for pounding cassava roots into flour. Sheppard told of another transaction:

> Our tent was so small and hot that we decided to buy two native bamboo houses. They were built of poles, the sides of large bamboo mats, roofed with long palm leaves sewn together and put on overlapping very much as shingles. These houses resemble very much tiny cottages

eleven feet square and nine feet high. The owner of the house started with a very high price and we with a very low bid. He came down and we advanced in our offer. Soon we agreed on a price, a straw was picked up by the owner and handed to us. . . . The straw was broken between our fingers, he spat on his end of the straw and threw it over his shoulder and told us to do the same with the end we had. The bargain thereby was sealed. We counted out our native money, cowrie shells, and paid for the house. . . . Their houses are built in sections and we soon had them taken down and moved on our land and reconstructed. We bought and planted palms, bananas and plantain trees, and in front of our houses had the way nicely swept. In the pleasant evening we would take our promenade up and down this beautiful walk.[123]

Describing the way he and Lapsley went about accommodating their eating habits to the environment, Sheppard wrote: "With the help of the natives we began to clear the forest, take up the stumps, and clean up generally. A chicken, parrot and monkey house was soon built, for . . . they were all good for food."[124] There were also other foods that the missionaries learned to like. Sheppard told about "delicious" crickets: "The cricket was four times as large as the American one and sang four times as loud and long. They live in the ground and come out at night to cut and eat grass, and the natives, with torches, capture and roast them for food."[125] Sheppard also reported on other special treats:

Every season brings its blessings. In November there are millions of caterpillars; these are gathered, dried and put up for food. . . . Green grasshoppers are put in scalding water, dried in the sun and eaten after harvest. July, flying white ants. At about five o'clock every evening . . . these ants pour out of holes in the ground. . . . Every man, woman, child, chicken, animal, and bird, and sometimes a missionary, sits over these holes and catches and eats them by the handfuls, alive and raw. They have the taste of condensed milk.[126]

The missionaries joined the Congolese in eating a root vegetable called manioc or cassava. That main carbohydrate of their diet was introduced along with corn by the Portuguese from South America. The staple grows like a shrub; the tubers from one plant produce many pounds of starchy food each year and its leaves provide a green salad. This easily cultivated plant may be the best contribution of colonialism to Africa!

Sheppard preceded Lapsley in moving from tent to cottage, but he found that did not immediately prove advantageous. The day after he moved in, ferocious black ants attacked. Lapsley made this diary entry:

Midnight—a great commotion. Sheppard was moving about very rapidly, and even dancing, and addressing the people [several camp attendants] in impassioned tones. On inquiry, I learned that a column of driver ants had entered his house and taken possession. They even came under his blankets and covered him; hence his animation. They happened to be marching by and smelt the palm oil inside. We made various reconnaissances with torches and candles, found many columns pouring across the open space. . . . One line had reached my tent door just as I got up. A fire stopped them. I looked around and met another body of them making for the back of the tent, where there was a greasy spot, black with them. . . . Sheppard slept in the moonlight till day. . . . We found the columns condensed to two heavy lines, mostly making for home again, loaded with little grasshoppers, crickets, and such small game, by the thousand—a first rate entomological collection. . . . Where the column turned back on itself once, I watched it, a foot wide, almost solid, shoulder to shoulder, close as they could get, and marching quickly as they do, I guess they must pass at the rate of a million in about four minutes.[127]

Sheppard's explanation of his predicament contained none of Lapsley's detachment:

I was alarmed by a band of big, broad-headed, determined driver ants. . . . There were millions. They were in my head, my eyes, my nose, and pulling at my toes. When I found it was not a dream, I didn't tarry long. . . . In an incredible short space of time they can kill any goat, chicken, duck, hog or dog on the place. In a few hours there is not a rat, mouse, snake, centipede, spider or scorpion in your house, as they are chased, killed and carried away. . . . We were told by the natives that when there are triplets born in a family it is considered very bad luck, so one of the babies is taken by the witch doctor and put into a deep hole where these ants live and the child is soon scented by them and eaten. We scraped the acquaintance of these soldier ants by being severely bitten and stung. They are near the size of a wasp and use both ends with splendid effect.[128]

Those insects are also called soldier ants because they march in single file and, as I found, attack even in daylight. During my visit to Luebo, a horde crawled up my legs and bit off morsels of flesh to the amusement of the group standing around. In spite of the mixed company, I quickly stripped off most of my clothes before launching a counterattack.

Black ants, or soldier ants, less than an inch long, can even torment Africa's largest animal: "The elephant is so annoyed by their getting into his trunk that he lashes his trunk against a tree in his agony until blood streams from his nostrils."[129]

Termites, mistakenly referred to as "white ants," are another very troublesome insect that were continually encountered. Unlike the soldier ants, these pests are not carnivorous. Smaller than soldier ants, they devour far more forest flora than do the elephants. Also they consume artifacts and demolish homes. Sheppard recalled: "All of Mr. Lapsley's shoes had been eaten up by the white ants and worn out. He wore a pair of moccasins, made by his native boy from goatskin, and his best suit was his pajamas! But he was one of the happiest men in all the wide world."[130] Lapsley wrote: "The white ants infest the fresh, damp earth of my house. They crawled up the bedpost and chopped a hole in my mattress before morning big as my hand." After replacing parts of the damaged bed frame, he commented, "I have made a big fire around my bed-post tonight, and feel quite secure until morning."[131] Recognizing the highly flammable structure of his cottage, one wonders how his anxiety could have been lowered by the blaze!

A lamp was soon invented to chase off nocturnal intruders—ants, termites, scorpions, and snakes—as well as to provide light. Sheppard explained, "Mr. Lapsley tore off a strip from one of his garments, twisted it up into a thick string, placed it in an empty corned beef tin, filled the tin with native palm oil and lighted the taper, and so we had the first artificial light." This mode of interior lighting became standard for years to come. Even so, "shake before using" became a household rule, Sheppard said, with regard to towels and clothing![132]

The industriousness and pride of the people in the Luebo area prompted Lapsley to note:

> Busy folks. Very few without something to do. But the principal business outside of [manioc] bread-making . . . is the manufacture of plain grass cloth. It is not made of grass at all, but of the inner strips of the leaves of a small, dark palm. . . . I saw the manufacture in all its stages—boys stripping off the outside of the leaf blade, and leaving the delicate green ribbons within, and tying them into hanks like yarn. Men were separating it, threading the loom with the warp; and then came the clack of the simple, but complete weaving machine, the simple, silent passage of the long polished stick which does duty as shuttle, and thus the usual everyday waist or loin cloth is finished. But the women pound a few choice pieces in a mortar with flour of maize or manioc till it is soft and satiny to the feel. These are dyed and worn on special occasions. . . . I like the black folks very much. They are not stuck up, though they are ready to stand up for themselves, and they like much better to keep on good terms. They are very funny and lively, and make good company. They keep pretty clean, especially those that live by the waterside, who have skins like velvet, soft and smooth. They all believe in sweeping their yards and houses in the town. If any fellow is lazy about it, they call a town meeting, and make him pay the price of five chickens or a goat, and the rest have a feast at his expense, which make them all careful.[133]

Lapsley gave a fuller description of the Luebo people in a letter to
Robert Whyte:

> Men and women divide the work (unequally), the women finding the
> bread, of which cassava and millet are the main bases. They also flock
> to the river for fish, etc., in season. Where there is clay the women
> made the earthenware. The men divide among them the trade of cloth
> or mat-making, making the palm wine, hunting, and each man builds
> the house that shelters himself and family. They are very genial and
> good humored, as you know, and lying, stealing, and impurity are con-
> sidered disgraceful, but are universal, almost. They have an idea of
> God, the creator and preserver of all things, and a tradition that a
> closer acquaintance with him once existed.[134]

While trying to adjust to their new environment, the missionaries
relied on body language and pantomime for communicating. Lapsley
noted that Sheppard "is powerful on signs."[135] To improve on their
rudimentary vocabulary, each day they took notebooks into the adjacent Teke village to record the oral languages of upper Kasai. No
record had previously been made of them, so they learned words by
pointing to objects and asking for names. For example, "muntu" was
the response when a person was singled out, and "bantu" when more
than one was pointed to. Sheppard commented on this laborious
process: "After some months we had thus collected subjects, preposi-
tions, pronouns, verbs, etc."[136]

Sheppard noted that the Kete "had never seen a book, nor a piece of
paper of any description."[137] They marveled at the little marks the missionaries made with hand movements and at being told that thoughts
were being put there for preservation. When Lapsley sent a note to
Sheppard to pay a certain number of cowries to a seller, they were so
dumbfounded by the paper-transmitted communication that they
became eager to learn this new magic.[138]

Lapsley and Sheppard attempted to replicate the three-pronged
emphasis of Jesus' ministry: teaching, preaching, and healing. They
focused on teaching young people, realizing that they were more likely
to be receptive, and had longer lives ahead. To teach reading and writing, a smooth place was cleared on the ground for printing the alpha-
bet with a stick. "They showed marked signs of intelligence," Sheppard
observed, "and soon mastered their A, B, C's."[139]

Most of the students were redeemed Luba slaves who had been purchased back by the missionaries for several dozen bandannas each.
Usually they had been thrust into slavery by an intertribal conflict that

made them prisoners of war. The Christian message of liberation was especially significant to those who had been forced into servitude, and the original biblical meaning of "redemption" became apparent. Before the term became a theological metaphor, pertaining to rescuing individuals from perdition and to spiritual salvation, it referred to the release of the Hebrews from bondage in Africa during the time of Moses. Lapsley recorded the indentured servant policy that was related to redemption:

> The State forbids slave-holding, but has a provision whereby persons may ransom slaves, who then come under the control, "guardianship," of the ransomer for seven years; then the slave is finally at liberty. These liberes must be registered as such before the commissaire du district.[140]

The ransomed slaves at the APCM were not kept in legal servitude for any period of time.[141] The adults were paid wages along with food rations, and the children tended to marry within their new community. Before long, Luebo became a miniature Liberia, a colony of the emancipated. The redeemer might face unintended consequences because the process assumed the acceptance of buying and selling humans. Sellers might be spurred by the payment to seek more ransom by capturing more people. Tshiluba was the dialect of the Luba ex-slaves and was spoken more widely in the Luebo area than Tshikete, so the missionaries began to learn it.

Lapsley obtained one pupil from a cannibal chief who was leading a forced march. When the caravan was passing near Luebo, he noticed the slave gang. A continuous rope had been knotted around the marchers' necks to keep them within a few feet of the next in line. Lapsley was horrified to learn that the slavers had killed one of their captives and even her young daughter had helped to eat her flesh. He asked the chief for an explanation and was told that it was customary to eat those whose walking ability had failed. Lapsley then successfully bargained to exchange some foreign cloth for the orphaned girl named N'Tumba.[142]

Sheppard told how he and Lapsley sat beneath a palm tree daily to teach gospel stories to any who might be interested. One story about Jesus stimulated a girl to ask, "What is his Father's name?" Lapsley answered, "Here you call him Nzambi, the Great Spirit." Further questions, such as "Where is his native village?" produced more explanation.[143] That girl could have been N'Tumba. Decades later Sheppard published a children's story about how an ex-slave girl became an evangelist.

Gospel preaching was the second emphasis of the missionaries. Sheppard was encouraged when there was "no shouting, but an intelligent interest shown by looking and listening from start to finish."[144] To those fearful of divine powers, his assurance that God is love was indeed good news. From a study of several hundred traditional African tribes, Ugandan professor John Mbiti concludes: "There are practically no direct sayings that God loves. This is something reflected also in the daily lives of African peoples, in which it is rare to hear people talking about love."[145] After a sermon by Lapsley on God's love, a woman named Malemba, the leader of the town dances, said, "If we had known God loved us, we would have been singing to him." In the bedtime devotions that night, Lapsley prayed, "We thank thee, heavenly Father, for the first evidence of thy blessing." Years later Malemba became a Christian leader at Luebo.[146]

Lapsley would probably have expected Malemba's dancing to stop when she became a Christian. While he appreciated some African music, his response to dancing differed from his partner. Sheppard's delight in the art is displayed in his telling about "break-down" dancing at the birth of a child and in his description of dancing in the open square when Xilanc tribal musicians came to a village. He exclaimed, "Such jumping, twisting and cake-walking!"[147] He approvingly wrote: "The moon, large and beautiful red, rose in a little while. The townspeople brought out their tom-toms and ivory horns to sing and dance in the open."[148] But when Lapsley watched hundreds of women dancers at Kasenga, he evaluated them as "lascivious in intention and effect, as are the songs to which they keep time." He lamented that children who imitate "the immodest gestures" that are "often frantically obscene" will not be able to have a pure mind. Kete dancers show, Lapsley claimed, "a disgusting and saddening exhibition of their degradation."[149] He may here display the nineteenth-century aberration that caused white Americans to believe that a praying knee and a dancing leg were not part of the same body. In her study of dance in that period, Margaret Fisk Taylor generalizes: "All conventional Protestant Christians came to assume that religious dancing might be done by 'primitive savages' or 'benighted pagans,' but never—absolutely never—by Christians."[150] Sheppard's outlook in this regard was more in accord with that of the Hebrew culture, which sanctioned dancing.[151] By integrating the sacred and the secular, he saw humans as spirited bodies.

Since music is basic to African cultures, the Congolese were more impressed by song than by sermon. Lapsley admitted: "I managed to get a small and somewhat interested audience to listen to a summary of gospel truth. They took more kindly to my singing."[152] Illiterate people tend to develop phenomenal memories, and the Congolese quickly learned lyrics by heart. They especially loved to sing with Lapsley "We're Marcing to Zion," a hymn of Isaac Watts that he had translated.[153]

Much of the transmission of religion is through practical expression rather than through formal preaching. This is well illustrated by one of Sheppard's recollections:

> One morning as Mr. Lapsley's door blew open a native saw a strange sight. It was Mr. Lapsley on his knees by his couch with his face in his Bible praying. The native was anxious to know of me what it all meant, and so I had the pleasure of explaining to him that Mr. Lapsley, their friend, was talking to the Great King above, about them. The native was so pleased he ran back to the town and told it to the people.[154]

Healing was the third prong of the ministry of Sheppard and Lapsley. Finding many people suffering from various diseases, they were distressed to find reliance on some ineffective remedies. For example, parents of a very sick child called in a witch doctor to provide treatment. It consisted of wringing a chicken's neck and dripping blood on a fetish and on the child's body. Presuming that even without special training he could improve on some of the witch doctors' prescriptions, Lapsley administered medicines he had for common sicknesses. The people quickly learned that his therapy was often more effective than traditional medicine. Although he did not charge for medical services, many expressed their appreciation with food gifts. Lapsley was especially pleased when he was compensated with a string of perch by a laughing girl whom he had cured.[155] On another occasion, he noted: "There were nearly twenty sores this morning, some twice the size of a silver dollar. I find a solid satisfaction in easing somewhat their pains—something accomplished!"[156]

In a letter home, Lapsley wrote:

> You will be a bit surprised to learn that I have become something of a doctor. How, I don't know, unless by having first to take a good deal of physic [medicine] from others, and then learning to dose myself and Sheppard. On the steamer up, I had four patients (a dozen counting the black folks) who sang my praises on my arrival here, and helped to make us welcome neighbors. . . . I began to take a little medicine to the town, and now I have many cases a day, and they have all got well. . . . They have a song in my honor like this: "Mutomba Njila [path-finder] gives us medicine. Makes us see health." It is always a good means of interesting them in the "Balm of Gilead."[157]

Out of necessity both American missionaries had acquired simple medical skills from textbooks and from observing Dr. Sims's treatment of tropical diseases. Subsequently, when on a steamer run by the government, Sheppard was appointed the ship's doctor by the captain. He was kept busy taking care of the wounded when a fight broke out between Europeans and native workmen.[158] One medication Sheppard dispensed was "Livingstone Rousers" that appeared to be effective.[159] In any case it probably did no harm, unlike the ground-up yellow jackets that witch doctors placed in the eyes and nostrils of people with sore eyes or bad colds.[160]

After getting established in Luebo, one missionary remained at the station while the other traveled with native assistants. They were interested in learning about the geography and culture of Kasai as well as in communicating the gospel. After a two-month trip south of Luebo as far as Wissmann Falls, Sheppard reported:

> A lake was discovered; also new streams, and some large game was killed. We made friends and treaties with chiefs, and told the people that at some future day we would send them teachers. We saw native cows for the first time. At one of the markets . . . the people were cutting up a twenty-five foot boa-constrictor into round roasts for sale. . . . I found the country to be rolling land and alluvial soil thickly populated with good, industrious people.[161]

With some hyperbole, Sheppard asserted: "Buzzards are unknown, for the natives eat everything that dies, from a snake to an elephant. There are no carcasses except human, and in some parts of the country, even these are eaten."[162] He also put this fish story in a letter: "Coming upriver I caught a catfish weighing sixty-five pounds. You could put a kid down his throat."[163] After seeing Congolese catch a large one of that species, he commented: "The natives never fish with a pole. They bait the hook, throw in the line, and tie it to their big toe."[164]

Some photos in Sheppard's album show him hunting and fishing with the Congolese. In one snapshot he is with a hunting party that is carrying an antelope. Another shows admirers gathered around as he stands with his rifle over a slain python that had swallowed a goat. Still another shows him proudly holding up a larger catfish than he could ever have caught in Virginia. He may have snagged it with a hook and line or he may have used a seine, which was the usual native method. In addition to bringing in food for the APCM, Sheppard was developing camaraderie with those who engaged in similar activities for their tribe.

Lapsley then took an extensive journey to investigate the country and people to the southeast, going as far as Luluaburg. One purpose of the trip was to find construction workers from a wider area, because the Kete lacked interest in such. He saw many Luba and Lulua people who wore only monkey skins and lived in bark-walled huts with conically shaped roofs. In each village he sang and told the story of Jesus, which the people found strange. Yet at place after place they invited him to make his home with them and teach them more about his God. Inhabitants of two villages were surprised to see a different kind of white man, one who was not threatening and who was accompanied by well-behaved men. Lapsley explained that his divine King liked blacks as well as whites and so he also wanted to be friendly.[165] He became something of a Pied Piper: "All along the route natives who had fallen in love with him joined the caravan. In many cases men with their wives, children, goats, sheep, and all their belongings followed him to Luebo."[166] These were the vanguard of the thousands of Lubas who would migrate to Luebo.

Since the Lubas were downtrodden by other Kasai tribes, they were more open to the ways of people from other countries who accepted them with respect. Phillips Verner, a member of the APCM a few years later, provided this description: "The Baluba are by far the most numerous people in all this country, and they are universally the objects of slave raids. They are a simple, laboring, inoffensive people, very susceptible to Gospel influence, and the white man's best friends."[167]

Sheppard rejoiced when his partner returned, but was saddened to see the ravages of the long trip. He wrote:

> How happy we were when a runner announced Mr. Lapsley's arrival. With the big ivory horn blowing and the drums beating, we ran down the banana walk to greet and welcome him home. He was tired, worn, and weary, and walked with a limp. He had been scorched by the sun, beaten by the rains, and torn by the thorns; his coat was in tatters, and his last pair of shoes worn into holes. . . . Our cook killed a goat and a feast of the very best we had followed. I could bear the burning sand with bare feet easier and safer than Mr. Lapsley could, so the last pair of shoes of the camp, though two sizes too large, were brought forth and put on his feet. . . . Mr. Lapsley told me the evening of his arrival that every bone in his body ached, and that he felt as though he had been beaten with rods. A fever soon followed. I nursed him carefully and tenderly through it and he was much improved in color from the purges and quinine.[168]

After returning to Luebo, Lapsley reported on physical changes at the station, "I found Sheppard had improved the place greatly, cleaning and clearing up the ground and planting us a banana avenue up to our front door."[169] Also, Lapsley mentioned that there was a row of pineapple plants beside each home. Those whom Lapsley had recruited went to work felling trees, uprooting stumps, and building houses for a permanent settlement. By the end of 1891, Luebo had been laid out with two cross streets, named Boulevard de Paris and Pennsylvania Avenue! A pavilion was constructed in the middle of the compound that was used for a dining room, a sitting room, a physician's office, a sanctuary, and for palaver. "Palaver is a Portuguese word meaning a conference," Sheppard explained; "what the Indians call a pow wow."[170] The term was used for every kind of friendly or unfriendly gathering.

Sheppard had this to say about calling villagers to gather at the large shed, and about signaling for other matters:

> [We] told the natives, "This is for God's palaver house. When you hear the telephone, come to it and we will tell God's word to you." I had bought a native telephone; two long iron bells welded together, without any clapper. One of these a native will take, and beat out in dots and dashes—like a telegraph alphabet—any message he wants to send. . . . So when one village got on fire it signaled to all the villages within hearing, "Come help us put out the fire." Once a native came in from the country to warn the village that five hundred M'choco warriors were on the way to murder us. Queta seized the gong and sounded the alarm to the village; in a few moments all were there. "Get your wives and children into the bushes!" Then he sounded by the gong the call to the villages round. . . . Ten thousand assembled; the M'choco did not dare approach."[171]

Stanley Shaloff is struck by how well the cofounders of the Luebo mission worked together:

> Sheppard and Lapsley complemented each other perfectly. In the rough period of adjustment, Sheppard's physical endurance, practical skills, and ability to converse with the people enabled the evangelists to surmount many obstacles. Equally important to the survival of the mission were Lapsley's business acumen and finesse in dealing with representatives of the State. The enthusiastic duo was eager to succeed and content with what they were doing. Despite repeated sieges of debilitating sickness and the absence of any tangible signs of success, they remained confident. For as Sheppard explained to Dr. Henkel: "I always wanted to live in Africa, I felt that I would be happy, and so I am."[172]

Adding to this comparison, Walter Williams observes:

> Sheppard, with a gift for learning the African languages, skill as a hunter, and physical strength, was the primary contact with the

Africans and directed the practical needs of the mission. Lapsley, on the other hand, managed the finances and dealt with the white colonial officials. Racial proscriptions broke down, and they worked together as equals. Together they toured the Kasai, introducing themselves, preaching, teaching, providing medical aid, and ransoming slaves.[173]

By the time Lapsley was able to recover some strength after his Luluaburg trip, the *Florida* returned to Luebo. It brought an alarming letter from the governor, stating that the land on which the APCM had settled had been given to another party. Since the State officer in Kasai had already given assurance that the property was unclaimed and was assigned to them, Lapsley decided to make the long trip to the Congo capital to protest in person. He was aware that the government tended to inhibit the development of Protestant missions. Robert Benedetto writes, "The government's tightly controlled land policies were used to extend the state-owned Belgian monopoly companies and the Catholic missions, while restricting the growth of the non-Belgian, Protestant communities."[174] Because of the importance of the Luebo land claim, plus the need to obtain supplies and to consult a physician, Lapsley went downstream with the boat to a region of greater health risk.[175]

In January 1892, Lapsley was treated at Kinshasa by Dr. Sims, and the next month he made out his will, bequeathing most of his little property to the APCM.[176] A letter he wrote then told of his most serious malaria attack ever, lasting several days, and revealed his awareness that he might not have long to live.[177] But his last letter home was a cheerful one, telling of the success he had in Boma with the governor, who declared that the land the Americans had applied for at Luebo had been officially registered as APCM property.[178] The Lapsley file at the Presbyterian Historical Society contains the original document in French certifying the APCM ownership of twenty-five acres on the right bank of the Lulua River.

The disease that had ravaged Lapsley throughout his time in the Congo now took its final toll. Tunduwa, where he had suffered his first malarial attack, became the scene for his last. The high fever he suffered from while he was there two years earlier had caused him to realize that his life might have been terminated at the very start of his Congo mission. Such had happened, he was told, to a young Swedish missionary who died just as Lapsley would die. "She took a fever which shortly proved to be of the violent hematuric type. A few hours was enough; the temperature ran up to one hundred and ten degrees, and when evening came, she 'fell asleep.'"[179] Grenfell, who happened to be visiting Tunduwa then, was among the Baptist missionaries who attempted to provide healing medication for Lapsley. He died at age twenty-six and less than a year after the Luebo mission was established. He was buried in the Tunduwa cemetery, which he had described as "a sacred spot" because it was for Protestants "who pioneered this work." Sims wrote this bereavement note to Lapsley's parents: "I dearly loved your son, and regard him as a real martyr. I warned him to go home, but he wished to complete a definite work before that. Too much goodness for his strength!"[180]

Two months passed before the *Florida* brought notice of Lapsley's death to Luebo. The villagers then wept and wailed as though one of their own children had died because the one they called Mutomba Njila had, in Sheppard's words, "found his way into their country, their homes, their language, and into their hearts."[181] Profoundly grieved, Sheppard went into the forest to discharge his anguish. He then wrote Mrs. Lapsley about "my comrade and co-worker":

> I can . . . say conscientiously, "I have kept the charge you gave me; I have loved and cared for him as if he were my own brother." . . . I have nursed and cared for him in all his sickness, and he has done the same for me. When I was sick his eyes knew no sleep. By my side he would sit and give me medicine. . . . My friend and brother has gone to be with Christ, and I shall see him no more. No more kneeling together in prayer! No more planning together future work![182]

A generation later Sheppard eloquently recalled the pangs he endured from the loss of his partner:

> The wild and barbarous tribe with which I was living gave me but little concern. The numerous leopards, lions, and hyenas were only the common, daily enemies of the body. The hissing serpents, the stinging tarantulas, the centipedes, and the scorpions, which infested my house, caused no restless nights; but let me tell you what was crushing—it was when a steamboat came . . . and there was no message of cheer or helpfulness. Then my heart was broken.[183]

To the end, the two pioneer American missionaries had high respect and affection for one another. In his last letter, Lapsley described his companion as "a great favorite" wherever he went. In the Kasai he was called "Shoppit Monine," the great Sheppard.[184] In reporting to his home office, Sheppard wrote about "Brother Lapsley and I" and the two were referred to at the Nashville mission headquarters as "colleagues."[185]

Sheppard found comfort in reflecting on the Gethsemane experience of Jesus, when he submitted to God, saying, "Not what I will, but
what thou wilt."[186] The hymn "How Firm a Foundation," which Sheppard translated into both Tshiluba and Bushonga, contains these words
attributed to Jesus:

> When through the deep waters I call thee to go,
> The rivers of sorrow shall not overflow;
> For I will be near thee, thy troubles to bless,
> And sanctify to thee thy deepest distress.

3

The Kuba People

INTO THE FORBIDDEN KINGDOM

Plans had been made for an expedition to the Kuba capital after
Lapsley returned from the lower Congo. He and Sheppard had recognized the advantages of planting Christianity in the center of a
kingdom with a population of about 200,000 that was culturally
advanced, politically powerful, and economically prosperous. The
Kuba land area, larger than the state of Maine, was quite fertile. Sheppard gave this description:

> The soil is alluvial and productive, watered by the Lubudi River and
> among lovely brooks. . . . The first and principal production is Indian
> corn, which is planted three crops a year. . . . The next thing that they
> raise in abundance is black and white eyed peas. . . . I have made many
> a pot full of peas disappear for them. Peas cooked in palm oil, plenty
> of red pepper and a "hunk" of cornbread is not bad. . . . They have any
> quantity of peanuts. . . . They also have sweet potatoes.[1]

The Kuba king had prohibited all people from other lands coming
into his kingdom. From the time that white traders first came to the
upper Kasai nine years earlier, some of them had in vain sent substan-
tial gifts to the king in hopes of being invited to Mushenge (or Nsheng),
his capital. Portuguese ivory trader Silva Porto and explorer Ludwig
Wolf failed in their attempts to enter the area. In reaction to these
Europeans, the king had issued a stark warning to his subjects, "The
Bakuba who shows a stranger the road [to Mushenge] will be
beheaded." Even so, the American missionaries longed to see the heartland of the Congo's dignified aristocrats.

While Lapsley was away, Sheppard concentrated on learning the Kuba language. This was done by extending hospitality to Kuba traders and tax collectors when they came to the Luebo area.[2] Sheppard's hunting skills enabled him to offer them several choice meats: elephant roasts, python steaks, and buffalo burgers. He told of killing a forty-pound monkey and, undisturbed by thoughts of distant family kinship, sharing the Africans' enjoyment of eating the meat. The Rev. James Bridges aptly gave a biblical comparison for such cleverness: "Sheppard, Jacob-like, made savory messes, with which he enticed the passing Bakuba, and thus, while eating with them, he learned many words of their language."[3] When the Kubas came to dinner they not only enriched his vocabulary but informed him of the names of villages, along with their chiefs, between Luebo and Mushenge. He also learned about the distances between villages and the streams to be crossed.[4]

Lapsley's death gave Sheppard a stronger determination to fulfill plans they had jointly made, even though he realized that venturing out without a partner would be even more perilous. At a meeting in Luebo, he asked for volunteers to join him in a search for Mushenge. He warned them of the danger, saying, "We may be all marching to our graves." Even so, nine men agreed to take the risk.[5] After setting out, Sheppard soon realized that it would be almost impossible to find the way to the Kuba capital without having a guide who had been there before. There were too many winding paths to choose among, including those made by large animals in dark forests and through grass as high as an elephant's eye. Wading through jungle swamps and crossing bridgeless rivers added to the problem of following a trail. He knew little more than that the capital was in the highlands a considerable distance northeast of Luebo.

The xenophobic Kubas that Sheppard met along the way supplied no directions. They knew their ruler was serious in threatening decapitation for anyone who told a foreigner about paths leading to the capital. The stern king had even beheaded his own son who had violated his law that made robbery of tributes left on graves a capital offense. But Sheppard testified that he had no fear because he could affirm with a psalmist: "The Lord is the strength of my life, of whom shall I be afraid? Though a host should encamp against me, in this will I be confident."[6]

Village chiefs cordially received Sheppard's party but gave no hint as to Mushenge's location. However, he was able to learn of neighboring habitations by repeatedly having one of his men accompany travelers in order to obtain eggs in the next village. When he returned with trail

details as well as with eggs, the whole party moved to the nearby village. Consuming all the eggs sometimes posed a problem, but once
Sheppard managed to eat thirty small eggs at one meal![7]

For more than a month, Sheppard did not succeed in finding the
Kuba capital. While detained at one village for several weeks, he "had
the pleasure of preaching, praying, and singing for them in their tongue
daily."[8] But one day, three Kuba ivory traders passed by on their way to
Mushenge. Sheppard sent his head man to follow them at a distance
and to mark the crossroads. Sheppard afterward led the rest of his men
for two days along the designated trail to the village of Bishibing, a few
miles from their destination. However, the traders discovered what was
happening and reported at the capital that a foreigner was close.

The Bishibing village chief was friendly but insisted that the next day
Sheppard must leave. With earnestness he said, "You must return the
way you came; [otherwise] not only will we be killed, but you and all
your people." By way of conveying calmness to the uneasy villagers,
Sheppard strolled about, watched blacksmiths, and purchased six beautifully carved ebony cups. He admired the large cornfields with towering stalks and learned that the villagers raised about fifty bushels of corn
to the acre and two crops a year. Having never encountered a gun
before, they were frightened when he shot four guinea fowls to give to
the chief.[9]

Sheppard later told about the way his exploration incensed the Kuba
king, whose title was *Nyimi* in Bushonga, the Kuba language, or
Lukengu (or *Lukenga*) in Tshiluba:

> The king called for his sons; called for his forty fighting men, who use
> bows six feet high and can send an arrow through a buffalo; gave his
> spear and knife to his son Toen-zaida and said, "Go down to Bishibing
> and bring back the chief, the foreigners, the villagers—all—and I will
> behead them." The next morning, as I was reading a copy of the Daily
> News—a copy two years old—I heard a great noise out in the village.
> A herald of Lukenga had come storming in and was proclaiming,
> "Hear the king's message. The king commands you all to come before
> him; . . . because you have entertained a foreigner you are all to be
> beheaded." The whole village was in intense excitement. . . . It was too
> late to run away. I could not rescue my people by force, but I sent for
> the king's son. . . . I said, "These people are not to blame. I have had
> no guide; no one showed me the way. Last night the chief begged me
> to go away, but I did not go. I am the only one that is guilty."[10]

The prince was flabbergasted to hear Bushonga spoken fluently by
one who was dressed in the clothes of a distant culture. Also, he could

not figure how anyone could come so far into his hidden kingdom without a Kuba guide or why he was willing to sacrifice his life for a Kuba chief. The tall, bronze-colored, and fearless prince ordered Sheppard to remain in the village while he reported to his father. Sheppard took a large conch shell and said, "This we call the father of cowries; present it to the king as a token of friendship."[11]

The august king and his council puzzled over this friendly nonwhite foreigner who spoke their language, knew trails of the area, and sent a marvelous gift. They concluded that the large, mysterious person was a previous Kuba king whose spirit had become reincarnated in a foreign man. Toen-zaida and other princes returned to Bishibing to tell its anxiously awaiting people that Sheppard had been identified by their father's wise men, who declared, "He is no stranger, but Bope Mekabe of your own family, who has returned to earth."[12]

The appetites of Sheppard and his men returned as they prepared to be escorted to the capital. On the way they walked across a great tree trunk that had been cut down to form a bridge. As they passed over a swift and deep stream, one of the porters fell in.[13] The men later reported that Sheppard, at great risk of his own life, leapt in, and rescued him after a heroic struggle.[14]

Sheppard told of entering the walled city of Mushenge:

> I had seen nothing like it in Africa. . . . The streets were thronged, even out into the country, with people coming out to meet us with rejoicing. The people all wore clothes, even the children. They brought me to a house prepared for me. It had four rooms, cleanly swept, with fresh mats on the floor, a bedstead of carved wood, with a quilted covering, a sort of chair adorned with tusks of ivory.[15]

A bountiful supply of fruit, vegetables, and meats were brought to the royal guest quarters for Sheppard's party. He wrote, "The king sent greetings, and with it fourteen goats, six sheep, a number of chickens, corn, pumpkins, large dried fish, bushels of peanuts, bunches of bananas and plantains and a calabash of palm oil and other food."[16]

The next day a blast of ivory horns signaled to the Kubas that they should put on their best robes for a celebration. Sheppard, dressed from pith helmet to shoes in once-white clothing, was accompanied by officials wearing red kilts and feathers in their hats. They brought him to the broad open square at the city center that was surrounded by hangings of exquisitely designed cloth. Thousands watched as the elderly king was carried in on a palanquin that was shaped, Sheppard said, "like the body of a buggy."[17] The mobile throne was covered with antelope hides, and in front of it was a lion skin on which his feet rested. Many attendants held up the royal platform by means of two stout bamboo poles on the sides. *Lukengu* leaned against a backrest made of four carved ivory tusks lashed together. Leopard skins were spread along the ground where he was put down, over which he walked to a place for observation and sat upon a slave. His feet, painted with powdered camwood, could not touch the soil, because his majesty must be protected from the pollution that defiles ordinary mortals. When the king stood up, his eagle feather crown enabled him to tower over all. A blue kilt was draped neatly in many folds about his waist and a broad belt decorated with a large cowrie shell held it in place. He also wore brass ornaments around his neck and legs that were permitted only for the royal family.[18]

Joining the gala celebration were several hundred of the king's seven hundred wives, along with his revered sister—the mother of the next monarch. Princes danced to the music of drums and stringed instruments while brandishing big knives. Later the wives sang sweet praises to their husband. It would have been impossible for Sheppard to have witnessed anything like this anywhere else. Jan Vansina, a recognized authority on the Kubas, comments, "The Kuba kingdom remained the lone witness to the stately courts that had once flourished in equatorial Africa."[19]

Sheppard recounted his initial encounter with King Kot aMbweeky:

> The king's servants ran and spread leopard skins along the ground leading to his majesty. I approached with some timidity. The king arose from his throne of ivory, stretched forth his hand and greeted me with these words, "Wyni" (You have come). I bowed low, clapped my hands in front of me, and answered, "Ndini, Nyimi" (I have come, King).[20]

The following day Toen-zaida took Sheppard to the palace for a more exclusive audience with *Lukengu*. They passed through a number of guarded gates before arriving at the inner sanctum. Among the hundred or more buildings in the king's compound for wives, children, and slaves, was an audience hall containing massive pillars of artistically carved mahogany, and walls covered with smoothly woven mats. The king was seated on a low stool and his favorite wife was by his side. In accordance with custom, the courtiers responded to the king's every utterance. Sheppard joined the others in giving honor: "During all the interview we clapped our hands after every sentence. If the king coughed we coughed, if he sneezed we sneezed. Two slaves on their knees supported the king's back."[21]

The *Lukengu's* vast harem was unrelated to his sexual appetite. Many of his wives were inherited from his predecessor and were a means for maintaining allegiance to the crown from chiefs throughout the kingdom. Hezekiah Washburn, an APCM missionary who was later to live for many years with the Kubas, explains: "These were hostages placed there by their families as a guarantee to the king that their family would be loyal to him. If the family should refuse to obey the king's orders, these girls were punished until the family paid a fine."[22]

Sheppard was fascinated to see statues of four former kings carved from hardwood. Wearing royal regalia, they sat cross-legged and carried ceremonial knives. "Such statues were considered to be the doubles of the kings they represented and as such were revered if not actually regarded as sacred," Vansina explains.[23] In her article containing photographs of these Kuba figures, Jean Rosenwald comments that each effigy possesses "qualities of infinite calm, detachment, and dignity" that the living king should embody.[24] One statue was of their most famous king, who lived in the early seventeenth century. Another one has a game board on his lap, depicting his favorite amusement. Still another monarch has an anvil before him, showing his devotion to blacksmithing.[25] Sheppard was not offered any of those statues, but two were later purchased by Hungarian ethnologist Emil Torday, who was an agent of the British Museum. He was able to obtain the highly valued objects when he visited Mushenge in 1907 after the glory of the Kuba kingdom had declined. Eventually all four statues that Sheppard saw ended up either in the British Museum or in the Musée royal de l'Afrique in Belgium. Appreciative of their "sumptuous quality," Vansina comments, "All the statues testify to the artistic taste then prevalent: essential symmetry of volume, flowing lines that avoid angular effects except at the base, a serene expression of the faces."[26]

Lukengu Kot aMbweeky II, in insisting that Sheppard acknowledge that he was of royal Kuba descent, said:

> The people are rejoicing. You need not try to hide it from us longer. You are Bope Mekabe who reigned before my father and who died. His spirit went to a foreign land; your mother gave birth to it, and you are that spirit.[27]

Sheppard tried, to no avail, to convince the king that he had not had a previous life. The king smiled at Sheppard's ignorance of his royal background, for it was obvious to his court that only by carrying the spirit of an ancestral king could one have such great knowledge of Kuba language and geography. The Kubas shared with most African tribes south of the Sahara a firm belief in reincarnation.[28] They thought that when a good person dies, she or he first becomes a ghost in another realm and is then reborn in a human baby.[29] By way of confirming that Sheppard was part of his royal family, the king drew forth his own knife from his belt and presented it to him, telling him that it was an heirloom that had been passed down from one *Lukengu* to another for seven generations. The current king thus believed that he was returning to Sheppard what had once been his possession.

Toen-zaida then led a tour of the capital, on which Sheppard reported:

> The town is laid off in perfect blocks—it reminded me of a checker board. Each house has one or two high fences round it, nine or ten feet high, of bamboo poles set close, so that the fence is as solid as possible. . . . The blocks and streets are all named. The streets are broad and clean. You can see hundreds of little children playing leap-frog, hide the switch, rolling hoops made of withes, and playing with marbles made of clay. . . . In the evening there is such a stir of the people on their way to market. The hustle and bustle of men and women, the carrying of big and little baskets, the merriment, . . . all make one feel that he has again entered a land of civilization. How many markets do you think I counted in this town? . . . Eighteen.[30]

Around each block, which contained a mother's kinfolk, was a high fence. A block captain was designated for communicating the king's messages, and for seeing that they were carried out.[31] Each family was required to sweep the street in front of its own house and maintain a high standard of personal cleanliness. Sheppard told of a Kuba who made him feel ashamed by asking if he had no knife for keeping his nails cleaner![32]

Maxamalinge (or Mishaamilyeeng), another royal son who befriended Sheppard, is afforded this description:

> He was tall, weighed about 250, fine looking and had a splendid bearing. . . . He invited me to go with him to his house and have dinner. . . . His house was surrounded by a number of private fences. . . . His wife, Bulengunga, was busy cooking. . . . There were three large rooms to his house, a reception room, bed room (in which is also kept his valuables—tusks of ivory, cam wood and big balls of copper and iron), and the kitchen. The houses of his slaves were just beyond the first fence. Dinner was prepared for six, and we all sat down on mats and used our fingers, eating from the various pots fresh fish, buffalo, greens, and corn bread. The visitors as well as my host and hostess asked question after question.[33]

Sheppard told of being in Mushenge at the time of the annual festival:

> There were representatives from all of the king's villages throughout
> the land. They brought with them their musical instruments . . . [and]
> their best clothes in long boxes made from bark. . . . The women had
> been to the creek and rubbed the sides of their feet many, many times
> against a stone until there was a white stripe all the way around. They
> wore a copper ring on their big toe and walked pigeon-toed. . . . Gar-
> lands of ferns and flowers were on their heads and around their necks.
> Daily, for two weeks they gathered in the big square, sitting in a great
> circle. The king and a few of his wives and sons sat on an elevated cov-
> ered bamboo platform. The delegates from each town sat together
> with their chief in front. It was a beautiful sight! The master of cere-
> monies ran into the center, saluted the king with the royal mace, then
> laid it before the chief of a village. The chief arose, made a few acro-
> batic movements, and from the center of the circle saluted the king
> and in a loud voice reported the health and prosperity of his town, told
> of the crops, the births and deaths, and then danced alone to the
> delight and amusement of all the people. As the evening drew near the
> formal ceremonies broke up with the music playing, the people
> singing and everybody dancing.[34]

Lukengu gave Sheppard permission to tell everywhere "about the
Great Spirit, a great King." Moreover, he agreed to give nine acres at
Mushenge for a mission,[35] but his successor retracted that permission.
Sheppard immediately began preaching at the Kuba capital, a town
with a population of about 10,000. He recalled:

> We would sing one or two hymns, have prayer, and then, as slowly and
> simply as possible I would tell the new and wonderful story of Jesus.
> The audience gave excellent attention, no moving, talking or laugh-
> ing. . . . There were many, many questions which I had the pleasure of
> answering after each service.[36]

Had Lapsley still been alive to take care of matters at the base station, Sheppard would probably have taken advantage of the opportunity to begin a permanent station in the capital immediately. But
after spending some months there, Sheppard told the king that in
spite of his love for him and his people, he must return to his responsibilities at Luebo. The reluctant king permitted Sheppard to leave
only after he promised to return and agreed to leave two of his men
there as hostages.[37] Sheppard told how the king's calendar operated:
"He tied a long string inside his door. Every moon he ties a knot in
it, and when he ties twelve he will expect me."[38] There was a fond
farewell for Sheppard and his party, "Hundreds of men, women and

children followed us out on the plain, waving, singing and shouting a farewell."[39]

ART AND CULTURE

Sheppard has provided virtually the only information about the Kuba people before the twentieth century. His record is highly significant because it dates to an era when the delicate web of culture had not yet been torn by foreign imperialism. The Kuba culture that Sheppard saw was the dream of anthropologists because it had not been contaminated by Western civilization. Conway Wharton, who lived among the Kubas as a second-generation member of the APCM shows in his book *The Leopard Hunts Alone* a heavy indebtedness to Sheppard's record. A more recent study of the Kubas is anthropologist Vansina's *The Children of Woot*, written in 1978 following the author's fieldwork in Kasai. He judges Sheppard's description of the Kubas to be "extremely valuable" and cites it often in his excellent monograph.[40] Vansina classifies Sheppard's 1892 trip into the Kuba kingdom as "precolonial" because the colonial conquest of the area did not begin for another eight years.[41]

Sheppard's understanding of Bushonga was his key for perceiving many facets of the culture before colonialism changed it radically. "Their language is full, highly inflected and musical," he said appreciatively.[42] Ernest Stache of the Belgian Trading Company at Luebo wrote to the Presbyterian Foreign Missions Committee expressing appreciation for having Sheppard in their midst. Stache commented on Sheppard's popularity "among the Bakuba, whose language he alone speaks of all the Europeans."[43] This linguistic ability, plus his royal adoption, afforded him a unique avenue for understanding the culture from inside out.

The Kubas' inland and forested location isolated them from the overpowering impact of the Europeans on the West Coast and of the Arabs on the East Coast. Rather than having their tribe decimated by slavers, they developed their economy by bringing in slaves. Vansina writes:

> The Kuba remained on the extreme edge of the Atlantic trading area from c. 1750 onward. This allowed their kings to maintain firm central control over the activities of long-distance slave traders from Angola. They imported slaves, exported ivory, and derived great wealth from such operations, especially after 1880.[44]

Kuba weapons and clothing from this period display their ethnic conservatism. They were satisfied with the arrows, knives, and spears they made and, unlike most other Congolese, they did not wear foreign cloth; foreign weapons and cups were forbidden. Their use of iron rather than flint to tip their arrows shows how far they had moved from the Stone Age.

The most destructive contribution of Western civilization, the gun, had not arrived in Kuba culture before Sheppard's penetration. He found that even its noise caused consternation among the people, who had neither seen nor heard such a weapon. One day he ventured out to shoot some birds in an agricultural area. The *Lukengu* informed him of the trouble he caused: "He told me that farmers had come and complained that their crops of corn would die if I continued to shoot over their fields. I consented at once to shoot no more, explaining to the king that I would do nothing to offend them."[45]

Another example of Sheppard's respect for different cultural understanding pertained to the use of palm nuts. Once when he was entertaining himself by throwing them at a mark on a house, an alarmed man set off angry cries from others. On inquiring why they were upset, Sheppard learned that sorcerers used palm nut charms to curse a house, so his action might cause the occupant to die. On learning of the resulting fear, he regained their confidence in this manner: "Immediately I went over to the excited crowd and explained my ignorance of the fact and promised to make reparations. It was accepted, so I begged the man's pardon and presented him with a chicken and we became friends again."[46]

Some nonlethal practices for determining guilt were reported by Sheppard without evaluative comment:

> A man accused of breaking the rule of honesty, if there is no eyewitness, is tested by putting his right hand three times deep down in a pot of scalding water, and if the skin begins to peel off, he is guilty; if it does not he is innocent. The girl accused of misconduct is tested by the witch doctor putting a small piece of copper wire and a finger full of red pepper in her eye. If the copper wire falls out and the pepper does not burn her, she is innocent. If otherwise, she is guilty and must pay a fine.[47]

One divination implement that Sheppard collected was a carved wooden crocodile. That creature never lies, according to Kuba lore, so a diviner claims that he can become informed of the crocodile's judgment on the cause of a misfortune by rubbing a small circular wood piece with a flat base along the raffia attached to the back of the image. The diviner, having been paid by a client, recites names of possible culprits individually as he rubs the crocodile. "If the button refuses to slide, the witch-doctor tries it three times, and if the button does not reach the shoulders of the crocodile the person is counted guilty of witchcraft," Sheppard explained.[48] The witch doctor, who obviously can feign whether or not the button sticks, actually decides who should be accused. The poison test is then alleged to provide confirmation or denial of the verdict.

Other procedures of witch doctors observed by Sheppard appear to have given patients intense pain below the neck to make them forget about their pain above the neck:

> If a man or woman has a severe headache, they lie down before their door and the witch doctor walks up and down on their backs, kneading them with his feet; or the "doctor" will have a hole like a grave dug in the ground, sticks laid across the top, a hot wood fire built below, then cover the fire with leaves and the patient laid across the sticks to smoke.[49]

Sheppard learned from the king about Kuba religious beliefs. They had a vague belief in an invisible high God who was responsible for the creation and control of nature. According to their mythology, Sheppard reported, the "first people, man and woman, were let down from the skies by a rope, from which they untied themselves and the rope was drawn up."[50] Weather calamities and agricultural failures were interpreted as signs of the anger of this God, called Chembe, a name corresponding to Nzambi of the lower Congo. This Supreme Being was feared but not worshiped.[51]

One characteristic of Kuba religion was treated by Sheppard in a positive manner. In contrast to some other Kasai tribes who had tall cultic objects, he said:

> I have seen in no Bakuba village an idol. I mean a large piece of wood carved into an image to be dreaded or adored. The people wear charms around their necks, arms and ankles, and these have their local significance. A man has his charm on his wrist and before eating with his neighbor, drinking palm wine or smoking a borrowed pipe, he will lick this small charm to prevent any evil wish of his neighbor entering his stomach.[52]

Observing some people in the Kuba kingdom, Emil Torday gave some support to Sheppard's report on their religion. He found there a deistic theology:

Not only were there no "graven images" of God, but their ideas refused to attribute to divinity any human failings like lust for revenge, severity, etc. Bad actions were not punished by God; their opposition to the laws of nature caused automatically, without divine interference, some unpleasant reaction. . . . If a man broke the laws forbidding the marrying within his own clan, it was the blood of the clan in him that suffered from the pollution and made him suffer in his turn.[53]

In visiting Mushenge in 1907, explorer M. W. Hilton-Simpson was aware of the work of the APCM and commended any missionary who aims at supplementing rather than supplanting Kuba religion. Work among the Kubas is more effective, he discerned, if

the missionary knows their history and their religion thoroughly before he attempts to introduce his own faith among them. . . . [They believe in] one God, the creator, and a set of moral laws of extraordinary high character. . . . By tactful management a missionary might be able to . . . [find] points of similarity between the Christian religion and the Bushongo belief, and thus slowly letting the native regard the former as an amplification of the latter.[54]

"The Bakuba are morally a splendid people," Sheppard asserted; "I have asked a number of Bakuba what was their real ideal of life, and they invariably answered to have a big corn field, marry a good wife, and have many children."[55] Their general honesty was such that Sheppard did not have to secure his private dwelling at the capital. He found there effective laws against stealing, gambling, and drunkenness.[56] Torday likewise evaluated their moral code, together with their craftsmanship, as Africa's finest.[57]

Sheppard recorded the activities of non-Christian peoples with such appreciation that it is difficult to realize that he was describing those whom most Americans of his time would have labeled "heathen" and "savage." Because of such typical deprecations, Hochschild acknowledged on a *Booknotes* television interview that he had had a disdain for missionaries until he learned of Sheppard. The author of *King Leopold's Ghost* tells how Sheppard differed from the colonialist:

His writings show an empathetic, respectful curiosity about African customs radically different from the harsh, quick judgments of someone like Stanley. . . . [Sheppard has] provided a mine of information for later scholars, for the Kuba had one of central Africa's most sophisticated political systems. . . . His is a valuable, firsthand look at one of the last great African kingdoms unchanged by European influence.[58]

The Kubas were, according to Sheppard, "quite a different class of people" from other Kasai tribes. "They were tall and stout. . . . They had tapering fingers, firm noses, high insteps, and were dressed in longer loin-cloths than those at Luebo."[59] Sheppard was informed that they "migrated from the far north, crossed rivers, and settled on the high table land. And with many expeditions fought and conquered the surrounding tribes."[60] He speculated that there might be a link between the Kubas and the most outstanding of ancient African civilizations: "Perhaps they got their civilization from the Egyptians—or the Egyptians [got] theirs from the Bakuba!"[61] Although that was a fanciful association, there were similarities between the cultures. For example, Kuba kings were called "God on earth,"[62] a status similar to that of the Pharoahs.

John Mack of the British Museum agrees with Sheppard that the Kuba should not be viewed as "noble savages" for "by their own efforts they had achieved 'civilization.'" He also writes:

> The Kuba were temperamentally historians. Like many centralised states, theirs was a society obsessively interested in precedent. . . . They could recount king lists, locate events in time by reference to the kings in whose reign they occurred—they even talked of a solar eclipse and a passage of Halley's comet, thus providing a means of linking Kuba chronology to historical time.[63]

The Kuba griot could recite a list of more than one hundred kings in an unbroken dynasty, according to Torday. He figured that their history commenced in the fifth century of the Christian era and that they immigrated to the Kasai area from the north.[64] Vansina lists the names of dozens of dynastic rulers, beginning with Woot, who was both the legendary first king and first father.[65] Since theirs was a matrilineal society, royal succession did not go from father to son but from king to a son of one of his sisters.[66]

Washburn has described the prominence of Kuba women:

> The ultimate authority was that of the oldest woman of the royal family. She was more powerful than the king. . . . She had the authority, in her position, to go in and tell him to stop his actions. If he didn't stop she could go further and remove the royal anklet and take it to the king's council. The king's council was composed of about eighty men and women who sat together with all of the adult members of the royal family. They had the power even to dethrone the king. Their method of dethroning a man was to have him killed.[67]

The Kubas were better organized than most African tribes, and their method of governance fascinated Sheppard. They were the ruling class and composed a relatively small part of the whole kingdom. About seven satellite tribes pledged allegiance to *Lukengu*. What the early explorers found is succinctly stated by René Lemarchand: "A distinctive feature of the political organization of the Kuba was a council of elders representing various crafts and arts, which served as an advisory body to the king."[68] That council also oversaw the collection of taxes from the outlying tribal chiefs. Apart from paying taxes to the king of the federation, tribal chiefs were largely autonomous in administering justice in their villages. Revenue officers went from village to village at stated times to gather tribute for the *Lukengu* from every man in every tribe of the Kuba kingdom. All leopard skins and one tusk of every elephant killed belonged to the king. Fishermen and hunters sent a certain portion of the animals they had killed and dried. Some sent baskets of scalded locusts, grasshoppers, and caterpillars to provide the royal table with tasty morsels. An abundance of farm produce was also collected.[69]

Along with other missionaries, Sheppard gathered Kuba folklore that tells how the tribe came to be dominant. Once upon a time, so one story goes, there were several tribes living close together. The chiefs decided it would be good if all united in a kingdom. To determine who would be king they agreed to throw their axes into water and the one that floated would be selected. Kuba women are very shrewd, so one chief's wife schemed to make her husband the ruler. She made an axe of wood and painted it to look just like iron. When the contestants and their followers gathered at the river, all axes sank except that of the Kuba chief.[70]

Sheppard told of the guilds that formed the basic structure of the Kuba economy. One was for hunters, who became skilled in killing everything from birds to elephants. Among the other guilds was one for fishermen, who made nets and traps to place in streams as well, and one for the potters, who formed both utilitarian and artistic objects from clay.

There were role reversals in Kasai as compared with Western civilization. Phillips Verner claimed that "a woman is rarely seen with a needle and a man never with a hoe."[71] The manufacture as well as the sewing of textiles was done by a male guild. Fiber was taken from the rib of raffia palm leaves and combed into threads. Rugs, mats, baskets, and clothing were then woven on handlooms. Sheppard said, "As soon as a boy is large enough to work, he is taught mat weaving. He must first make dozens of balls of string from the palm fibre. Then day by day he cuts the long bamboo poles into narrow splits."[72]

Sheppard purchased twenty lovely mats made of palm fiber and compared the fabric to "fine velvet."[73] The textiles usually retained their natural cream color, but were sometimes dyed with fast colors. If crimson was desired, the threads were dipped into camwood root that had been pounded into a powder and mixed with water. When the dross from pulverized iron was boiled, a strong solution gave a black dye, and a weak solution produced purple. Yellow and brown were obtained by beating to a powder the root or bark of certain shrubs and trees, then steeping them in a pot. The cloth for a dress garment was about one yard wide and several yards long. It was gathered and folded at the waist, hanging somewhat like a Scottish kilt.[74]

Sheppard gave this further description of Kuba cloth:

> From looms of their own ingenuity they turn out smooth and nicely made cloth of the palm fibre. Some of it resembles coarse linen; some of it is much like plush. Not just a little, but thousands of yards are made by this people. They are very fond of dressing. Their cloths are usually twenty-seven inches wide, and from five to eight yards in length. Many of them ornament their nicest ones very tastefully, with cowries and beads. And with their dresses arranged much like the highlanders' dress, hat and walking stick, they do not make a bad appearance.[75]

A piece of raffia that Sheppard brought back to Virginia was one yard wide and eleven yards in length. He explained its use: "A young man's first duty after getting his hut and farm in order is to weave this long burial mat. He wraps it with palm leaves after rolling it tight . . . and fastens it to the inside of his house until it shall be needed."[76] Sheppard also described how it fit in with Kuba funeral customs:

> When a man is buried all the cloth he owns is wrapped round and round till he looks like a bale of cloth himself—then a hole is dug and he is rolled in and a mound is made over him, and then plates and cups and saucers are set all round it for the use of the spirit. Every cup and saucer and plate has a hole made in the bottom . . . to make them use-less to living people, so that no one would carry them off.[77]

Sheppard also acquired a sample of Kuba tapa cloth. To make it, the inner bark of the mulberry tree had been stripped off and soaked. The pulp was pounded together, dyed, and dried. This cloth, which could be used as a blanket or dress, was pieced together with inch-long tri-angular pieces of varied colors, like a patchwork quilt.[78]

Embroidery was done in two-dimensional designs from memory without the aid of a pattern drawn on the cloth, resulting in intriguing variations. In the Sheppard collection of Kuba artifacts at Montreat, I have seen a hat and a fan that were intricately designed and splendidly woven. Art historian Harold Cureau gives this description of the pieces that Sheppard collected:

> The surfaces of almost everything were decorated by utilizing a vari-ety of techniques (i.e. carving, modeling, applique, embroidery, weav-ing, chasing and incising). Many of the patterns are geometric in character, and were influenced by a variety of natural and man-made forms such as animals, plants, houses, basketry, and flowing water.[79]

Sheppard was fortunate to have arrived in Mushenge when the Kuba kingdom was at the peak of prosperity. This was signified by "the increasing profusion of decorative patterns on all available surfaces of luxury objects."[80] He was struck by the way the Kuba lavished designs, even on their own bodies. Abdomens displayed a variety of decorative patterns. Sheppard photographed the ornamental scarification pro-duced by rubbing a soil and organic mixture into skin lacerations. He gave these illustrations of creativity in commonplace objects:

> Sometimes it takes them a year to hew out a canoe from an enormous tree in the forest, miles from a river. When it is in good shape . . . they take a chalky substance, trace a design, and proceed with a small adz and knife to carve the design. . . . Their clay pots for cooking and the large water pots are decorated, and knives as well as spears are carved. Their baskets . . . are woven in figures on both sides. . . . Even their hoes . . . all have patterns made by the blacksmiths on both hand and blade.[81]

Artistic designs were carved within many Kuba homes. Figures were found on door jambs, on trunks, and on the ends and sides of beds. Sheppard observed, "In the centre of their double room houses (and some have four rooms) is a large centre post, measuring from twenty-seven to thirty inches in circumference, and from fourteen to seventeen feet high, beautifully carved from top to bottom."[82] Vansina writes that "houses were really basketry work fixed to poles and decorated like mats." At the time when Sheppard was in Mushenge, "the walls had become very elaborate to build, or, more accurately, to plait, stitch, and sew together. . . . Sliding doors had been invented as an improvement over the mats that unrolled to perform the same function in simpler buildings elsewhere."[83]

Metalworking was an important Kuba craft and often a marvel of ingenuity. Iron and copper ores were found that appeared like pebbles on the surface of hills, or like dead moss in the sluggish streams.[84] After smelting the ore in charcoal ovens made hotter with bellows, blacksmiths produced a wide variety of useful objects, including axes, bells, and razors. Sheppard deposited at the Montreat Historical Society a ceremonial copper ax on which figurines were engraved. When the Belgians saw Kuba copper art, they investigated and found rich malachite deposits in the region. Subsequently, they opened a large mining operation southeast of the Kuba kingdom.

The Kuba manufacture and use of distinctive knives got them their name. They referred to themselves as "Bushongo," meaning "knife-throwing people." "Bakuba" is a Luba word, meaning "lightning people." The Luba were presumably impressed by the lightning-like strokes of the knives developed by their military superiors.[85] Sheppard's "virtuoso piece"[86] was a large knife given him by Lukengu that may date back to the seventeenth century. The two-edged copper blade has an oval design. The coil on the brass inlaid handle represents the bowels, and the bell shape of the handle end represents the navel. This signifies close kinship ties and assures the knife owner of protection by members of the royal family.[87] It was called an ikul, or peace knife, because Shyaam aMbul, the Kuba king, instituted it to replace the more lethal shongo or branched throwing knife.[88]

Another ornate knife Sheppard brought back was for executions, but it was not old, he explained, because it contained no notches on the blade to record killings. It resembles a headless human figure with arms raised above the neck, although Sheppard saw curved buffalo horns in the art. Sara Lane, in her article on Sheppard's metal artifacts, notes the "delicate design through the center of the iron blade" and adds:

> One wonders whether there is any reason for the numerous curves other than a love of beauty—beauty even in a beheading knife. Offenders against the king or chief were executed in Dr. Sheppard's day in Africa by a public executioner, a witch doctor disguised by a mask.[89]

Sheppard described the decapitation method:

> The victim's hands and feet are bound, his arms strapped to his side; a strong sapling is bent down and his head is so tied to it that his neck

is stretched and held taut. The executioner whirls the knife . . . and with one stroke severs the head from the shoulders and cuts the cord that holds it, so that it is flung, ghastly and horrible, at the feet of the awe-stricken spectators.[90]

The artifact given to Sheppard that displayed the highest degree of smithing technique was a ceremonial sword. The crafting skill exhibited by the bands of braided brass and embedded strips of coiled iron in the center of the blade illustrates how far the Kubas had developed in technology. The sword symbolized authority because it had been possessed by Kuba royalty for generations. Prince Maxamalinge took it when he had to flee the capital, and later gave it to Sheppard in appreciation of his protection and hospitality.

From the artifacts and notes that Sheppard left at the Hampton Museum, Lane gathered these comments:

> No man of importance among the Bushongo tribes is considered well dressed unless he wears in his belt a knife or carries one in a sheath at his side. Some of these are merely ornaments; others are carried for protection against man or beast. One can readily understand the pride and joy of carrying one of the shining copper blades or one of bright steel with a delicate design cut on it, especially if the man himself designed it. . . . The metal inlay work in the handles gives an outlet for individual expression in design and in choice of material, brass and copper, brass and lead, and lead alone being used. . . . The sheaths are made of thin pieces of wood or reeds bound together with cane, often woven into some design.[91]

Lane also describes the skill shown by the spears that Sheppard collected:

> Spears are used both in war and in the hunt, and men of importance always carry them when walking or when in council. Spear handles are made of strong heavy wood and balance well in the hand. . . . In spears used for hunting the hippopotamus or forest animals, the iron head or point is loose and is fastened to the handle by many strong cords which are twisted about it but which uncoil when the point is caught in the animal. At one end is fastened a cork. If a hippopotamus is being hunted and the barb enters the thick skin, the animal runs. The bobbing of the cork frightens him and he makes for deep water where he dies. The floating cork marks the spot. If the hunted beast is a deer or other forest animal, the cork catches in the branches and impedes progress.[92]

Forming still another guild were Kuba carvers who worked with wood and ivory. From a solid block of ebony, a chair might be made.

Sheppard obtained a wood headrest featuring a servant supporting the sleeper. The Kubas produced wooden eating implements and musical instruments. Sheppard described a kind of xylophone played by two men with sticks, having "a narrow table-like frame with strips of a special kind of wood laid across it and gourds of different sizes tied under these strips to produce different sounds."[93] He brought back a huge trumpet made from an elephant tusk, along with drinking horns and wooden mugs. He explained, "The natives drink water and palm wine, their only beverages, from cups of various shapes made of mahogany or ebony and elaborately carved."[94] Also in Sheppard's possession was a wooden bowl carved with a geometric design and finished with palm oil.

Pipes for smoking were Sheppard's first Kuba purchases. On one a man's head was featured on a finely carved bowl; it had a two-foot stem and a mouthpiece made out of the leg of a large bird.[95] Sheppard eventually came to possess several treasured pipes with elaborate designs. Pertaining to smoking habits, he noted:

> The pipes of the Bakuba people are almost sacred, many of them being blessed by the witch-doctors. . . . If the smoker in traveling gets tobacco from a village and some enemy wishes the smoker harm through the tobacco, the wish is made useless because of the witch-doctor's blessing. . . . Some pipe bowls are made from very hard wood and are left to the son as a legacy. . . . The Bakuba smoke tobacco. . . . The cannibals smoke hemp. The Bakuba women never smoke.[96]

Sheppard appreciated the talented singers who used a variety of musical instruments in their serenading. He recalled: "Many nights the Bakuba gathered around my house and, with harps and voices made sweet music. The harps are something on the order of small crude mandolins. . . . Around the home, in the field or on a journey they always whistle, hum or sing."[97] In the Sheppard collection at Montreat is a kalimba, which has metal reeds over a wooden sounding board. Harmony can be produced by depressing and releasing the reeds with the thumbs, so outsiders have called the instrument a "thumb piano." It takes considerable skill to play one, because I have not succeeded in making much music on my kalimba after years of trying!

Complicated procedures for salt extraction and soap making were developed by the Kubas. Lacking natural salt deposits, they cut, dried, and burned reeds from certain swamps. The ashes were then boiled and a salt deposit collected. For making soap, the oil extracted from smashed palm nuts was heated with an alkali that came from the ashes of banana leaves.[98]

Even though they were all pagan when he first encountered them, and not until several years later did any profess Christianity, Sheppard gave the "highly civilized" Kubas this tribute:

> I grew very fond of the Bakuba and it was reciprocated. They were the finest looking race I had seen in Africa, dignified, graceful, coura-geous, honest, with an open, smiling countenance and really hos-pitable. Their knowledge of weaving, embroidering, wood carving and smelting was the highest in equatorial Africa.[99]

Torday was also bold to assert that the Kuba "are undoubtedly the greatest artists of black Africa; as weavers, embroiderers, carvers in wood and as workers of metal they have not their equals in the whole continent."[100] Vansina supports Torday's high rating of this art: "The Kuba achievement has been underrated in the history of Africa. . . . In many ways it was comparable to that of the kingdom of Benin from about 1500 onward."[101] The British stole much of the Benin art after conquering the West African kingdom over a century ago, resulting in its bronzes becoming widely known in European museums. Western-ers are more likely to be knowledgeable of various West African king-doms than they are of the Kuba kingdom, even though the latter produced a lion's share of Congolese art.

Sheppard observed patterns of maturation and gender interaction. Pubescent boys were instructed in tribal mores while in seclusion, and this education was concluded with a ceremony before the king. He placed a conical cap on the head of every youth, attaching it to a tuft of hair by a long iron pin with an ornament in the end.[102] He charged those coming of age to go out and build a home, cultivate land, and marry someone desirable.

A young man, rather than his parents, usually took the initiative in finding a mate, and a girl had the right to refuse his proposal. The courting procedure was described by Sheppard in this way:

> A young man sees a girl whom he likes; he has met her in his own town or at some other, or perhaps at a market place or a dance. He sends her tokens of love, bananas, plantains, peanuts, dried fish or grasshop-pers. She in turn sends him similar presents. . . . He asks her to have him, if she has no one else on her heart, and tells her that he wants no one to eat the crop that is in the field but her.[103]

To seal the marriage contract, the fellow gives the bride's mother and uncle a payment, which could be cowries, cloth, or goats.[104] The couple sits before a judge who warns the groom, "You must have but one, or you will be beheaded," since only the king can have more than one wife. To the girl the judge says, "This is your husband; you are to love him." He charges them both not to beat each other. Sheppard claimed that Kuba husbands tend to show more affection to their wives than did the men in other tribes.[105]

The wedding celebration and subsequent gender roles were given this treatment by Sheppard:

> The young man and girl, with their young friends, all dressed in their best robes, meet and march Indian file through the open market and receive congratulations from everybody. The new bride and groom continue their march to the already prepared house of the young man. A feast of goat, sheep, monkey, chicken, or fish, with plenty of palm wine is served and all is ended with a big dance. . . . The husband knows that he must cut down the forest and assist in planting corn, millet, beans, peas, sweet potatoes and tobacco, hunt for game, bring the palm wine, palm nuts, make his wife's garments, and repair the house. He is never to be out after eight o'clock at night unless sitting up at a wake or taking part in a public town dance. . . . The wife is expected to shave and anoint the husband's body with palm oil, keep his toenails and fingernails manicured, bring water and wood, help in the field, cook his food, and take care of the children.[106]

Shaving by one's spouse was needed because there were no mirrors before Sheppard arrived. Dim reflection in the water was the only means for the Congolese to see their faces. He caused a sensation when he gave out many small, silvered glass mirrors. No gift that he could have bestowed was more coveted.[107] Not impressed with the dull implements used by the Kubas for shaving, Sheppard testified: "I borrowed a native razor. . . . You wet your face with clear water and by many painful downward strokes you 'chisel' off your beard."[108] He brought back to America some iron and brass "razors" that do look like chisels and were used for removing whiskers as well as protrusions on leather or raffia.[109]

The matrilineal status of royalty increased the dignity of all mothers. Sheppard recorded these observations: "A man never meets face to face his mother-in-law on the highway. The man steps off and hides or turns his face. He never sits near or eats with her at any time. He must always act shy. He honors her in this way."[110]

The Kubas projected the centrality of family relations onto their stories about the heavenly bodies: "The sun was the father of the heavens, the moon was his wife, and the stars were their children."[111] The moon,

which beamed with exceptional brightness near the equator and supplied virtually all the light in towns at night, was scrutinized because it
allegedly portended important happenings among earthlings. Sheppard observed:

> Gardens and fields were planted on the light and dark of the moon,
> and children born under certain moons were fortunate or unfortun-
> ate. . . . The new moon was carefully watched whether it bore good or
> evil tidings. If the crescent lay with both points upward, this was a sign
> of peace. If it stood on the point, drums were beaten, horns blown,
> arrows dipped afresh in poison, for there was going to be blood shed.[112]

Ceremonializing the dead was among the Kuba rites of passage that
Sheppard studied. He described the treatment given a man whom he
had been visiting during his terminal illness. When his family discerned
his condition, they bathed him and put on burial clothes. Sheppard
advised them against being too hasty, but they continued preparations
by shaving his upper body and anointing him with palm oil. The wife
asked her dying husband about any debts he owed that were unknown
to her. He was able to communicate that he owed none but that certain
debtors, whom he named, had not repaid him. After his family and
friends watched him expire, a scream was initiated by his wife. "Then,"
Sheppard said, "all the town came with slow steps and moaning song,
hands extended in the air or folded over the head to weep with the
bereft. They all cried; those who really could not cry squeezed out
tears, anyway. They must cry." Mourners passed in review before the
deceased, who was placed in an armchair, with a new hat on his head
and an elephant tail in his hand to show strength. The next day there
was an all-day dance "to cheer up the bereaved family and to run away
evil spirits." The funeral was concluded on the third day at a graveyard
outside of town when pallbearers lowered the "oblong telescoping coffin" into the ground. On top of a layer of banana leaves the women put
in clay with their hands; this was followed by men who closed the grave
completely. For the next year the widow was expected to remain away
from the public and secluded with friends.[113]

Although Sheppard generally lauded the high standards of the Kubas,
he was not uncritical of some of their practices. He expressed a mixture of anger and revulsion with regard to the killing of innocent persons. Along with many African cultures, the Kubas presumed that
there is a human cause for every bad happening. Sheppard provided
these illustrations:

A woman crying and holding her hands over a bruised eye came to my place asking for medicine. She said that early in the morning she and her husband had a quarrel, and he on his way to his cornfield was bitten by a snake. He returned home and beat her for it and said that she had sent the snake to bite him. The capsizing of a canoe, the falling out of a palm tree, a hunter or traveler killed by elephant or leopard—these are caused by some enemy.[114]

In another of Sheppard's examples, the Kubas blamed outsiders for damages resulting from a violent storm. The upset king accused Sheppard's people of causing the storm by stirring up the water at the creek the day before. The missionary calmed the king by explaining that the suds produced by foreign soap when clothes were washed could not cause a storm cloud. Also, witch doctors searched for the person who caused lightning to strike a person.[115]

The nonscientific causality that Sheppard found intolerable was the pervasive trial by poisoning. He asserted:

In the native mind no one dies an ordinary death: they have been bewitched by an enemy. The witch doctors are paid by the relatives of the deceased to hunt out the guilty one. Early in the morning with painted bodies, feathers in their hair, leopard skins on their bodies, big war knives in their hands, they proceed to run, leap, scream, ring iron bells up and down the streets, stopping and hooting at every door, until by some imaginary force they are held at someone's door. A great shout goes up from the chasers. The person is called out and accused. Of course, they declare their innocence, but they are taken to a shed called the witch's house.[116]

An old woman whom Sheppard knew at Mushenge was seized and accused of killing a child. She protested that she did not even know the child was sick. Her belief in her own innocence and her faith in the witchcraft ordeal was such that she willingly downed the bowl of poison. Sheppard saw her stagger and fall in agony about ten minutes after drinking the potion. Wood was then piled up and her body was burned to ashes.[117]

Sheppard gave these details regarding the theory and practice of the ordeal:

The condemned sits from one to three days in the house made for that purpose and always on the most prominent street, to receive the visits and expressions of encouragement or condemnation of friends or enemies. The supreme test comes when the victim, followed by hundreds of villagers, is led by the witch doctor out of the town to a large plain. Bark is scraped from a poisonous tree, pounded in the presence of the excited people, mixed with water, poured into a cup or bowl, and then the witch doctor calls to the people for silence. He says to the condemned that if he is surely guilty he will die when he takes the poison; if not guilty he will vomit it. The accused never refuses to drink the poison and he seldom remains to tell the tale of innocence or guilt. The victim is told to walk and in about ten minutes the poison has its effect. If it acts as an emetic, a great shout of joy goes up from friends of the accused. The victim is allowed to be carried off to a secret place by friends and the excruciating heaving goes on for hours. If the victim, from the effects of the poison, staggers and falls, a shout goes up from enemies and the witch doctor leaps upon the neck of the fallen and crushes out the remainder of life. The body is borne by friends to a pile of dry wood and brush and placed upon it. Palm oil is poured on freely, then a torch is applied, and the body of the victim is burned. The fire, they believe, destroys both body and spirit and the person cannot come back again.[118]

As a modern person, Sheppard regarded witch hunts a travesty in any religion, whether the hunters were in a New England colony or in an African tribe. He told of his efforts to convince the Kuba king that witchcraft was wrong: "I tried to prove to him that the poisonous cup was a very cruel and unjust practice and there were no witches. . . . The king thought me very foolish, saying, 'If a person is innocent they can never die.'" The king and his people were unwavering in their dogma. Once the king used this ordeal on those whom he suspected of attempting to poison him. Sheppard reported that of those compelled to drink poison, one hundred died.[119]

Sheppard was also indignant over the way in which the Kuba royalty ruthlessly disregarded the sacredness of human life. Slaves were buried with their dead owner to increase his or her prestige in the afterlife realm; consequently, the more important the person, the more numerous the victims. Whereas animals had become substitutes for humans in the sacrificial rites of many peoples, among the Kubas nearly all the focus was on the sacrifice of humans. Slaves made up a large portion of Mushenge's population, and most of them were Lubas.[120] As has been characteristic of some other cultures from ancient times onward, the more affluent Kubas believed that the dead should be buried with utensils, clothing, and servants so they could continue their same lifestyle after death. "You can't take it with you," was not their proverb! "Slaves are kindly treated in life," Sheppard admitted, "but are often killed when their master dies." When a son of Kot aMbweeky's sister died, forty-seven slaves were buried with the Kuba heir apparent.[121]

The burial rites of a woman who had been helping at his Mushenge house was recalled by Sheppard:[122]

> On the burial day of one of the villagers I saw a number of men com-
> ing down the street with a slave woman, whom they were having trou-
> ble forcing along. I stepped out and inquired [about] the trouble, and
> they explained that the owner of the slave had died and they were
> going to bury her with the dead. I protested and ventured to rescue
> the woman. For about ten minutes the Bakuba, my people and I were
> tied up in a scramble. We were overpowered and on they went with
> their victim.[123]

Sheppard complained to the Kuba king about this practice of killing
slaves at funerals of important persons. He told the king that "it was
wrong without the least shadow of justification." Rather than being
embarrassed at the practice, the king bragged that his people honored
the dead more highly than the Kete, who sacrificed only goats.[124] At the
capital a number of slaves were kept "like cattle for slaughter" to
accompany the aged king when he died.[125] The Kubas thought that the
dignity of the deceased could be indicated by costly burial objects, and
in this regard they displayed the transcultural constant of using a
funeral for conspicuous consumption.

At the royal cemetery, Sheppard became fully aware that the massacre of innocents was not an empty boast of the nobility:

> I was shown the grave of Lukenga's mother in a grove of palms. It was
> marked with tusks of ivory and surrounded by a great many other
> graves. "Whose are these other graves?" I asked. "Oh those are the
> slaves who were sent with her." "What—so many?" "Yes, the people
> loved her, and all the villages around contributed slaves."[126]

Trial by poison and funeral homicide made Sheppard especially
aware of the need for a religion that championed social justice and
Christian mercy. He concluded: "Seeing these awful customs practiced
by these people for ages makes you indignant and depressed and also
fills you with pity. Only by preaching God's word, having faith, patience
and love will we eradicate the deep-rooted evil."[127]

Sheppard was soon given international recognition for his exploration
of areas previously unknown to Europeans. Within a year of his departure from Mushenge, he lectured on his expedition to the Kuba kingdom and exhibited some exquisite artifacts in London's Exeter Hall.
The prestigious Royal Geographical Society, the oldest scientific association of its type, recognized him particularly for the discovery of a
lake in the Kasai region, which they named Lake Sheppard.[128] On June
23, 1893, that Society elected him a Fellow, an honor earlier conferred

upon David Livingstone, Henry Stanley, and George Grenfell when they returned from Africa, and upon Charles Darwin when he returned from his Beagle voyage. At the age of twenty-eight, Sheppard was one of the youngest members ever inducted into the Society as well as the first African-American member.[129] Henceforth his status was much enhanced by having the F.R.G.S. initials placed after his name in publications. Subsequently, Sheppard discovered in the Kuba kingdom another lake and named it in honor of Mary Baldwin, the distinguished educator of Staunton, Virginia.[130] His appreciation of Baldwin may have been due in part to her liberal contributions to PCUS foreign missions.[131]

When Sheppard returned to the United States, he gave Americans their first view of Kuba art. He explained the details of mat making and told of leaving a handsome mat at the White House:

> The bamboo is first gathered, and from it are then prepared splits generally 180 to 220 in number, three to four yards in length. They then prepare their twisted threads, and dye them in different colors, and weave them in the splits artistically with their hands. When finished, such a mat is a lovely piece of work, and, as my wife says, "an ornament to any floor." I had the pleasure of presenting to our honored President, Mr. Cleveland, one of these mats, which he accepted for his floor.[132]

At Virginia Hall in Hampton, where a decade earlier Sheppard had attended classes, he gave an illustrated lecture featuring extraordinary Kuba knives and battle axes, native foods, and textiles with delicate pile. He had begun collecting artifacts for his alma mater as soon as he arrived in the Congo and continued to do so for his two decades there. He informed President Armstrong, in a letter written on September 1, 1890, of obtaining many objects for the Curiosity Room at Hampton.[133] Armstrong had convinced Sheppard that exposure to native artifacts was one of the best ways of inculcating appreciation of other peoples. Having been delighted by examining expressions of alien cultures as a Hamptonian himself, Sheppard was eager to provide such stimulation for subsequent students.

Cureau observes that "as a class, art collectors in the Western World were: (a) white Americans, and Europeans; (b) persons of high socio-economic status; and (c) persons with sufficient leisure and wealth to travel at will." He finds it noteworthy that the Sheppards, although outside that class, amassed art objects of considerable merit "from Africans at all levels of their society, and in the context of their daily existence and relationships with these peoples."[134]

Many years passed before the enlightenment Sheppard gave the Western world about the Kubas corrected distortions that many colonial people had about African culture. For example, Diedrich Westermann, director of the International Institute of African Languages and Cultures, wrote decades after Sheppard's discovery: "No African people or group of peoples have ever formed a nation . . . bound together by a common language, civilization, and history. . . . Since they have never had a national consciousness, they could not feel humiliated by foreign rule."[135] Actually, the Kubas had a well-formed culture and government before the Belgian nation was formed and they resented the encroachments of Leopold's agents on their sovereignty.

4

Mission Developments

Not long after returning to Luebo from the Kuba capital, Sheppard headed for America to begin a well-deserved year's furlough and, as he said, "to marry a very sweet Christian woman." George and Margaret Adamson, members of the Free Church of Scotland, took charge of the APCM during his absence. They came to Kinshasa as lay missionaries, where machinist George helped build the steamer *Pioneer* for the Bololo mission. They had both studied at Guinness's London Institute for Missions. Thinking that the APCM could make good use of the talents of a couple with a Presbyterian heritage, Lapsley and Sheppard recommended their employment, and they arrived in Luebo shortly after Lapsley's death.[1]

During the absence of Sheppard from the APCM, the Kuba king invited the Adamsons to visit him. They reported that "their reception and impressions seem to have been much less favorable than Mr. Sheppard's, and they only tarried one day." Adamson preached to the king and asked if he wanted a missionary to settle in his midst. The king curtly replied that he wanted Sheppard to come but not the "Bula Matadi."[2] In the latter he probably included not only Belgian officers but all white people. Adamson, unfortunately, lacked the ability to carry on as Sheppard's partner.

While awaiting his ship at Matadi, Sheppard met four additional APCM appointees, the Rev. Arthur Rowbotham from England and his wife Margaret, as well as DeWitt Snyder, a druggist from America, and his wife May. Sheppard helped the newcomers make the difficult trek to Kinshasa and then walked more than two hundred miles back to embark for Europe. Arthur observed: "Brother Sheppard is just a whole team in himself. He has the natives well in hand, and they like him. He has a good way with him in being friendly with the carriers, and yet having them do as he says." Sheppard walked along with Arthur, who was riding in a hammock because of illness. "Brother Sheppard is a fine doctor of fever, and a splendid nurse," Arthur acknowledged. He told of the various medications he had received from Sheppard and added, "The rubbing he gave me . . . was worth having the fever!"[3]

After witnessing the effectiveness of the drugs dispensed by Sheppard, a hammock man requested some medicine to make his wife love him. Arthur noted about that native: "He had bought her from a neighboring village and she would not live with him, but at his approach ran away into the tall grass and hid from him. Sheppard told them we had no medicine to give, but talked to her. The next day the carrier said it was all right."[4]

Near Kinshasa the trekkers visited Makoko, a chief with whom Stanley had made one of his treaties. Both Stanley and the missionaries were amazed by the beard he wore in two coils.[5] When unrolled it was six feet long and hit the ground when he stood! The once powerful Makoko was subdued by Leopold's agents, and Rowbotham reported that "now all his people have gone away on account of the burdens imposed on them by the state people."[6]

The Congo was especially unkind to white women. The first one to enter the Kasai basin, Margaret Adamson, became the first to be buried in the missionary cemetery in Luebo. Then Margaret Rowbotham's chronic illness caused the Rowbothams to decide to leave the Congo mission with her infant son four months after arriving in Luebo. The Snyders continued on until 1896, when May died of malaria. More personnel who could withstand the rigors of life in the tropics were desperately needed.

Sheppard was engaged to Lucy Gantt, an Alabaman two years younger than himself. She was born in Tuscaloosa to a former slave, Eliza Gantt, who had been abandoned by her impregnator prior to the baby's birth. Since Lucy's pigmentation was light brown, her father may have been white. When this only child of Eliza was old enough to go to school, the mother joined her in order to learn to read the Bible. Lucy later recalled that schooling was limited during a year to the three months between cotton seasons. At eleven she was admitted to a school for blacks at Talladega, Alabama, which had been started along with Hampton and Fisk by the Missionary Association of the Congregational Church. (Talladega College was the first in Alabama to be opened to blacks and it offered degrees regardless of race. It continues to be affiliated with the United Church of Christ.)

Each month during Lucy's nine years at Talladega, Eliza sent eight out of the ten dollars she earned as a domestic to pay Lucy's tuition. Among her teachers were graduates of Yale, Oberlin, Wellesley, and Mt. Holyoke. Dr. Du Bois discerned that the contribution of these idealistic instructors from the North was "not alms, but a friend." They "came not to keep the Negroes in their place, but to raise them out of the defilement of the places where slavery had wallowed them." They lived and ate with their students, putting them in touch with the best American traditions.[7]

When enrolled at Talladega, Lucy engaged in her first missionary work. Her summers were spent in spartan conditions while teaching basic literacy to blacks.[8] Her school was "one-room with backless benches and no equipment." When she later read about Du Bois's teaching in rural Tennessee, she recognized the similarity between their work in adjacent states at the same time.[9] He had assisted African American children struggling against the "barriers of caste" as they sat on rough planks in a log hut.[10] When the teenaged Tuscaloosan returned to her hometown for holidays, she and Sheppard met and fell in love.

Lucy developed a beautiful singing voice under the tutelage of the skilled wife of the president of Talladega. She participated in the college choir and was featured as a soprano soloist on special occasions. After graduation, Lucy accepted an invitation to tour for a year with the famous chorus that introduced Negro spirituals in the Northern states and in Europe. Lucy agreed with Du Bois that those folksongs were "the most beautiful expression of human experience born this side of the seas; . . . the Fisk Jubilee Singers sang the slave songs so deeply into the world's heart that it can never wholly forget them again."[11]

Having completed Talladega's "normal school" program, Lucy obtained a good teaching position in a Birmingham city school in 1887 and retained it for six years. She became engaged before she knew her fiancee was planning to become a missionary to Africa, and that calling necessitated a long wait for an opportune time for marriage. Their correspondence was handicapped by the nine months it sometimes took for an exchange of letters between Alabama and Africa. In 1893 she was elated to receive a London cable from "Sheppard, F.R.G.S.," announcing that he would see her in a few weeks.[12]

The wedding took place in Jacksonville, Florida, where Eliza Gantt had gone to live. In February 1894, on the day before the ceremony, Sheppard spoke at a Florida school about his Congo adventures and concluded by saying, "The man who did these things is to be married tomorrow right here in your own city." Consequently, those children filled the Laura Street Presbyterian Church, where William and Lucy were married amid bouquets of orange blossoms.

In addition to attending to personal matters while on leave, missionaries have the vital responsibility of publicizing their work with hopes of obtaining more support from their constituency. In his home state, Sheppard's address at Hampton Institute entitled "Into the Heart of Africa" was published in 1893, providing the first written record of the Kuba culture. He received an enthusiastic hearing at a meeting of the PCUS Synod of Virginia. Bridges reported that Sheppard "has been speaking to crowded houses, capturing all by his eloquence, fund of humor, and histrionic qualities." That reporter, a white minister, concluded, "A Virginia Negro, through the power of Almighty Grace, is our hero."[13] Sheppard also went on a lecture tour in the North with President Hollis Frissell of Hampton Institute, and spoke in Chicago in response to an invitation from the McCormick Seminary faculty.[14] Pertaining to his itinerating in Kentucky among predominantly white churches, this record was made, "Sheppard told the story of his experiences in numerous churches and before church assemblies so vividly and so appealingly that the whole church took the Congo mission to its heart and new impetus was given the entire missionary enterprise."[15] In his article "When Black Missionaries Opened Africa," E. T. Thompson notes that "Sheppard's genial nature and tactful conduct made him a universal favorite."[16] Indeed, this was the case among both Americans and African tribes! Sheppard's ability so impressed a Mr. Graham of Asheville, North Carolina, that he arranged to pay his mission salary.[17]

Realizing that the APCM might close unless the Luebo staff were increased, Sheppard was eager to recruit new personnel for the mission. A white Southerner reported on the interest Sheppard awakened: "The people of his own race listened with deepest interest to his accounts of Africa, and the sad condition of her millions of people. A strong desire was kindled in their hearts to do something to aid in the great work of their redemption."[18] The Sheppards persuaded two fellow Talladega alumnae, Maria Fearing and Lillian Thomas, to join them. In addition, Sheppard recruited Henry Hawkins, a Mississippian who had graduated from the seminary in Tuscaloosa.

Maria Fearing had been a slave on a cotton plantation for the first twenty-five years of her life. Amanda Winston, her mistress, selected her as a house-girl and included her when engaged in religious education with her children. After Fearing heard stories of children in other lands who did not know of God's love, she hoped that some day she could share the Good News with Africans. She united with the Presbyterian Church in Gainesville, Alabama, to which the Winstons belonged and where Charles Stillman was the pastor.[19]

After the Civil War, Fearing found employment with someone who was willing to assist her in the rudiments of literacy. A minister, noticing her determination to become educated, enabled her to enter the preparatory school operated by Talladega College. At the age of thirty-three, she began elementary school and excelled in her studies. After completing the ninth grade, she became a teacher and earned enough to buy a home in Anniston. She then returned to the college as a residence hall matron and became the roommate and the chaperon of the youngest student, Lucy Gantt. While together at Talladega, the matron probably shared with Lucy her dream to go serve in Africa.

Fearing heard Sheppard speak about Africa when he visited Talladega in 1894, causing the spark kindled by her former owner to burst into flame. She eagerly responded to Sheppard's appeal for volunteers to assist him in the Congo. However, the Mission Committee turned down her application, probably because they presumed that it would be too difficult for a fifty-six-year-old, Pygmy-sized person with less than a high school education to learn a new language and have the physical vigor needed to cope with the tropics. She then told Samuel Lapsley's father of her desire to go even if she paid her own way, and begged him to buy her house. Judge Lapsley agreed to purchase her home in Anniston, the town where he now also lived, and to intercede on her behalf with the Mission Committee. Fearing's application was then approved and a few days later, as the first self-supporting PCUS missionary, she joined in New York the other missionaries Sheppard had recruited.[20] Maria Fearing and Lillian Thomas, both Alabama natives, became close companions for life and they had remarkably little sickness during their Congo years.

Lucy Sheppard did not feel well for most of the trip to Luebo because of seasickness and pregnancy. She did manage to get out in London to pay homage at Livingstone's tomb and to hear the children's choir at St. Paul's Cathedral. Julia Kellersberger, Lucy's biographer, states that "she was woman enough to be keenly interested in shopping for a year's supply of food and clothing, and in packing their tropical garments in termite-proof tin trunks." During a month in what was then the world's leading international capital, her husband addressed the public in a variety of places. He wrote, "I was invited and spoke to large assemblies in Y. M. C. A. room, Bishopgate, Exeter Hall, Congregational Church, St. John's Wood, East London Tabernacle and Presbyterian Church, Regents Square."[21]

While they sailed on another Dutch ship southward from Europe, a heavy gale brought waves crashing over the deck for many days. The Sheppards were not only seasick but anxious over whether the steamer would stay afloat. Their most gratifying experience was seeing—a hundred miles before entering the river's mouth—the brown water from the Congo as it contrasted with the blue ocean. In elegant prose, Lucy described the Congo's color as

> a symbol of the people whose bodies reflected its deep, dark sheen; whose souls had been as unfathomable as its depths; whose struggles for centuries had been as varied and as consuming as its rush to the sea; and whose future still remained as unknown as the depths of the river's bed in its whirlpool regions.[22]

Reality overcame romanticism on their dreadful trip upcountry. At Boma, Lucy saw for the first time her husband delirious with malaria. As a milestone along the way, they visited Lapsley's grave where Sheppard had made a neat cement covering, and they planted there some American flowers. At Matadi, Lucy got on the Congo "rapid transit," as a picture of the three-mile-per-hour hammock transportation is captioned in Sheppard's photo album. She is shown suspended from a large bamboo pole while on her long journey to Kinshasa. Her husband taught her words for "stop" and "go" in the native language, but she confused the terms. Consequently, when she grew stiff from constant jogging, her command to the carriers only resulted in greater speed and more bumps! To complete their caravan journey before the rainy season began, they arose before dawn and covered twenty-two miles daily, the men on foot and the women in hammocks. At night they gathered around a campfire and had their one hot meal of the day. One night they stayed at the American Baptist station at Banza Manteke, where the Sheppards had the delight of being awakened by graduates of Spelman College in Atlanta who brought them freshly baked biscuits.

The new missionaries quickly learned that some Europeans had made life difficult even for black Americans. The carriers were on the verge of deserting or killing their passengers in the mountainous jungle after finding that white traders had left in ashes a village along the way where families of some of the carriers had lived. Sheppard averted their mutiny by speaking to them in their language and convincing them that all foreigners should not be blamed for the disaster. Hawkins wrote that "the road from Matadi to Lukunga was a kind of hospital of the meanest kind, in that it had no inmates to attend upon the afflicted and dying." In addition to frequently seeing the discarded bodies of carriers, they observed women and children dying of hunger and disease. Sheppard administered medicine to credulous natives who believed that "God's men" have a "balm" for every illness.[23]

At Kinshasa the Americans began the difficult voyage upriver on a steamer, which was probably the same one that Snyder described:

> Our steamer . . . is a long narrow boat and very tricky, given to upsetting at the least provocation; her boilers are old, her decks rotten, her cabins small and dirty and, as usual with state steamers, her cuisine abominable. . . . The captain ran us into the bushes growing along the side of the river, scraping one deck of the steamer from stem to stern and carrying away a big monkey which was tied to the rail. . . . Another time the captain lost control of the steamer and we floated sidewise, steamed backwards, and for an hour or more went every way but the right way. A large steamer belonging to the Dutch Trading Co. coming over the same route two days behind us was overturned by the swift current, resulting in the complete loss of the steamer and a rich cargo of rubber, besides the loss of some of the crew.[24]

Continuing upcountry on the steamer, they found that Leopold's agents had continued to cause life-endangering antagonisms. The women lay for hours on the floor of the dining salon over a period of two days while the boat was hit by arrows from hostile villagers who were retaliating because State officers on the preceding riverboat had attacked them.[25] Congolese patience was coming to an end, even though, as a London periodical at this time stated, they had shown remarkable restraint:

> The natives of the Congo have consistently refrained from shedding white men's blood. They have been shot down ruthlessly, by the score, since Stanley's days, when European governors or explorers deemed their destruction necessary; but though they have often offered fight in self-defence, they have never taken the initiative, as far as we are aware, in molesting the invaders.[26]

The Luebo-bound steamer ran short of food, so the passengers lived for days on meager fare. Lucy boiled leaves of sweet potato vines in a

tin can to provide something green to supplement the hardtack crack-
ers.[27] The workmen aboard dealt with their hunger in a different way.
After one of them drowned, the captain told his fellow workmen to take
the recovered body ashore and bury it. After they went out of sight,
Sheppard learned, they "actually ate their dead comrade."[28] A more civilized feast occurred after Sheppard—who had acquired the name
Ngela, meaning "hunter"—shot a hippo and supplied steaks for all
aboard.

Since the rainy season had not begun, the water depth was not sufficient to permit the steamer to go up the Lulua River to Luebo. An
overloaded canoe transported the five missionaries and some of their
possessions up the Kasai tributary for the last lap of their trip, soaking
all aboard. In the light of a tropical October moon, the Sheppards
arrived bedraggled at their destination and the "honeymoon voyage of
ten thousand miles was over."[29]

On returning to Luebo, Sheppard found that the station that had been
left under George Adamson's oversight was now nearly in shambles.[30]
Following the death of his wife, Adamson had resigned from the mission. The Snyders were the only missionaries left in Luebo, and there
were no professing Christians among the natives. Sheppard now
worked with the new missionaries from Alabama to revitalize the
APCM.

The Sheppards' first residence was a hut made of sticks and mud
with a leaky thatched roof and rotting mats on a dirt floor. The damp-
ness and the darkness within was depressing. They found the infesta-
tion of snakes in their house similar to what might be expected of rats
in an American barn. When a python crawled over the bed in which he
and Lucy were sleeping, Sheppard was more concerned about his wife
being terrified than about being harmed by the snake. Moving with serpentine quietness so as not to alarm her or scare away the intruder, he
slithered out of bed and killed it.

At the time of year when Jesus' birth in a stable was being commemorated, Lucy brought forth her firstborn in a similar setting, and
named her Miriam. There was little joy because the mother "came very
near death."[31] Snyder was called on to deliver the infant even though he
had never seen a baby born. He did not know what to do when he found
that the placenta had not been discharged. The medical text he consulted simply advised that a physician should be called if such a
complication arose, but that was impossible. Fortunately, there was no
hemorrhaging and the placenta was expelled naturally three agonizing

days after the delivery. Although Miriam was six weeks premature, she appeared to be in good health until her sudden death a few weeks later.[32] Poignantly, the baby was buried in a bamboo coffin lined and covered with her mother's wedding dress.[33]

Snyder's attitude toward Africans made life especially difficult for him at Luebo. He wrote home that he was "entirely outside the limits of civilization . . . among the . . . degraded savages of Africa." He stated that his message was to "tell them of the wonderful words of Jesus; how He came not only to save the enlightened people of America but also this benighted, untutored black people, living in sin and darkness."[34] Snyder recalled the line "naught but man is vile" from a missionary hymn on seeing "half naked men and women and children keeping time to the tomtom, a native drum, in figures lewd and disgusting." From that spectacle, he concluded, "One cannot help but think, none but the Devil reigns here."[35]

Snyder had ambivalent feelings toward Sheppard. On the one hand he found him to be "a wonderful helper and a good companion" and relied on him to engage in French conversation with the Belgian traders in the area.[36] His wife referred to William and Lucy Sheppard as "refined, gentle, and deferential in manner to us" and she appreciated the eight nights he attended her when she had a high fever. "Mr. Sheppard was indeed a brother in every sense of the word," she said; "this sickness has brought us all very close together." Yet DeWitt was unable to overcome his racial prejudice. During his wife's illness he felt bereft that even though the Sheppards were mulattos, they were "not such companions as white people make." He gave this stereotypical judgment about the APCM African Americans: "It is my opinion that they will do well if they always have white help at the head. I don't think our colored brethren are capable of doing good work by themselves."[37] For DeWitt, racial consciousness was so dominant that even blacks whom he acknowledged as sharing similar religious orientation, educational attainment, and social graces were not fully acceptable as friends.

Sheppard built a new five-room house for Lucy and himself that was comparatively more comfortable. A hard floor was made by spreading dust from pulverized termite mounds, trampling it down smoothly, and building a fire on it. The walls were constructed of woven palm fronds that were then covered with mud and washed with white clay found in the streams. Vines served as door hinges since there were no nails or hardware. In lieu of window panes, muslin or defective kodak film was fastened to the bamboo frame to let light in and keep bugs out. Palm leaves from the swamps were used for roofing. Regarding this spartan residence, Lucy wrote:

> All of the furniture that I had was made from packing boxes of various shapes and sizes. . . . My cooking was done out of doors, the kettle or saucepan resting on three stones, or upon several hard anthills. I managed to bake by putting live coals above and beneath a clay pot. . . . Lights were another problem. Candles were a luxury. . . . When I was finally able to obtain a glass lamp in which I could burn palm oil, I was so overjoyed that I felt certain no light in the homeland was any brighter. Congo girls took their turns, by twos, working in my home learning new methods of more abundant living. The laundry work was especially difficult for them, since their own washing was always done by beating their loincloths on boulders by the river's brink. Boys were trained in my kitchen to cook, for I had ever in mind the future home-making of young Christian men and women.[38]

The Sheppards found that even their new home was an inviting place for other creatures to set up residence. "Innumerable frogs, insects, and spiders of tremendous size moved in with the Sheppards and set up their own housekeeping with a vengeance," Kellersberger states. One night they were awakened by sounds of crunching on the roof thatch, and the next day they found the intruder's footprints. Phillips Verner related what had happened:

> Once Mr. and Mrs. Sheppard enjoyed the novel sensation of hearing what proved to be a leopard walking over the thin palm leaf roofing of their house just over their heads. Soon after the visitor made way with eleven goats on the place in a single night. His practice was to break the necks of one after another as fast as he could, and then to carry each one off and hide it in the forest. The powerful beast was strong enough to jump over a six-foot wall with a hundred-pound goat in his mouth.[39]

In the Montreat archives there are several photos of leopards killed by Sheppard. He shot them more for self-protection than for sport. On his Kasai expedition a decade later, Torday shows that leopards continued to be a hazard to humans as well as to domestic animals. He wrote, "The country is simply infested with leopards, and as many as five people have been killed by these beasts in one day."[40] When Sheppard was asked in 1893 about the danger of wild animals in the Congo, he coolly replied, "I have known of only five persons carried off by any since I have been in Africa."[41]

In June 1895, Sheppard prepared for a week's march from Luebo to revisit the Kuba king in Mushenge. Against his better judgment, Lucy decided to accompany him. He explained:

> My wife would not listen to anything that I said about hardships and dangers on the road. I told her of big elephants, little elephants, big leopards and other animals, but she simply replied, "Well I would like to see some of them." Her head was set that way, and there was no use talking, she just had to go. I have found out a few things since marrying—when women set their heads to a good work, they are not easily dissuaded.[42]

In a jungle so dense that the sunlight could not penetrate, they passed through an area thick with elephants. Sheppard scouted with his rifle in front of Lucy's hammock along a path where elephant tracks were fresh. They sang and talked as loud as they could, hoping that the elephants would seek a quieter place. "My wife was quite brave," he reported; "one of my regrets was that she did not know how to climb a tree."[43]

Sheppard's pet monkey again proved to be an asset to the evangelist. At the end of a day's march he brought forth Tippo Tib to amuse the villagers while tents were being set up. Following this, Sheppard said,

> We quietly moved Tippo on the inside, and we had a full congregation for a Gospel service. They give excellent attention while you are speaking and singing; but when you say "let us pray," and have concluded your petitions, and open your eyes, you will be surprised, and also amused, to find the greater part of your congregation away up the street.

At those services Lucy started off with the hymn "E Jisus kusa"—"Yes, Jesus Loves Me."[44]

At a village near the capital, the Sheppards encountered a son of Lukengu. They admired the handsome five-inch knife he carried in his belt; it had a brass blade and an ebony handle inlaid with copper. The prince said it was given to him by his father to show that he was empowered to collect taxes. Sheppard was later given that knife.[45]

A royal honor guard came out of the capital to escort the Sheppards, and many Kubas greeted them along the entry pathway. That evening they were serenaded by musicians who were using instruments resembling mandolins. The next morning there was a crowd of five hundred outside the guest house to say good morning.[46]

In a letter written while at the capital, Sheppard told of a private meeting with his old friend. The *Lukengu* was not seated on his throne as before, but reclined on leopard skins. He grasped Sheppard and exclaimed: "My son! my son! do you still love me, and have you come at last! I sent message after message for you, but no word came." The king was disturbed because he knew that Sheppard had been back in Luebo for eight moons before coming back to visit him.

At a formal reception in the public square, one of Sheppard's men preceded the delegation from Luebo; he carried a staff flying the Congo Free State's lone star, the United States' stars and stripes, and the ensign of the APCM. When the king entered in his best robe with a spotlessly white eagle plume on his head, "a shout from 5,000 voices ascended in one chorus." The aged king, who was unable to walk without assistance, greeted Lucy, noting comparative heights, for she could stand erect under her husband's arm.

Sheppard presented *Lukengu* with gifts from people living in several American states, including medicine, an album showing buildings at the World's Fair, a silver cup, and a pocket knife. The king was pleased to know that people in a foreign land were thinking of him. Sheppard also said to the king, "The highest honor which I can do you and your people is to commend you in prayer to the King of kings."[47]

Sheppard's pleasure of returning to Mushenge and introducing Lucy to the Kuba culture was diminished by a happening that he noted: "Last night, about midnight, I heard screaming and moaning. . . . The evening before a child of royalty had died, so the parents had had four slaves—two women and two men—killed, to honor, as they believe, their little one!"

While in Mushenge, Sheppard was at liberty to do evangelistic work. In doing so he gave attention to the "wicked custom" of killing Luba slaves to be buried with someone of prominence. Preaching, for Sheppard, was not a one-way proclamation, but a combining of listening with speaking. "All of my preaching to the king was in the way of conversation," he said.[48] These discussions with the king about God's expectations pertaining to human rights seem to have affected him. Lucy watched him "lean forward, drinking in every word that was said to him of Him who came to 'seek and to save.'"[49] Sheppard wrote, "I have a promise from Lukenga's lips that this cruel murder shall be stopped."[50] However, the practice continued with subsequent Kuba kings for another decade. Fearing reported that when this king died, even a boy living at Luebo who had become a Christian was taken by his former slaveowner to be sacrificed.[51]

Back in Luebo, the Sheppards continued their evangelistic work. Lucy reported on the first APCM baptismal service, explaining the requirements for becoming a church member: "In April 1895, five young men wanted to profess faith. . . . These were carefully instructed and trained, and after some months when we had seen evidence of their changed lives, we received them into the church. At once these five started out as missionaries of Jesus." One of those youths, Kachunga, was unusually intelligent and was selected to go to America to assist in translation work.[52] Hawkins later gave this report from Luebo: "Sheppard preached a feeling sermon on 'The Prodigal Son.' Soon after, four prodigals gave notice that they desired to return to the house of their Father."[53]

These natives then went to ten Kasai villages to teach and lead Christians, Sheppard reported, and they were "received kindly."[54] Although they were literate, they relied on what they remembered because no textbooks or Scriptures had been translated. As the dissemination of the gospel became the responsibility of converts, an indigenous self-propagating church developed.

Having Sheppard as the senior missionary at the APCM pleased his sponsoring church. In the 1897 report of the Foreign Missions Committee to the Presbyterian membership, much attention was given to his effectiveness with white State officials as well as with blacks. Tribute was also paid to the women who had joined him three years earlier: "If he has been worthy of his high trust, no less can be said of the three devoted women who have been his fellow helpers in all this time of trial. Surely our Church has reason to be devoutly thankful for her colored missionaries."[55] Walter Williams has noticed that Presbyterian officials consistently referred to their black personnel as "Reverend," "Mr.," "Mrs.," or "Miss" and gave them not only respect but an influential voice in the making of mission policy.[56] The respect shown Sheppard had a reciprocal effect, as is displayed in what he wrote to those Presbyterian executives: "I am proud of our Southern Church, which is doing so much for the evangelization of the Negro in America and in Africa. I owe all that I am, or ever expect to be, to that Church."[57]

Because of her former training and experience, Lucy had oversight of the APCM educational work. She first had to learn Tshiluba, of course, and for that there were no manuals. As her husband had done several years earlier, she mingled daily with villagers in the market place, straining to pick up every nuance of inflection. Her ear was so sensitive that the vocabulary she compiled was published in the first Tshiluba dictionary.[58]

A chief called Luebo "God's Town" and sent some from his tribe to be part of the community.[59] Actually, Luebo was now not one town but a number of villages spread over several miles, with a local chief in each. It had become a magnet for runaway slaves owned de facto by State officials and by some villagers who lived outside the Luebo area. The missionaries upheld the biblical law declaring that fugitives should not be returned to bondage but should be permitted to dwell in freedom wherever they had taken sanctuary.[60] Since the masters from whom the slaves had fled had an investment in what they presumed to be their property, maintaining a freedom sanctuary demanded continual vigilance by the Mission. State Inspector Paul LeMarinel, who became the next governor of the Congo, visited the APCM to charge it with illegally liberating a fugitive slave girl. He took her away to be returned to her master.[61]

The students at Luebo continued to be mostly former slaves who had been redeemed by the mission. The place for teaching had no walls, roof, textbooks, pencils, slates, or desks. Like Jesus, Lucy wrote with her finger on the smooth ground.[62] Much of the instruction was necessarily oral, but this was rewarding because of the excellent memories that were common among preliterate people. Knowing dozens of hymns by heart was not uncommon, and Lucy marveled at the ability of some to repeat a sermon almost word for word.[63]

In 1897 Lucy reported that there were forty-five students enrolled at the Luebo school where she was principal.[64] She found them just as talented as American children in the three R's and many of them "eager for every new idea we are able to convey to them." Especially gratifying to her was the response of the girls. One of them was able, after ten months of instruction, to read from Paul's difficult letter to the Romans.[65]

At Luebo, Maria Fearing mixed well with the natives, and after a year she knew their language well enough to teach a class and translate hymns. She took charge of the girls who had been kidnapped from villages and brought to Luebo to be sold. She taught them sanitation, sewing, cooking, child care, and how to read the Gospels. Several of the early converts came from the girls she had trained. The Mission Committee in America came to realize that Fearing was worthy of full support, and after two years she was compensated with the regular missionary salary for the next two decades. She spent little on herself and used most of her personal funds to assist liberated slave girls who resided in a building named Pantops.[66] She was called Mamu [Mother] by the dozens in her family who had been orphaned, abandoned, or redeemed from slavery.[67]

Maria Fearing and Lucy Sheppard focused on giving women equal educational opportunities, hoping to liberate them from becoming domestic drudges. African women had traditionally been expected to carry quite literally the burdens of the household. William Sheppard was amazed at their strength to do heavy work, including farm hoeing. It was not unusual, he said, to find a woman with "two children tied on her back, a pot of water balanced on her head, a basket in one hand, and a large child held by the other."[68]

After Lapsley died, it was five years before another man of his ability was sent to the Congo mission. William Morrison, from Sheppard's presbytery in Virginia, shared the spirit as well as the mental ability of Lapsley. He grew up in the Shenandoah Valley near Lexington in a home of devout Presbyterians, where blacks were respected. When as a boy he saw an ex-slave chopping wood, he threw chips at him. The old man told William to stop, but finding words had no effect, he turned him over his knee and spanked him. Humiliated by being punished by a presumed inferior, he reported the incident to his mother with an expectation of her sympathy. However, his mother had watched the episode from a window and she also disciplined him for his inappropriate behavior. When Morrison told this story as an adult, he quipped, "Africa made quite a lasting impression on me the first time we came into personal contact."[69]

Both Lapsley and Sheppard would no doubt have endorsed much of what Morrison came to see as the missionary's role:

> Both Protestant and Roman Catholic missionaries are in the same work. . . . We desire to be open minded and charitable toward all who come in the name of Jesus Christ. . . . There are enough great essential principles of doctrine and Christian living to teach without wasting time and creating disturbances by emphasizing denominational differences. We should remember first and last that the natives should be treated as kindly and courteously as white people. We should always keep in mind that we are their servants and not their masters. Under their black skins they have feelings and sensibilities similar to ours, which ought to be respected. If we laugh at their customs, appearance or fetishes, we destroy their confidence in us and repel them. . . . If you make a mistake it is best to confess it in their presence. Conform to the dignified customs of chiefs and dignitaries where no morals are involved. Be ready to receive the natives without becoming impatient when you are busy.[70]

Morrison arrived at Luebo sick with fever and was carried to the home of the Sheppards. He had not met any of the APCM missionaries before, but a letter after his arrival indicates that he quickly felt at home there:

> Mr. and Mrs. Sheppard have been mine hosts, and most royally do they entertain—generous, refined, kind—a typical home, even if it is in Africa where it is no small task to have a real home. . . . This palatial residence is built of posts and sticks, daubed with mud inside and out, with roof of palm leaves, and dirt floors covered with native mats.[71]

Sheppard, now called an architect, took charge of having a larger chapel constructed in 1896 to replace the one he had built several years earlier to seat three hundred. But the new structure was soon overflowing too, and a year later he added on another thirty feet.[72] After observing Sheppard leading a Luebo church service, Morrison was struck by the veneration he was given: "Whenever he lifts his hand there is silence, whenever he speaks there is closest attention—he is a chief, a prince, an apostle among this people." In that same letter Morrison also wrote about other roles a missionary needed to play:

> I find that the duties of the missionary's daily life are a most varied character—he must be at once preacher, teacher, lawyer, judge, farmer, gardener, doctor, mechanic, accountant, scientist and last but not least, a general, who commands the confidence and obedience of all about him.

THE IBANCHE STATION

Shortly after his 1897 arrival at the APCM, Morrison wrote:

> I find the mission work on this station, Luebo, in what I regard as a most flourishing condition, due, in great part, to the faithful labors of the past. Today the chapel was crowded to its utmost capacity, many standing at the doors and windows. It was built by Mr. Sheppard only last summer. . . . Mr. Sheppard and I expect to start for Lukenga's. . . . It is a sacrifice, in a sense, for Mr. Sheppard to leave Luebo and go to found a new station, yet I believe he is glad to go to the Bakuba, and I really think it is best for him.[73]

Two months after Morrison joined the APCM, he and Sheppard set out for the Kuba capital. Sheppard's royal patron had died a year earlier and his nephew Mishaape was establishing himself as *Lukengu*. All

Kuba kings were generically called *Lukengu*, even as all Egyptian kings were called Pharoah in the Bible. To eliminate potential rivals, Mishaape murdered seven of Kot aMbweeky's sons and drove his uncle's other intimate associates into exile. Sheppard's close ties with the deceased *Lukengu* was now a liability and the Kuba royalty were never again as open to his influence. His relationship with Kuba monarchs was similar to that of the Hebrew Joseph with the Pharoahs. Just as new ones arose who did not care about the bonding that alien Joseph had established with a former Pharoah, likewise Sheppard was *persona non grata* to the new Kuba king.[74] Previously, Sheppard's reincarnation of Bope Mekabe, presumed by the earlier *Lukengu*, saved his life, but now his honorary membership in the Kuba royal family made him suspect in the eyes of Kot aMbweeky's successors.

Sheppard and Morrison waited at Ibanche (also spelled Ibaanc, Ibanj, Ibanshe, and Ibonge!) on the border of the central Kuba area, about forty miles from Mushenge and forty miles north of Luebo. There they received a message from Mishaape that he would invite them to his capital after his formal coronation. This could be celebrated only after the chiefs of all the towns in the kingdom pledged their allegiance by sending presents to the king. In addition, new elders had to be appointed and a new capital needed to be constructed to which treasures of his predecessor would be brought.[75] The death of Mishaape's mother months earlier had caused another disturbance in the Kuba kingdom. Her body lay unburied pending the slaughter of six hundred slaves for burial with her so that she could be served in a royal manner in her life after death.[76] After these conditions were met, the *Lukengu* could then crown himself simply by putting an eagle's feather in his hair. Sheppard optimistically assumed that the APCM would be able to open a station there after the political situation settled.

However, Mishaape had no interest in showing favors toward Sheppard. He was especially peeved because Maxamalinge, who was under suspicion as the son of the preceding *Lukengu*, was being sheltered by Sheppard at Ibanche. The king's agents went there with orders to assassinate Sheppard as well as Maxamalinge. However, the prince learned of this and foiled the scheme. The king then informed Sheppard that he wanted to talk with him at Mushenge. Intrepidly, he made the long journey; after arriving he was instructed to come alone to the king's palace at midnight. Sheppard told of the tense confrontation:

> I went into the presence of Lukenga. We sat down, turned face to face, folded our legs, and began talking. He said, "I am glad you have

come," and I answered, "I am glad to be here." "Do you not know,"
he said, "that it is the custom when the crown passes from one family
to another to murder all the sons of the old king? Were you not told
that you were to be shot with poisonous arrows?" I said I had heard it
but did not believe it. The king said, "It is true." Then he added, "Can
we settle this thing now?" I said, "I hope so," and I could see murder
in his eyes. He called for a man. The man brought a small pouch of
leopard skin. The king called another man and asked him for a banana
leaf. He put it over the fire to make it pliable. Then he took some
strong medicine out of the leopard skin and put it into the banana leaf.
After sitting awhile he had it tied up and gave it to a servant, telling
him to throw it into the Lingadi River. The king said, "Do you see
that?" I said, "Yes." The king said, "It has gone into the Lingadi, from
that to the Ligadi, then to the N'gala. I cannot call it back and it will
not come back. Just so everything is gone that was between us which
I had in my heart against you. He said, "Now, what are you going to
do?" I said, "If you will allow me I will kneel here on the mat with you
and pray." After prayers we went to our houses. I stayed with him a
week and then went back to Ibanj.[77]

The APCM reluctantly decided that Ibanche was as near to the Kuba
heartland as a station could safely be established. After Sheppard and
Morrison visited in some Kuba villages, Morrison reported:

> All . . . received us most kindly. . . . The people want us to come, only
> the king is in the way, but his authority is practically absolute. I have
> faith to believe that the door of the tribe is now open, and God has
> used Mr. Sheppard as the human means with his unusual tact and wis-
> dom, in the management of the natives.[78]

Back at Luebo, Lucy attempted to combine starting a family with her
school responsibilities. Her second baby, Lucille, lived only a few
months longer than her first. Then Wilhelmina was born at a time
when Luebo was threatened by a nearby uprising. Native soldiers
armed with modern rifles had revolted against the State officials and
had vowed to kill every foreigner in the district. This threatening situation, along with Lucy's exhaustion from illness, caused her to take the
advice that she should return to America with her child. Dr. Sims
thought foreign workers should take an extended break every three
years to recover from tropical illnesses, but Sheppard was content to
remain in the Congo while Lucy and Wilhelmina left.

In 1898 Sheppard accompanied his family on their trip down the
river; they arrived in Leopoldville just as the rail line was completed.[79]
That city was developing alongside Kinshasa and a monument was

erected in its central public square to honor the Belgian king who had overseen the railway construction. By special permission the Sheppards rode on a freight flatcar to Matadi, thereby becoming the first passengers to ride over the narrow-gauge rail line. The engineering marvel included ninety-nine metal bridges and steel crossties to foil the ubiquitous and ravenous termites. When passing through the gorges, it seemed at times that they could reach out on either side of the train and touch the Crystal Mountains. Having several times previously taken weeks to walk along the path that paralleled the rail line, Sheppard was thrilled to relax while the train snaked through the difficult terrain in only two days. During his brief stay in the lower Congo, he consulted with the Governor at Boma about obtaining local self-government at the APCM.[80]

While the Sheppards were away, Morrison wrote: "We all miss Mr. and Mrs. Sheppard very much. We trust that Mrs. Sheppard has reached home safe, and that Mr. Sheppard may be permitted to return to us. There is no man in all this country who has the influence over this people that Sheppard has."[81] Morrison was especially impressed with his command of Bushonga and he recorded in his diary while in Ibanche: "Sheppard conducted the service this morning—about half the congregation was Bakuba and the other half Baluba. He preached in both languages."[82] Morrison's concentration on Tshiluba eventually resulted in his *Grammar and Dictionary of the Buluba-Lulua Language* being published at Luebo. In the preface of that text, which became basic for all subsequent APCM personnel to study, Morrison expressed his appreciation to the Sheppards for their linguistic assistance.

Soon after Lucy returned to America for her first furlough, Rebecca Davis of *Harper's Bazar* found her so fascinating that she interviewed her for the style-setting fashion magazine. Davis reported that Lucy was a quadroon (offspring of a mulatto and a white) and that her husband was a mulatto. She could not understand why someone with her graces and education would not be content to work with blacks in America who desperately needed to have such qualities transmitted to them. Lucy affirmed that her calling was to African missions, while confiding that no adult Kuba had yet been converted to Christianity. "The hope is in the children," she said, by way of pointing to her role as a religious educator.[83]

Lucy had a long visit in Staunton with her in-laws, who had moved a decade earlier to the booming county seat. Rail lines connecting the city with all points of the compass had made it a mercantile center. In

1887 this notice had been published in the newspaper for Augusta County: "William Sheppard, an experienced barber of Waynesboro, has moved his shop to No. 216, North Augusta Street. . . . The shop is well fitted up and is for the accommodation of white people."[84] William Sr. operated one of the two dozen black businesses in Staunton on a street in the center of the city, and resided at 3 Academic Street. The Augusta County population was about two-thirds white, and the senior Sheppards always worked for whites. For thirty summers William's mother was employed in Warm Springs, fifty miles west of Staunton. There she made bathing gowns and taught swimming while working as the women's pool attendant. The wooden structure housing the spa, where Thomas Jefferson once bathed, still stands in the hill country of Virginia. Sometimes Fannie was assisted at the resort by her daughter Eva, but Eva's main work was as a beautician and masseuse in Staunton, where she had an all-white clientele. She had married James Anderson, a schoolteacher, and their three daughters helped care for their cousin Wilhelmina.

The senior Sheppards had transferred their church membership to the First Presbyterian Church in Staunton, and that congregation gave financial support to Dr. and Mrs. Sheppard's work in the Congo.[85] In October 1898, Lucy spoke to the Women's Society in the church building that is still in use across the street from Mary Baldwin College. Her presentation, as reported in the Society's record, was typical of those given to supporting congregations:

> [Mrs. Sheppard] gave interesting sketches of different phases in African life, showing us both the encouraging and the discouraging features. She seemed thoroughly happy in her work, and can even speak cheerfully of leaving her little baby here in the home land when she returns to her post in Africa. Her voice is naturally very sweet, and it is highly cultivated, so every one enjoyed her delightful singing. She had with her a good many interesting curios, some of which show marvelous skill on the part of their makers.[86]

During her stay in Virginia, Lucy took time to compile a book that she could carry copies of back to Luebo. After she translated forty-six hymns in 1898 for APCM use, they were published by Curtiss Press in Richmond. The hymnal, entitled *Musambu ws Nzambi* (Songs of God) became the first printed material ever made in the Tshiluba language.

After seeing off his family for their Atlantic voyage, Sheppard returned to Ibanche and, as the lone American on the new station, worked with the natives to transform brush land into a village. In 1899, when he was serving as chairman of the APCM, with Morrison as treasurer, Sheppard reported that he had supervised the construction of a number of buildings. One was the church in Ibanche that he named the Lapsley Memorial Chapel, which had a "goodly number" of members. On its completion, Morrison said, "Mr. Sheppard has had so much experience in African architecture that we are sure it is a model."[87] Some who were attracted by the Mission were natives whom Sheppard had rescued from being poisoned by witchcraft.[88]

In 1899 Mishaape was in a desperate predicament because "the State had sent soldiers and killed a number of his people, and had taken his town."[89] With spears, bows, and arrows, the Kubas unsuccessfully attempted to defend their capital. In 1900 the State returned to Mushenge to kill the *Lukengu* and most of the Kuba royal family. During the period of mourning and bewilderment, the Kubas trusted Sheppard and left their valuables in his custody at Ibanche while fighting with the State officers. Hundreds were killed and captured during the conflict, but no harm was done at Ibanche. Massive looting of ivory and other treasures by Leopold's agents resulted in decimating the once prosperous Mushenge. The Kubas, who had a history of independence, felt much degraded as the period of control by the European colonialists began.[90]

The clash with forces from outside the Kuba culture compounded the violence that always accompanied matrilineal succession to the throne. According to custom, none of the king's sons from his large harem could succeed him, but his eldest son served as interim ruler until a new *Lukengu* was established. The transition period provided the monarchy a good opportunity for eliminating undesirables. Persons who were disliked could be included among those buried with the deceased king.[91] After Mishaape's death, it was several years before a victor emerged from the battle over which one of his nephews would permanently replace him. The great insecurity of the monarchy during those years was evidenced by there having been three on the Kuba throne between the *Lukengu* who was fond of Sheppard and the one who managed to establish himself more permanently in 1902.

Mbop Kyeen, the immediate successor to Mishaape, was friendly toward the American missionaries and invited them to move their station close to Mushenge, hoping that the move would give the Kubas better protection from the State.[92] Before his death from an epidemic that ended his reign of less than a year, Presbyterians were quick to follow up on this *Lukengu's* welcome. Samuel Chester, on behalf of the

PCUS Committee of Foreign Missions, wrote to Leopold, requesting that he permit the establishment of a new station and thereby overrule the rejection of the same request by his officials in the Congo. Chester, who confused the title of the Kuba king with the name of his capital, received no reply to this letter:

> The town of Lukengu is one in which we have long been interested. Our missionary Rev. W. H. Sheppard has made several visits to the place and the consent of the people of the village has finally been obtained to his going there to live, and work it as a mission station. The present chief is very anxious for Mr. Sheppard to come. The people at Lukengu have suffered much from the effect of their superstitions and from the disturbances that have come to them from the outside. We feel sure that Mr. Sheppard's presence there, with his remarkable gifts for dealing with the African people will tend to restore the condition of peace, order, and security, and make Lukengu a much more desirable place in the future than it has been in the past. We ask therefore for a concession at Lukengu. Our Mission wishes to purchase sufficient grounds on which to erect their mission buildings and to give them a quiet home while they carry on their work. . . . Our missionaries in your dominions will be devoted only to elevating and improving the character of the people among whom they labor, in which good work they are actuated only by the motive of love and loyalty to the King of Kings, and their desire to advance His kingdom of peace, truth, and righteousness in Africa.[93]

King Kot aPe, the survivor of the internal purges and external conflicts, was convinced that Maxamalinge had concocted lethal medicine, put it in a goat's horn, and buried it in the ground at Ibanche. This, the *Lukengu* believed, had caused the illness [probably smallpox] that had killed two Kuba kings in a brief period of time. Kot aPe enticed Maxamalinge to visit the capital and then the king persuaded the State to arrest him on a trumped up murder charge. Steadfastly viewing Maxamalinge as a friend and refugee who needed protection, Sheppard traveled a long distance to defend him in court and to denounce the superstition that had brought on his persecution. Sheppard was able to secure the release of Maxamalinge, but not before he had been tortured.[94] Had Sheppard given prime consideration to political expediency rather than to the principle of saving an innocent life, he would have advanced his own status by sacrificing the pagan prince.

Sheppard, with strong backing from the Kuba people in the Ibanche area, sent a strongly-worded message to the new young king that the innocent men he had tied up to be beheaded must be freed. Accordingly, the *Lukengu* liberated the victims and invited Sheppard to his capital. Sheppard realized that the king was probably resentful at this point over being denounced, and that he might be setting a trap. Sheppard "felt shaky" in going to Mushenge until he recalled the biblical assurance, "The king's heart is in the hand of the Lord, as the rivers of water; he turneth it whithersoever he will."[95] As it happened, Kot aPe was charmed by Sheppard and extended to him a bountiful hospitality when he visited the capital. Lukengu listened at his palace as Sheppard voiced his disapproval of the killing of slaves at a royal funeral, the poison ordeal, and the king's determination to eliminate potential rivals.

Kot aPe gave Sheppard permission to conduct evangelistic services at the capital. "At our departure," Sheppard reported, "the king begged us to send to him people of God to continue the work, saying that he would build a 'big house' and support Bantu ba Nzambi, God's Messengers."[96] Moreover, he said he wanted his and other children at his capital to be taught by Christians and agreed to provide land and a school building.[97] Henceforth the difficulty of working at Mushenge was due not to the Kubas but to the State being wary of allowing the establishment of another APCM station that might be critical of State policies.

When Lucy returned to Kasai in 1900, she left her daughter in Staunton with the Andersons. The Sheppards took up residence at Ibanche in a comfortable home with whitewashed mud walls and a thatched roof. Lucy was the first foreign woman to enter this area and for two years she did not see another American woman. There she learned another language, set up another school, and gave birth to another child.

The Sheppards' only boy baby was officially named William Lapsley Sheppard, but he was always called by his African name, Maxamalinge, in honor of the Kuba prince who had come to live with them. They continued to enjoy their friendly relationship with the prince and his beautiful wife even though the royal couple did not become Christians. When "Max" was two months old, Lucy followed the local custom of presenting the baby to the villagers and they responded by giving the mother gifts, usually chickens. She learned that neither mothers nor fathers in the community expressed a gender preference in bearing children.[98] The *Kassai Herald* later reported that Sheppard called his boy "Speaker of the House" because of his lusty cries, and added, "He talks the native language entirely, can't speak a word of English."[99]

Lucy took a major leadership role at Ibanche, as she had previously done at Luebo. In 1900 there were fifteen students in the school she opened, but two years later she reported that more than a hundred were enrolled.[100] For mothers and daughters, Lucy started a sewing class that provided both hemming instruction and Christian fellowship. The members especially enjoyed singing Christian songs in their own language.[101] Lucy also formed the first APCM women's group, called "the Sunshine Band," whose aim was to care for the sick, look up indifferent church members, and lend a helping hand to all. They met in her home to pray and to sing; she used her musical talent to teach them Negro spirituals. The native women took full charge of the weekly meetings.[102]

A boon to education came when a hand-operated "Benjamin Franklin" printing press was obtained in 1900 and housed in the publication building in Luebo. The Congolese were soon trained to set type and, beginning in 1901, the APCM published the *Kassai Herald* for distribution among southern Presbyterians in America. Both of the Sheppards frequently contributed articles to that quarterly journal. In 1902 the first book to be printed and bound in Luebo was an enlargement of the hymnal in Tshiluba that Lucy had earlier compiled. She credits "Xepate," one spelling of her husband's African name, for the translation of ten of his favorite English hymns. The Luebo press published mathematics, science, and elementary reading texts as well as books containing scriptural selections.[103] Lucy also wrote a Bushongo reader, the first work to be printed in the Kuba language.[104]

To establish rapport between children of Africa and America, Lucy wrote to inform boys and girls of her homeland that on moonlit nights their Congo counterparts played hide-and-seek and, when the moon did not shine, they told creepy animal fables while sitting around a fire.[105] With funding from a patron in Richmond, the Sheppards established in Ibanche a home for girls, which demanded much attention from the limited mission staff.

For several years the mission at Ibanche did well and Kot aPe remained amicable. Motte Martin, a new APCM missionary who visited this king with Sheppard, reported:

> Throughout the length and breadth of his land the superstitious drinking of poison as a test of witchcraft has been positively forbidden. . . . In repartee they [the Kubas] are witty and brilliant, getting the best in many cases of even our shrewd and gifted Sheppard. . . . Sheppard, who knows these people as no other man has ever known them . . . says that in consultation he has found them so practical and reasonable that in times of crisis, when he has been in doubt, he relies largely upon them for advice.[106]

Sheppard told about the results of his landscaping at the second APCM station:

> Our Ibanj station is a very attractive one. Its scores of stately palms, lovely grass, the way the station is laid off, the broad boulevards, long walks lined with pineapples and other fruit trees, the strong and well-made houses of the missionaries and people—all these things have caused more than one passing trader or State officer to say that this is the prettiest station in the Kassai.[107]

Judging from Sheppard's description of Ibanche's flora and fauna, the station resembled a Garden of Eden:

> We have lots of roses and other pretty flowers. The trees and the grass are always beautifully green except for a few weeks during the dry season. We hear continually the sweet songs of the happy birds that sing among the branches of the trees in our yard. We have lots of cunning pets, too. Parrots, hawks, eagles and monkeys. Also a little jackal. All of them are very tame and make such lovely pets.[108]

Explorer Alfred Pearce complemented Sheppard's assessment:

> During my eight years of travel on the Congo . . . nothing which I have as yet seen could compare with it. . . . It is only a little over a year since the buildings were commenced. There is now a fine church building, lofty and well supplied with ventilation by numerous sun-shaded windows. . . . I witnessed the [baptismal] sprinkling of fifteen natives one Sunday [in the church with 113 members]. . . . For many miles around Ibanj, the natives consider Mr. Sheppard their father and friend.[109]

The Lapsley Chapel, built of bamboo to seat two hundred and fifty, was replaced in 1900 by a much stronger church built of clay to seat four hundred, but a year later it too was overcrowded.[110] In 1902, when Sheppard presented to his Ibanche congregation the need for a larger church, he found this enthusiastic response:

> Every eye flashed with delight at the idea of having a real big church, which would seat a thousand people. . . . The following day there were enough posts (brought in from the forest), fifteen and twenty feet long to begin work. Mr. Phipps and I laid off the place. . . . The next day the posts began to go up, a hundred men . . . [were] making a building for Nzambi (God), and all to be their own, made by their own muscle. . . . Every moonlight night we would ring the bell and a crowd would gather to carry dirt and make mortar and plaster till a late hour. They generally ended up in a mud battle, and their faces and bodies did look a sight. So the work went on for about four

months. Soon we had the windows put in, and they are real church
windows, twenty-two in number. . . . We have had five hundred men,
women, and children hard at work at one time. The women went off
about two miles and brought whitewash, and soon the church was
beautifully white, inside and out. In the meantime benches had been
made by volunteers.[111]

Sheppard obviously did not think of the Congolese as being generally lazy; on the contrary, he found them eager to work with him on projects they believed to be important. Confirming that judgment, Vansina
notes: "In 1892 most Kuba worked from six in the morning to eight at
night. A work ethic definitely existed. Kuba mythology as taught to boys
in initiation equated laziness with the supreme evil: witchcraft."[112]

By contrast, a frequent complaint from white missionaries was that
the Congolese shunned labor. While Morrison was also at Ibanche, he
reported, "My hardest task . . . is to overcome the force of gravity that
seems to exist so powerfully between the earth and the bodies of my
work people."[113] Verner likewise said, "Work is the pet abomination of
the savage African; nothing but brute force, or the power of grace can
change this."[114]

The lack of rapport of some missionaries with the natives may have
caused some of them to work grumblingly and only if driven to it.
Sometimes the presumed laziness was due to faulty perception by visitors. When outsiders pass through a village, Sheppard observed, they
only see natives taking a break from their work to gawk at the strangers
in their midst and conclude that they are habitually idle. After living
with villagers for some time, he was favorably impressed with their
industry.[115]

At Ibanche, the Kubas were becoming receptive to Christianity, and
in 1903 they made up more than half of the 280 who were received into
the church. Sheppard noted that one of King Kot aMbweeky's grand-
sons was preaching there to his own people. He was proud to report
that native evangelists "have been taught reading, writing, spelling, and
arithmetic in our mission schools" and that "many of the villages in
which they live and preach give them their entire support." As a result
"some have flourishing churches and schools far away in the interior."[116]

For the entire APCM operation, Sheppard started the Young People's
Society of Christian Endeavor, an organization that was popular in
America. In addition, he reported:

There are two organized churches and several outstations and a band
of earnest native evangelists who travel for miles and miles around the

country, proclaiming to their brethren the glad news. Schools flour-
ish, books are written and printed, and the whole Bible will soon be
translated. In the two churches there is a membership of over fifteen
hundred.[117]

Other African American missionaries assisted in the development of
the APCM. They numbered six men and five women during the first fifteen years of the Mission, and there were usually more blacks on the staff
than whites. The Rev. Lucius DeYampert and the Rev. Joseph Phipps
were close associates of the Sheppards at Ibanche. Except for Phipps,
who was a northern Presbyterian, all of the black men were graduates of
the seminary at Tuscaloosa. DeYampert was the first member of the
APCM with some formal medical training, so he took charge of the phar-
macy and the dispensary. He met and married Lillian Thomas after coming to Ibanche; they adopted three Congolese girls. Phipps had been a
rum distiller on the island of St. Kitts in the West Indies before his conversion and education, which included study at the Moody Bible Institute in Chicago. Because his grandfather had come from the Congo to
St. Kitts, where African languages continued to be spoken, Phipps had a
familiarity with some of the African tongues before joining the APCM.[118]

Thanks to Phipps, the racial prejudice of Verner was diminished.
When they both came to Africa on the same ship, Verner was disgusted
at having to nurse Phipps when he was seasick. "Oh, the helplessness
of that race is appalling!" he exclaimed. But while they served together
on the same station, Phipps helped save Verner's life after he fell into a
game pit and had his thigh penetrated by a poisonous stake. He judged
Phipps to have three important qualifications for missionary service:
humility, teachability, and a strong physique.[119]

Dr. Sims, who had been in the Congo for many years, noted that no
black missionary from any church had died there.[120] He realized that
such persons more easily adapted to the climate and resisted tropical
diseases. Moreover, Sims said, "A colored man could stand the rough
life and shanty dwelling much better than a white man."[121] For these
reasons, Rowbotham and Verner recommended to the PCUS Mission
Board that a search be made for more blacks for Congo service.
Africans have an affinity for a missionary like Sheppard, explained
Verner, because he is "a living proof of the possibilities of their race."
He "inspires in them hopes and aspirations which they might never
otherwise know."[122] Livingstone had earlier advanced the notion that
blacks would be better missionaries in Africa and gain more converts.[123]

In 1903 the Sheppards received more help for their expanding work when a new missionary, Althea Brown, was assigned to Ibanche. Although her parents had been slaves on a Mississippi cotton planta- tion, her brilliant intellect resulted in her achieving the highest aca- demic honors at Fisk University in Nashville. Like Lucy Sheppard, she was among the Jubilee Singers. She was stationed at Ibanche and was impressed to find a thousand members in the church. Also, she was pleased that Lincoln Park was part of the station as well as tree-lined streets with names such as: Grand Boulevard, Palm Avenue, Chester Avenue, and Rankin Avenue. She noticed in front of the Sheppards' home four flags flying: the American, British, French, and Belgian. She also observed that when Sheppard wanted the sexton to ring the church bell he would give a special whistle. However, his parrots imitated his whistle so well that the bell was rung more frequently than desired![124]

In an article entitled "Our Ibanj Physician," Brown wrote about Sheppard:

> He not only builds churches and preaches the gospel, . . . but, like
> Luke, he is also the beloved physician with a genial smile and a heart
> full of love for everyone. He is known, loved, and reverenced by the
> natives far and wide. Although he is gentle and kind in his manner, he
> is firm and resolute in his speech, and all trust him. . . . Often he hears
> the midnight cry: "Come, father, my wife, or my child, or my husband,
> is sick," and none has ever been turned away. . . . He is famous for his
> dental surgery. . . . When asked where he obtained his knowledge of
> dentistry he said that he was indebted to Dr. S. H. Henkel, of
> Staunton, Virginia, in whose office he worked for some years. The
> natives, traders, all throughout the Kassai District, come to him to
> have their teeth extracted.[125]

Althea Brown met Alonzo Edmiston, a Stillman graduate, after he joined the APCM in 1904, and they married the next year. The Edmis- tons served at Ibanche until it was abandoned in 1915; they then resided at Bulape, nearer the center of the Kuba kingdom. Together they achieved seventy-two years of service with the APCM. Alonzo pioneered in providing agricultural training for youth. Althea was an outstanding linguist, and her six-hundred-page *Grammar and Dictio- nary of the Bushonga or Bukuba Language* was eventually published in 1932 at Luebo. She also translated textbooks, folk tales, songs, and proverbs. While on furlough she delivered the commencement address at her alma mater in which she emphasized the importance of blacks becoming involved in developing Christianity in Africa.[126]

A dozen African Americans, equally divided in gender, served the APCM, and nearly all of them were recruited by the Sheppards. They were: Henry Hawkins, 1894–1910; Maria Fearing, 1894–1917; Lillian Thomas (DeYampert), 1894–1918; Joseph Phipps, 1895–1908; Althea Brown (Edmiston), 1902–1937; Lucius DeYampert, 1902–1918; Alonzo Edmiston, 1903–1941; Adolphus Rochester, 1906–1939; Annie Taylor (Rochester), 1906–1914; and Edna Atkinson (Rochester), 1923–1939. During the Sheppards' last year in the Kasai, there were slightly more black than white missionaries with the APCM. The respect they gained for their race brought far more equitable treatment while working abroad than they would have received in the southern United States. Shaloff comments:

> At no time . . . were they ever officially called upon to assume an inferior posture. . . . The black evangelists had given evidence that self-reliance, initiative, and dedication were not peculiarly white traits and that contrary to Verner's assumptions they were quite capable of assuming all of the burdens of a foreign missionary. The lesson, which was lost on some, was that if they were able to succeed abroad then they most certainly were capable of comparable attainments at home, if only they were given the chance.[127]

A year after Brown arrived, the Sheppards went on a long furlough—his first in a decade. Shortly after they left in 1904, hostilities between the State and the Kubas resulted in the destruction of Ibanche and several other villages. The conflict began after Kot aPe was treated "with utmost contempt" by a "pompous, tyrannical, blustering" State officer named Captain DeCocke.[128] He summoned *Lukengu* to Luebo for the payment of taxes and fined him for being tardy. When the king was unable to pay the large fine with what he had brought with him, he was arrested. At the king's request, the missionaries at Luebo loaned him the 100,000 cowrie shells needed to purchase his release. Ethel Wharton, who lived for many years among the Kubas, comments on the outcome:

> The chains were later loosed, but the proud Bakuba never fully recovered from the shock of seeing their king reduced to imprisonment. It was the beginning of the slow disintegration of a unique primitive culture, full of both beauty and horror, before the relentless march of modern civilization.[129]

Incensed by the imprisonment, *Lukengu* issued a decree on returning to his capital "to kill everyone, both friend and foe, who was not a subject." His rage was directed toward the State officers and the traders who worked under their protection, but his warriors struck out indiscriminately against all foreigners. Unfortunately, Sheppard was not on hand to use his persuasive powers to moderate the insurrection. There was a State-operated rubber trading station close to the Ibanche mission, and Kuba troops burned the whole area in a general reprisal. When the strike on Ibanche was imminent, the missionaries escaped by night to Luebo. A band of Christians then came from Luebo hoping to protect the mission property but found the station was a smouldering heap, including the newly expanded Lapsley Church with a seating capacity of fifteen hundred that had been used for worship only twice. After the Kuba calmed down, Ibanche was gradually rebuilt and the mission work resumed.[130] When Phipps visited Kot aPe a year after the Kuba attack on Ibanche, he found a friendly king who attended Christian services held at Mushenge and invited the APCM to establish a mission station there.[131]

The Sheppards spent much of their furlough in Staunton with their daughter and his parents. Wilhelmina and her three-year-old brother Max had difficulty becoming acquainted for the first time because they spoke different languages. Her father brought her some parrots that also caused a linguistic problem. He gave one of them to the Staunton Y.M.C.A., with the assurance that it was quite tame and willing to learn English, although its native language was Bushonga![132]

The senior Sheppards were proud when a large number assembled at their church to hear their son speak, and they were pleased when the local newspaper reported that Lucy sang at the service in African dialect with a voice that "was full of tenderness and sympathy." Sheppard also gave a lecture on the Kubas to hotel guests and to black servants in the Warm Springs ballroom. It was a familiar place for him because, beginning at the age of twelve, he had accompanied his mother there for several years to serve in the dining room and at the bathhouse. After he gave an inspiring speech, Lucy sang several familiar hymn melodies, using lyrics her husband had translated into Bushonga.[133] Years later he returned to that ballroom to speak to hotel guests and people from the community.[134]

After their family reunion, Lucy and her husband traveled widely to tell of APCM developments. In city after city they spoke to overflow audiences in large churches. She continually charmed congregations by singing songs of Kasai and by telling of her work with African women.[135] On one day in Lynchburg, Virginia, Sheppard spoke to immense crowds at three Presbyterian and Methodist churches while Lucy "sang with simple pathos and deep feeling hymns that, though in the dialect of an African tribe, were also in the language of the heart."[136]

After the Sheppards visited Hampton Institute, the *Southern Workman* published not only his address but the words and music of "Chimpoong Galoo," an African folk song Lucy had sung for those in the teacher training program.[137] At the Monteagle Chautauqua in the Cumberland Mountains of Tennessee, Lucy gave a fascinating talk and sang for a large number who gathered in an amphitheater. The *Independent* characterized her in this way: "Thoroughly unaffected, . . . able to adapt herself to any surroundings, and with a faultless sense of propriety, she elicited admiration from all with whom she came in contact."[138] Lucy also spoke at Fisk University in Nashville and addressed her alma mater in Alabama on the topic "From Talladega College to Africa."

Newspaper reports told of the response given Sheppard during this furlough, or home assignment, as more appropriately designated. At the First Presbyterian Church in Charleston, West Virginia—then the largest in the denomination—many could not be seated for his presentation. The report told of "spellbound" listeners and concluded, "His experiences have been even more thrilling than any recorded by the great African explorer, Henry M. Stanley."[139] Sheppard noted that he was giving "on an average of six or seven lectures a week."[140] A Boston newspaper reported that he delivered in Nashville "one of the most powerful addresses" at the largest international student convention ever held.[141] When he spoke at the Central Presbyterian Church across from the capitol in Atlanta, an editorial called him "probably the greatest Negro of his generation."[142] Sheppard then spoke to overflowing audiences at a large church in Montgomery and to students at Tuskegee Institute.[143] Writing from Tuscaloosa, he reported, "I am just [back] from Cuba."[144]

"The black Livingstone of Africa" was the way Sheppard was referred to when he was on a northern speaking tour. "At Princeton," Alfred Wilson testified, "I heard him thrill the students and faculty with the stirring story of his experiences on the Congo."[145] He was probably invited to that university by Woodrow Wilson, perhaps because they had similar roots. Wilson, then president of Princeton, was also born in Augusta County. His father was the minister of the Staunton church that Sheppard and his parents later attended. Both could recite the Westminster Catechism and believed that "man's chief end is to glorify God and to enjoy him forever."

In 1906 the Sheppards tore themselves away from their daughter, whom they left with relatives in Staunton, and returned to the Congo by the usual circuitous route. In London they joined William and

Bertha Morrison, who had recently married in Mississippi. Also traveling with them were two black missionary recruits: Annie Taylor, a Tuscaloosa native of high ability, and Adolphus Rochester, who became her husband. Bedinger, a later white missionary, described that couple:

> Mr. Rochester was born in Jamaica and therefore was a British subject. As a young man he emigrated to Brazil, where he became an orderly in a hospital. There he learned much of medicine and the care of the sick, a knowledge which he used to good purpose in the Congo. Leaving Brazil, he came to America and later graduated at Stillman Institute. Mr. Rochester spoke the most beautiful English. . . . He also had a good grasp of the native dialect. Mrs. Rochester was a most charming lady, well-loved of both natives and her fellow missionaries. . . . The most cordial and harmonious relations existed between the two races. Undoubtedly, this close relationship was a strong factor in the remarkable success of our Congo Mission.[146]

On their last Congo assignment, the Sheppards enjoyed more comfortable transportation to Luebo. At Matadi the American missionaries made reservations to Kinshasa on the one "first-class" railway car, which contained a total of twelve seats, six on each side. Then, at Leopoldville, they boarded the long-awaited new APCM riverboat. After Lapsley's death, his longing for a steamboat operated by the APCM had resulted in church folk deciding that such a boat would be a fitting memorial. During Sheppard's first home assignment he had formed an interdenominational "Congo Missionary Society" to receive monetary aid that was used in part to buy a steamer.[147] As chairman of the Congo Boat Fund, he was pleased to report in 1898 that money was on hand to build a steamer sufficient for APCM's needs. The *Samuel Lapsley*, built in the Trigg shipyard of Richmond, became the first American-made steamer in the Congo. But in 1901, less than three years after it was put into service, it capsized in the notorious swirling currents above the mouth of the Kasai. A new missionary and a number of Congolese were drowned; in addition, a year's supply of food and barter goods were lost. In response to this tragedy, contributions abounded for the construction of a sturdier vessel. A larger and stronger *Lapsley* was soon built in Glasgow and reassembled at Stanley Pool. It could steam upstream from Kinshasa to Luebo in half of the twelve days that the old *Lapsley* took. It did well on its maiden voyage until, because of the low water, it grounded on a sandbar when within one hour of Luebo, where thousands waited to meet them. The natives were especially interested in seeing Bertha Morrison, the only white woman in a thousand-mile radius, who had hair "like a cow's tail."[148]

When the Sheppards finally arrived at Ibanche, they found virtually nothing left there to represent the arduous toil they had given to build the splendid station a few years earlier. Hawkins commended Sheppard for "his natural aptitude to adapt himself to the ever shifting conditions, which forms no insignificant part of the Congo life."[149] The Sheppards saw a largely rebuilt Ibanche and moved into a house that replaced the one destroyed when the village was burned. It had large mats covering the entire floor and the luxury of glass windows. But it was not secure from invaders and sometimes Sheppard killed as many as seven snakes a day of different sizes and kinds. He wrote about this to a friend in Hampton, and added, "We have had elephants to come out of the forests surrounding us, step over our low fence and eat banana leaves in our front yard."[150] More pleasantly, Sheppard reported, "We have a bamboo tree in our front yard with no less than five hundred birds' nests in it. These birds are yellow and just like canaries and sing from morning till night."[151]

Shortly after the Sheppards returned to Ibanche, Kot aPe visited the Mission with a large retinue. He apologized for his soldiers burning down the station during the period of their absence by not distinguishing more carefully between different types of foreigners. *Lukengu* recognized that he needed to ally himself with the APCM, and with Sheppard in particular, in his effort to defend his people. Brown pointed out that "he despised being a tool in the hands of the Congo Free State" and being required to "exact from his own people tons of rubber annually."[152] Kot aPe showed that he had already done much to help restore Ibanche, and Sheppard expressed his forgiveness by presenting him with a pair of peafowls he had brought from America. The regal strut and flamboyant tail feathers made the peacocks an appropriate gift. The Sheppards requested that the king supply some girls for the Maria Carey Home, which was being developed along the lines of the Pantops Home at Luebo. The king had become convinced of the advantages of literacy and health training, so he commanded his villages to send to Ibanche one girl each. When forty girls arrived a day later, Sheppard asked him to send fifty boys to the station for instruction. Again, this was immediately accomplished, and among them was a nephew of the king who became a Christian.[153]

Kellersberger thinks that this term may have been the Sheppards' most fruitful, "They were now proved veterans, wounded in the fight, but returning to the front from sheer love of hard places and challenging opportunities."[154] The emotional wounds consisted mainly of the death of half of their children and the separation from their daughter.

"Prepare ye the way of the Lord, make straight in the desert a highway for our God"

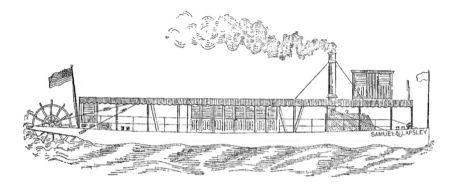

A sketch of the 70 by 12 foot *Samuel N. Lapsley*, which was built in Richmond in 1900 and shipped to Leopoldville. The frail craft soon sank in the swift current at the mouth of the Kasai River. A second *Lapsley* was then manufactured in Glasgow and was used for decades. It had two decks and a more sturdy construction.

The many bouts with tropical sicknesses had also inflicted battle scars.

Many boys were enrolled in the Industrial School at Ibanche and lived in a dormitory constructed for them. Half of the students were Kubas, three being from the royal family.[155] A band was begun with instruments that a benefactor had given the Sheppards; a photo shows natives playing several Western brass instruments and Sheppard with his banjo, perhaps participating in a jazz number.

The Sheppards set up in Ibanche a press where Lucy had a Kuba hymnbook printed. Her husband contributed twelve translations, more than half of the total, including "Come, Thou Fount of Every Blessing," "My Jesus I Love Thee," and "Take My Life."[156] Subsequent editions of the hymnals continued to use some of Sheppard's translations, with his African name spelled "Shepete."

During all the years that the Sheppards were with the APCM, there was never a certified physician on the station where they resided. The first one arrived in Luebo in 1906, but he was days away from Ibanche. Lucy worked in the Ibanche clinic, administering the simple medicines that were available. Once she traveled forty miles to Luebo by herself to nurse Bertha Morrison, debilitated by high fever.[157] After serving for only a few years, Bertha also became another malaria martyr. She was honored when a new mission station was given her native name, "Mutoto," meaning "star."

In an article entitled "How It Strikes an Outsider," British consul

Wilfred Thesiger responded to the skepticism that often arises over the authenticity of alleged conversions to Christianity. After visiting APCM stations in 1909, he wrote:

> Many instances of considerable self-sacrifice on the part of the native converts in behalf of their religion could be quoted to show that in numberless cases the conversion is genuine enough. No one could fail to be struck by the evident earnestness of the crowds which filled the large church buildings of Luebo and Ibanj, or pass unnoticed the fact that wherever the teaching of the mission has spread the natives are putting up of their own free will and at the expense of their own time and labor buildings which serve as church and school combined.

Thesiger marveled at the way in which Presbyterians had developed what they do best. He reported:

> As regards to education, the work of the Luebo Mission struck me as having been astonishingly successful, especially among the Lulua and Baluba, who seem to be animated with a passionate desire to learn to read and write. Everywhere I found schools crowded during the work hours, and I must have received a score of petitions during my tour from the smaller villages, asking that I would give them a letter to the Mission in order that they, too, might obtain a teacher.... Under these circumstances it was not surprising to learn that the mission schools and printing press were unable to keep pace with the demand.... A large number of their mission-taught boys find good employment on the steamers, railways, and with the trading companies.... As many of the boys are sons of chiefs and headmen, who will ultimately take their fathers' places, the beneficial effects of this branch of the station work can scarcely be overestimated.[158]

Paget Thurston, who was also with the British consulate, told of what impressed him on visiting Luebo in 1909:

> The machine shops, the brick [pharmacy] store, printing office and book binding department, the carpenter shop, the new schools and brick kiln all speak of the busy daily life. The church building is immense—bigger than any church in America or England. On Sunday . . . the great church is packed.[159]

The two APCM stations, Luebo and Ibanche, had a total of 7,705 members and over 20,000 adherents by 1910. Most of the 5,700 in the weekday schools and the 8,000 in the Sunday schools would eventually become full members. This increase was not due to the requirements for membership being lowered, for candidates for baptism were required to complete instruction that took almost a year.[160] At that time the largest congregation connected with the southern Presbyterian Church was not in America but in Luebo. In the Congo, the number of Presbyterians was greater than the number of Protestants in any other mission, and they made up approximately 15 percent of all Christians in the colony.

The large numerical Christian growth came from the combined efforts of the missionaries and the Congolese Christians whom they had educated. Missions authority Stephen Neill acknowledges that the system of village evangelists in Protestant missions in Africa was developed first and with the greatest success by the APCM.[161] Slade likewise states:

> It was in the Kasai that the system of native evangelism and missionary visitation won its most striking successes. . . . Luebo and Ibanj became training centers from which increasing numbers of evangelists were sent out to the villages, and the outward movement spread in ever widening circles.[162]

As early as 1876 the PCUS mission policy declared that native churches "have the inherent right of self-government." Before the APCM was established, its controlling General Assembly set the goal of "raising up natives to fill the settled and permanent pastorate, both in the ruling and teaching sphere." It stated:

> We ought not to seek to propagate our own distinctive Presbyterian body in various parts of the world, but rather to disseminate simply the principles and doctrines that we hold. . . . The foreign missionary, with the blessing of God, may set the ball in motion, and for a time shape its course. But it is for men raised upon the soil to continue and extend the work.[163]

Even though Sheppard and other missionaries expressed paternalism at the beginning, their long-term goal of an indigenous church came to fruition. They attempted to diminish their leadership role as soon as the young Christians could assert mature initiative. Their objective was subsequently stated as "the establishment of self-governing, self-supporting, and self-propagating native churches."[164] Sheppard commented on fifty Congolese Christians involved in indigenization: "We believe this is the plan that the Master would have us carry out: educate the natives and send them out to preach to the others. They are quick on the road, do not need a long caravan to go with them, speak the language fluently, and know the trails." By 1907 a number of church officers could be found on the Presbyterian mission stations, marking "the beginning of turning over to the native Christians the management of the internal affairs of the native church."[165] In 1909 Sheppard told of six Kuba towns that fully supported between them three teachers and two evangelists. He exclaimed, "What a blessed change! Many more of the chiefs of other villages have asked for evangelists and teachers, assuring us of their entire support."[166] Sheppard claimed that there were 400 educated evangelists being supported by the Kuba villages, where their churches were located, and that many people affiliated with the APCM were literate and made use of Bibles and hymnbooks printed in their own language.[167]

Sheppard must have been gratified to realize how rapidly the APCM developed in the second decade of his efforts, especially in comparison to the first decade when there was only one struggling station at Luebo with few converts. Scholars at the Hoover Institution have commented, "He had the satisfaction of seeing the mission he had founded attracting converts by the hundreds and growing and expanding until it was one of the most important centers of Christianity and civilization in Central Africa."[168]

5

Atrocities Protest

IVORY AND RUBBER

Foreign traders were first attracted to the Congo by their lust for ivory. Centuries before the European arrival there, the "Arabs" penetrated from East Africa as far west as the upper Congo River. These people were actually negroid Africans who had adopted Islam and dressed in Arab clothing. Humans were needed to carry ivory to the east coast for export because the domestic animals used elsewhere had a low survival rate in the tropics. Also, unlike its Asian counterpart, the African elephant cannot be domesticated. Few Africans would willingly go long distances from their home areas as porters, so slave labor was regarded as indispensable to business. After capturing Congolese natives, the Arabs organized them to find ivory and carry it to Zanzibar; those surviving were usually sold there to the highest bidder and exported to Arab states.

Africans recognized that their firearms were puny for confronting elephants, so they often had to be forced to hunt the dangerous animal. Those who did not produce their ivory quotas might be given the Qur'an-sanctioned punishment of hand severing.[1] Arab chiefs sometimes required the presentation of chopped-off hands as evidence of a soldier's effectiveness in administering penalties. Finding that a hand could more easily be removed from a corpse, the soldiers sometimes first killed a victim. The amount of ammunition issued was compared with the count of hands presented in order to determine if a gun was used for the purpose for which it was issued.[2] Arab traders usually did not permit villages to survive if they interfered with the business of gathering and transporting tusks.

When Stanley was establishing stations in the Stanley Falls region in 1883, he found whole villages wiped out by slavers. At one camp he found 2,300 women and children fettered. He figured that for every one enslaved, six were killed. Deciding to stay on good terms with the slavers, Stanley did not protest their ghastly atrocities while in the Congo, and he even worked with notorious slaver Hamidi bin Muhammad, better known as Tippo Tib, for control of the natives.[3] But Leopold soon realized that coexistence was not possible with the Arab competitors for ivory. Leopold's agents supplied repeating rifles and machine guns to their native soldiers, enabling them to overwhelm the Congolese who had Arab-supplied one-shot muskets. By 1894, Arab slave-trading in the Congo was mostly wiped out and Leopold's reputation as a humanitarian was enhanced.

At that time few realized that Leopold surreptitiously adopted the Arabs' methods for extracting valuable products from the Congo. His private correspondence displayed a willingness to use forced labor as a means of civilizing "indolent and spoiled people." He seemed to think of the people in the African wilds as nondomesticated animals who needed to be treated harshly to break them in for "civilized" purposes. Leopold's policy was made explicit in 1897 when his Governor-General Wahis ordered his agents, "Where the natives refuse obstinately to work, you will compel them to obey by taking hostages." A certain percentage of each village was conscripted to work for the government, either in commerce or in the army. Villages were assigned quotas and had to sell ivory to State agents at a price far below the world market.[4]

Since slavery was officially forbidden in the Congo Free State, some villages were forced to surrender those who had been slaves in the traditional culture. Those "liberated" people were then forced to become workers or soldiers for the Europeans. Beginning in 1891, some of the State troops were orphans of former slaves who had been reared in Catholic boarding schools. Stanley's officer Edward Glave wrote in 1895 of seeing such children at a Jesuit mission in Kinshasa. Their health was so poor that three hundred died in a two-year period. He commented that "if the Arabs had been the masters, it would be styled iniquitous trafficking in human flesh and blood; but being under the administration of the Congo Free State, it is merely a part of their philanthropic system of liberating the natives!"[5] Boys had several hours of military exercises daily as a part of their "Christian" training. At fourteen they were inducted into the *Force Publique*, having learned effective ways of threatening and killing their fellow natives.[6] These soldiers received low wages but handsome commissions when they were able to collect from villages, by persuasion or terror, products for export that exceeded the quota.

Leopold's agents continued the Arab practice of receiving severed hands to determine whether soldiers had disobediently sold or used for hunting their cartridge allotment. For each right hand brought in, District Commissioner Leon Fieveza, for one, gave two more bullets.[7] Some European post commanders accepted baskets containing smoked hands of children as well as adults. The more humane soldiers took hands from the living without killing their victims. Collecting marketable goods was also encouraged by cat-o'-nine-tails floggings, which were usually not fatal. State officers apparently had no reluctance to use cannibals who engaged in an orgy of man-eating after a village raid. Sometimes bones were broken before the victim was killed on the belief that suffering was a meat tenderizer. Even some European commanders developed a taste for human flesh.[8]

The Belgian king looked beyond the ivory business to other lucrative products in the forests of the Congo. Following the invention and mass manufacture of bicycles in 1888, and motor vehicles in 1895, rubber prices on the world market soared. The same year that Sheppard arrived in the Congo, John Dunlop of Scotland began producing inflatable rubber tires that were indispensable to the new vehicles.

Before 1890 most of the crude rubber had been coming from a South American tree, but then a vine was discovered in Congo that produced gum of the same quality. From his observations near Luebo around 1900, Verner wrote:

> I have seen vast illimitable growths of this vine, clambering up gigantic trees and almost obscuring the light of the midday sun. This vine grows to the height of perhaps two hundred feet, is as thick as a man's body, of a spongy porous texture, with numerous branches, and a beautiful foliage. . . . An incision in the vine is followed by a free flow of the milk-white juice. . . . A large vine will produce thirty pounds of crude rubber per year, and an acre of forest will average two hundred vines, thus giving three tons of rubber per acre of forest. . . . A small forest is as profitable as a gold mine and surer of returns upon the capital invested.[9]

Verner found an abundance of wild rubber vines in rain forests and figured that little would need to be paid to workers who were involved in the rather arduous task of preparing the rubber for market. After an incision was made, sap was collected in a gourd tied beneath the cut. This was then boiled in a pot and the dehydrated paste was kneaded under foot. The solid rubber was then cut in strips, rolled into balls, and dried in the sun. Verner figured that the upper Kasai forests could annually produce about 20,000 tons of crude rubber and that a rubber investor could enjoy a profit of 900 percent after all expenses of purchase, transportation, commissions, and duties were paid.[10] The high return on investment was due to having no cultivation or specialized equipment expense, and the availability of cheap labor for harvesting.

Leopold took advantage of this new rubber market, and exports from the Congo quadrupled in the last years of the nineteenth century. By eliminating competition, the king guaranteed his burgeoning profit. After his monopoly went into effect, the purchase price dropped from thirty to five cents a pound, even though world demand was rapidly increasing.[11] By 1903, rubber constituted 87 percent of Congo's exports and in the Kasai an investment produced a profit of 1,875 percent in three years.[12] Annual rubber exports increased from 241 tons in 1893 to 6,000 tons in 1906.[13] In subsequent decades, cultivated rubber trees in Liberia, Brazil, and Malaysia supplied the demand after Congo's wild vines were destroyed.

Climbing up trees to make incisions into vines and to collect sap was a grueling and dangerous work. Brass wire and colored beads did not provide sufficient incentive to get workers voluntarily into swampy forests where man-eating leopards roamed. Heavy force needed to be applied to obtain rubber. Taking wives and children hostage was one effective method; they would be released only after their husbands or fathers met a rubber quota. Meanwhile, guards routinely raped the attractive women. Ludwig Bauer describes the Congo business organization:

> Leopold had two thousand agents in the country, sharers in his interests, and at the same time confederates; under their orders were 20,000 blacks, many of them cannibals, as soldiers, let loose to work their will upon alien tribes. Children of the wilderness, with firearms thrust into their hands, were allowed to give free rein to their murderous impulses, and punished if they did not extort a sufficiency of rubber.[14]

Europeans first became aware of the torture and slaughter in procuring rubber by the testimony of E. V. Sjoblom, a missionary from Sweden who joined the American Baptists in the Congo after being trained at Guinness's London Institute. He stated, "I saw . . .

dead bodies floating on the lake with the right hand cut off, and the officer told me . . . it was for the rubber."[15] Sjoblom's on-the-scene accounts of atrocities were published in 1896 in several European journals. Leopold's response was largely a smoke screen to overcome protests in the press. He stated that the Congolese found his agents "powerful protectors of life and property, the kindly guardians they need so much." To dissipate charges against his methods, Leopold ordered Governor-General Wahis—who was the target of some of the accusations—to make an investigation.[16]

In 1896 Leopold instituted a Native Protection Commission with members appointed from outside the rubber-producing areas. It was composed of three Baptist and three Catholic missionaries as well as State representatives. George Grenfell was made chairman, probably because he was known to be uncritical of Leopold's policies. For work in the Congo, the king had decorated him with the Legion of Honor medal. The Commission was unable to get a majority together to make recommendations, in part because no compensation was provided to cover the expenses of members who in some cases would have had to travel for many days to attend a meeting. Even if the Commission had met and made recommendations, it was a sham; it had no authority to deal with reported abuses. "The appointment of the Commission was a huge success for Leopold's image-makers and propagandists," Benedetto observes.[17]

Some of Leopold's supporters launched a counterattack against Protestant missionaries. They were accused of meddling in public affairs, of being scandalmongers, and of having personal animosity toward the Belgian king. These supporters also viewed missionaries as subversive to colonialism because they were diminishing the awe that natives had of whites as superior beings. But most of the status quo allies of Leopold saw missionaries as underminers of the traditional functioning of capitalism. The bottom line for the Belgian officials was that "they wished to preserve at any price the system for exploiting the rubber resources which was transforming the Congo into a profit-making enterprise."[18] While they did not actively favor mass killing, return on investment was the paramount concern. Shareholders in the bloody-red rubber enterprise were indifferent as to whether profits might result from their company's elimination of competition and refusal to pay a living wage to the menial laborer. They insulated themselves from the negative and far-off results of economic production, such as depriving future generations of raw materials and damaging the environment. Bauer writes:

> The returns accruing to the various joint-stock companies at work in the Congo State increased enormously; . . . annual dividends were declared ranging from fifty to several hundred percent. . . . We have no reason to suppose that the shareholders . . . were anything but . . . humane persons, who would have apologized most politely if by accident they had trodden on a neighbor's foot.[19]

Leopold's promises to correct possible excesses on his Congo commercial operation effectively diminished criticism for several years. Even though there were more than two hundred Catholic and two hundred Protestant missionaries in the Congo at that time, nearly all of them cravenly kept silent. In 1900 the APCM became the lone whistle-blower to colonial cruelties carried out in pursuit of quick profits.[20] The international attention that Sheppard initiated with regard to the Zappo Zaps eventually caused Leopold to lose his private Congo state.

SLAVERS AND CANNIBALS

In the Kasai district, Leopold's agents allied themselves with the Zappo Zaps, a subtribe of the BaSonga Menos. Sheppard explained the tribal name and described the appearance of those he called cannibals: "'Ba' for people, 'songa' to file, and 'meno,' teeth—the 'filed teeth people.' Their teeth were all filed to a sharp point and their faces tattooed. They carried large spears and quivers of poisonous and steel arrows. Two tiny pieces of palm fibre cloth was all they wore."[21]

Although the Zappo Zaps were not a large group, they gained influence by working as mercenaries of whatever power was dominant. The deadly iron weapons they had long possessed gave them an advantage over most other Africans, and the guns they were supplied with made that advantage overwhelming. Bedinger gives this description:

> The Zappo Zaps derived their name from Zappo Zap who revolted from the Basonga chief and worked for the Arabs. Long before the coming of the white man their slave raiding parties were scouring the country, leaving a trail of burnt villages and half-eaten bodies, while hundreds of slaves were annually exchanged with the Arabs for guns, ammunition, cloth, and other articles of European manufacture.[22]

Hermann Wissmann told of meeting Zappo Zap and his well-armed men in 1887. In token of having worked for Arab traders, Zappo Zap dressed in Arab fashion with a turban, a shirt, and a pair of pants. He had obtained guns in exchange for ivory and slaves. After the Arab slave trade was suppressed, Leopold's agents brought the opportunist Zappo Zap warriors to the Luluaburg area from outside the Kasai region.[23]

At Luluaburg, Lapsley met Prince Zappo Zap, a young adult, who was named after his father. He wore shoulder-to-knee clothing and had a folded cloth rakishly tied about his head. Zappo Zap gave several young slaves to Lapsley in exchange for his gift of blue cloth and brass wire. A slave had less worth to the Zappo Zaps than a pig. Lapsley was grateful to be given slaves, for they could be released and educated at Luebo. He learned that the Zappo Zaps numbered about eight hundred and were "part of a tribe of cannibal marauders" who had recently immigrated into the area.[24] Lieutenant Paul LeMarinel had brought them from the eastern Congo around 1890 to assist in enforcing government policies. The Zappo Zaps resided at the administrative headquarters for the Kasai district, where they were used in offensive and defensive activities for the State.

The Zappo Zaps unwittingly rendered a valuable linguistic service. They enslaved many Lubas from southeast of Luebo and sold them in other tribal areas in the Kasai basin. The slaves tenaciously retained their own language, Tshiluba, and their captors and masters became familiar with it. The slave language extended wherever the Lubas were found in tribes scattered over an area of one thousand square miles. It became the most widely understood and spoken tongue in the large region, so the APCM decided to concentrate on providing a written form of Tshiluba. Thus Tshiluba became the dominant regional language from then onward.

Independent observations of the Zappo Zaps were published a decade later by scholars exploring the upper Kasai. Englishman M. W. Hilton-Simpson was interested to find that this group deviated from the usual type of cannibalism. For the Zappo Zaps, partaking of human flesh was not a ceremonial feast at special occasions. Hilton-Simpson also found it surprising that they stalked and captured humans to eat when the forests teemed with game animals. He observed that meat carved from slaughtered slaves was fried like bacon, and was not crudely eaten in the manner of a lion tearing at raw flesh.[25]

Zappo Zap was more affluent when Emil Torday talked with him than when Lapsley had visited him about a dozen years earlier. Obviously, the State had rewarded him for the bloodthirsty acts of his men. Torday describes and evaluates the leader:

> When he saw that things were against them [the Arabs] he turned traitor and sided with the Europeans. . . . I consider him the greatest

scoundrel unhanged. . . . He is very rich and very powerful. . . . His harem is one of the grandest in the Congo. . . . He was responsible for the [military] rising of the Bushongo.[26]

Ethnologist Alan Merriam has made the most thorough study of the Songas. He shows that they ate human flesh not only as a way of terrorizing their enemies but because they considered it a delicacy. He states: "The flesh was roasted, and all parts of the body were eaten except the hair and nails. Brains were considered especially good, and frequent comparison is made between the eyeballs and boiled eggs."[27] Rowbotham noted that natives of the upper Kasai reckoned the power of this cannibal tribe "by the number of slaves already eaten, or by those in their possession who could be eaten at any time."[28]

At Luebo, Lapsley observed caravans of Zappo Zaps leading "slaves laden with baskets of the little rubber balls." He stated, "I know not how many droves of hungry slaves have been marched past the door of my hut. Most of these were sold for goats, which were driven by with at least as much consideration as the human cattle were."[29] During that first year on the APCM station, Sheppard wrote Dr. Henkel about the Zappo Zaps:

> This a powerful tribe. The men are . . . young giants. Their weapons are guns, battle axes, clubs, bows and poisonous arrows. About two months ago, we had an attack by night from them, but only a few of them appeared and we stood as firm as you please, and the trouble was soon over. . . . I received a nice battle axe from a wealthy Zappo Zap. It is a beauty and if you should like it, I will bring it for you.[30]

After getting to know these fierce mercenaries who worked for the State, Lapsley wondered if the APCM was at a disadvantage in having to deal with a regional government of this sort. "It is doubtful whether missionaries get more immediate good than harm from 'State protection,'" he wrote.[31] He described the warriors and their activity in this manner:

> Their houses, like themselves, are both tall and big, and square, with the corners rounded. They made on me the impression of being peculiar, not like others. Their mode of living has been to hunt a town weaker than themselves, surprise it at daybreak, catch all the people and kill those too strong to make slaves of; then sell the slaves for guns or anything that is current, goods, goats, ivory, or rubber.[32]

One of Leopold's high officials issued this ominous order to his Congo commanders:

I have the honour to inform you that from 1 January 1899 you must succeed in furnishing four thousand kilos of rubber every month. To effect this I give you carte blanche. You have therefore two months in which to work your people. Employ gentleness first, and if they persist in not accepting the imposition of the state, employ the force of arms.[33]

Accordingly, that same year the Zappo Zaps invaded the Kuba kingdom, causing a heavy loss of life and property. The proud Kubas were hit hard because they stubbornly refused to gather rubber for the State.

The Zappo Zaps who adopted the ways of the foreigners were successful in subjugating the highly cultured Kubas who attempted to retain their indigenous values. The APCM recognized that the government of the Congo discounted any hearsay reports of the cruelties toward Congolese that had gone on for years. Lachlan Vass stated: "The State [agents] . . . absolutely refuse to take or consider any evidence except the evidence of a foreigner, and what he reports must be seen by him. The natives' evidence is worth little or nothing."[34] The APCM commissioned Sheppard to visit the Kuba area under attack and make a firsthand report. "It honestly wished to ascertain whether these Zappo Zaps were acting simply under their own brutal instincts, and if so, it wished to call the attention of the State authorities to these outrages."[35] At this time the Presbyterians presumed that State agents had not approved the carnage. Least of all did they think that Leopold, who had accepted Lapsley so cordially, would knowingly tolerate, much less command, such brutality.

Another reason why the missionaries at Luebo asked Sheppard to investigate was because the scene of the Zappo Zaps' current activity was near the village of Pianga, which was not far from his Ibanche station. Even before Sheppard received this request from the APCM, refugees from invaded villages had begged him to help alleviate the devastating attacks they were receiving from the Zappo Zaps. He had not responded because he assumed that they would surely murder him. He sagaciously told his people, "There is no use in exposing myself in that way and tempting Providence." Years earlier Sheppard had expressed wariness of getting near those unprincipled people, "You can trust them as far as you can see them—and the farther off you see them the better you can trust them."[36] So it was with much trepidation that Sheppard responded to the APCM directive.

Sheppard had difficulty recruiting anyone to accompany him in this investigation of reports of killings and arson by the Zappo Zaps. He assembled about five hundred natives at Ibanche and informed them of the situation. He then made this appeal: "You who are willing to go, stand in line. You who are not willing, go to your homes." He was understanding of this result:

> I looked away for a moment and when I looked up everybody had gone! And to tell the truth I also wanted to join them, for I did not want to go to Pianga at all. But I was compelled to go, so I walked around and got eleven men to follow me.[37]

In the journal Sheppard kept in September 1899, he tells of passing through more than a dozen burned and deserted villages. Then he notes: "At a curve in the path through the forest we met face to face sixteen Zappo Zaps, who with lightning speed cocked their guns and took aim. . . . I leaped forward, threw up my hands and cried out in a loud voice, 'Don't shoot; I am Sheppard!'" Chebamba, the leader of the patrol hunting for slaves, recognized Sheppard because they had frequently encountered one another before. Two years earlier the Sheppards had treated a wound that was threatening Chebamba's life. Due to gratitude for the medical attention, he was quite friendly. He freely talked about the raiding, burning, and killing he had done. Chebamba reported on "his big friend" to Mlumba Nkusa, his commander, who soon approached with a large number of armed men. Sheppard described him as "a most repulsive looking man," in part because his teeth were filed to sharp points. Also, his eyebrows were shaven and his eyelashes plucked out.[38]

Mlumba escorted Sheppard to a stockade that was quartering hundreds of Zappo Zaps and was flying Leopold's lone star flag. The commander assumed that all foreigners were allies of the State, so he trumpeted his brutality, disclosing what would have been beyond imagination. Sheppard was taken to a large confinement where slaughter had taken place, which was reeking with the stench of corpses. He was brought water by a soldier whose "hands were even then dripping with the crimson blood of innocent men, women and children." Mlumba told of inviting men and women into the stockade and giving them the choice of paying their Kasai taxes or being killed. The exorbitant demand included sixty slaves and much rubber from tribal leaders, but only eight slaves and 2,500 balls of rubber had been received. "I think we killed between eighty and ninety," Mlumba acknowledged, "besides those in other villages to which I sent my people."

Sheppard counted forty-one bodies and was told that the rest had been eaten. He noticed that the cannibals had carved steaks off of the lower parts of three bodies. The forehead of one decapitated person had been used to make a bowl for rolling tobacco. Sheppard saw sixty women prisoners huddled together; they were being kept as hostages and for satisfying the sexual appetites of the warriors. Seeing the corpse of a young woman lying nearby without her right hand, he asked for an explanation. Mlumba stated that they always cut the right hand off to give to Leopold's agent on their return. Sheppard was then taken to a shed where hands of victims were being heated over a slow fire. He counted eighty-one hands and saw human flesh being preserved by being dried out on bamboo sticks. Mlumba said, "I don't like to fight, but the State told me if the villages refused to pay to make fire." He informed Sheppard that in addition to the Pyaang people whom he had just assaulted, the State had sent him to collect tribute from other areas of the Kuba confederation. In particular, the Kuba capital and the Kete villages in the Luebo area were to be invaded. Mlumba told Sheppard specifics on the ammunition and about five hundred rifles he had received from the State.[39]

Sheppard's investigating party remained for two days in the sickening company of the armed Zappo Zap raiders. Although it took two days to get there, they returned to Ibanche in one day. The first matter of urgency was getting the women hostages released. Due to Sheppard's findings, they were soon freed by the State, but Mlumba was not arrested until he was again accused of atrocities five years later. At that time the puzzled Mlumba said to his superior, State officer DuFour, "You have sent me to do this and yet you have put me in chains!"[40]

To document the deplorable conditions, Sheppard took snapshots with his Kodak camera, which amateurs were beginning to use widely. He was among the first to use it as a powerful instrument of social reform. In his album at the Presbyterian Historical Society there is a photograph that provides visual proof of three alive young men without right hands. The label, "Some of the evidence of Belgium atrocities," expresses Sheppard's judgment that the Belgian king was ultimately responsible. Another photo is of a young woman with a locked chain about her neck. Beneath is the inscription: "Rescued by Sheppard from the cannibals." As Hochschild observes, Sheppard "recorded a scene he came across in the Congo rain forest that would brand itself on the world's consciousness as a symbol of colonial brutality."[41]

The APCM realized that Sheppard's story was too shocking and inconceivable to be widely accepted without supporting testimony. Accordingly, Vass went out and also witnessed the barbarity and carnage of the Zappo Zaps. He told of seeing many corpses with right hands removed and added more data regarding the terror. "The whole country is pillaged and not a village left standing," he wrote; "in a radius of about seventy-five miles, there are probably over 50,000 people sleeping in the bush, unsheltered and in the midst of the rainy season." In the first report to church people in America of these outrages, Hawkins of the APCM commented that "the State authorities at Luluaburg are endeavoring to shield their agents and possibly bring odium upon our missionaries."[42]

As soon as the APCM received the second report from Vass, they attempted by every means possible to stop subsequent brutality. Morrison, whom the APCM had elected to serve a term as its legal representative, sent Sheppard's findings to DuFour, the district chief at Luluaburg, whom he presumed had authorized the slaughter. After a superficial investigation, DuFour concluded that no district official was responsible for the Zappo Zaps' conduct. Morrison then wrote Leopold in October about the massacre; in February he was informed that the matter had been turned over to authorities for consideration, but no further response was forthcoming. Leopold did exclaim to his cronies: "Cut off hands—that's idiotic! I'd cut off all the rest of them, but not the hands. That's the one thing I need in the Congo!"[43] When the APCM protested to the Native Protection Commission that Leopold had established to hear charges of kidnapping and enslavement by the State, Father Emeri Cambier, a Commission member and the head of the Catholic mission in Luluaburg, responded that forced labor was legal and that the officers were doing their duty. Unpersuaded, Morrison asserted, "You know that every important stipulation of the General Act of the Conference of Berlin has been publicly violated and illegally trampled under foot."

Cambier then wrote the Governor of the Congo that the alleged inhumanities reported in the vicinity of Luebo were exaggerated and might be no more than disturbances in Morrison's brain.[44] Although Cambier was in Belgium when Sheppard visited the scene of the brutality, he accused Sheppard in Belgian journals of fabrication and claimed that Mlumba had been the victim of an attack.[45] In 1900, other Belgian journals accepted Sheppard's report as accurate but explained that the Zappo Zaps were armed by the State in order to protect the Catholic missions. Also they claimed that those guilty of the atrocities had been severely punished.[46]

David Rankin, the Associate Secretary of the Presbyterian Mission Board, immediately presented in an American national magazine Sheppard's full account of the Zappo Zap episode, with this introduction:

> As the work of the Mission was being seriously disturbed and the lives
> of its adherents threatened, the Mission dispatched the Rev. W. H.
> Sheppard on a tour of investigation. He was the oldest member of the
> Mission, knew the country best, and was best known by the natives.
> Moreover, his tact and heroism in the past indicated that he was the
> proper man to send on this perilous journey.[47]

Morrison was outraged over the whitewashing or indifferent
responses by Leopold and his agents. He boldly asserted that the State
had "turned out to be a gigantic slave and trade company, whose philanthropy had been turned into greed."[48] Appealing to world public opinion
with the concrete evidence obtained by the APCM was the only way left
to try to effect change. Morrison thundered in a leading American journal, "The slave-raiding of the Arabs was better than the butcheries of the
cannibal army of Leopold today."[49] In the Congo there was no American
consul to whom he could appeal, but that office would soon be established, largely because of Presbyterian overtures to Washington.

The Aborigines Protection Society of Britain was determined to halt
the "systematic slave-raiding" of Leopold's officials.[50] That powerful
lobby had been formed in 1838 to carry forward the humanitarian work
started by William Wilberforce and other slavery abolitionists. Henry
Fox Bourne, Secretary of the Society, was invigorated by the APCM
reports and made use of Sheppard's account of the Zappo Zap raid in a
book he wrote on the Congo atrocities.[51] The Society corroborated
Sheppard's testimony by issuing a statement by Edgar Canisius, an
American, about a Belgian officer:

> Last year I was on a rubber expedition with Major Lothaire, and dur-
> ing the six weeks it lasted, nine hundred natives were killed and scores
> of villages burnt. Knees were hacked off, hands severed at the wrists,
> limbs broken with revolver bullets, rubber collectors tied to stakes and
> exposed to the burning sun.[52]

Sheppard's eyewitness account of eighty-one severed and smoked
hands was the most widely quoted information about Congo atrocities.[53] That sensational testimony did much to shift public opinion in
Europe and America. The *Times* of London, the leading English-
language newspaper and one that Leopold read daily, introduced it in
this manner: "We have heard reports for years past of the terrible affairs
in the Congo; . . . yet, as they have often been based on second-hand
native stories, they have been difficult to verify. Now the case is different." Mention was made of the high character and education of the
source, stating that Sheppard was a Fellow in the Royal Geographical

Society, and an "accredited missionary of one of the leading Christian churches in the United States."[54]

Some State officers acknowledged mutilations that had been made during this period but knowledge of this became available to the public only after the demise of the Congo Free State,[55] and only with the publication of *King Leopold's Ghost* in 1998 have they become widely known. For example, Belgian Commissioner Charles Lemaire admitted after retirement that he informed the State, "To gather rubber . . . one must cut off hands, noses, and ears."[56]

Disgusted at the slowness of the movement to counter Leopold's excesses, Joseph Conrad wrote: "It is an extraordinary thing that the conscience of Europe, which seventy years ago has put down the slave trade on humanitarian grounds, tolerates the Congo State today. It is as if the moral clock has been put back many hours."[57] In 1899 Conrad published *Heart of Darkness*, telling of his Congo experiences in a true but fictional form. That masterpiece is a wrenching tale of exploitation by European traders. The main character is Mr. Kurtz, a two-faced top colonial official who writes the report for the International Society for the Suppression of Savage Customs. In it he states that "by the simple exercise of our will we [Europeans] can exert a power for good practically unbounded."[58] Kurtz's brand of savagery includes placing African skulls on stakes in front of his house. In order to pile up ivory for export, the sadist works through cannibals who extort the product from Congolese and who oversee chain gangs that bring it to the steamer. The tale's concluding phrase sums up Kurtz, who symbolizes Leopold, as having "the heart of an immense darkness."

While Sheppard's testimony was causing reverberations in England, Henry Wellington wrote a book glorifying Leopold's Congo enterprise. He attacked Morrison's accounts of alleged mutilations and other outrages because they were merely hearsay.[59] Wellington cunningly did not mention the man from whom Morrison obtained his reports, no doubt recognizing that he could not so easily dismiss the graphic detail of the prime witness.

Booker T. Washington wrote an article in which he quoted extensively from the Zappo Zap account written by one he had known at Hampton Institute. He judged the atrocities against blacks in the Congo Free State to surpass anything previously known of slavery in Africa or in America. He discerned that "one of the most unfortunate results of this method of dealing with the African is the heritage of misunderstanding, mutual distrust, and race hatred that it inevitably leaves behind."[60]

The Anglo-American publicity given Sheppard's report caused repercussions in the Belgian legislature. In 1900 Georges Lorand was virtually the only Belgian to denounce those who were massacring and pillaging under the "pretext of civilization."[61] Ruth Slade states:

> Lorand reproached Belgian Catholic missionaries for keeping silence about what they must have seen and heard around their stations. A Catholic deputy, Colfs, came to their defence, saying that they would speak out if they could—but they feared lest their mission work should suffer and the name of Belgium be brought to shame.[62]

The European and American protests had little immediate result in Kasai. Soon another devastating attack was made by the State soldiers in the Luebo area. About it, Morrison testified:

> I have seen a number of times thousands of people fleeing into the forests to escape from the cannibal soldiers of King Leopold; I have seen these soldiers scouring through the forests and, after catching a number of men whom the government wanted as laborers, going away with the captives tied together by ropes around their necks. Raids upon villages are being constantly made, some of the people are killed and eaten, others are carried away into captivity and sold, others are forced into military service.[63]

Villages under the protection of the Luebo mission were swelling in size with Lubas as a result of the large number of slave killings by the Lukengu and the enlarging slave operation of those in the business of extracting Kasai products.

It would be misleading to maintain that all Presbyterian missionaries were of the same mind regarding humane treatment of the Congolese. Phillips Verner had no formal theological training before beginning in 1896 his several-year term with the APCM. He was born on a South Carolina plantation owned by his slaveholding ancestors, and his father responded to the "Yankee Invasion" by being a leader of the White Supremacy Party after the Civil War. Following in his family tradition, he became primarily interested in supplying raw material for industry regardless of the bondage involved. Verner was aware that the Zappo Zaps were cannibals, and he included in his 1903 book a picture of a pyramid of human skulls and other bones which he titled "a cannibal grave-yard."[64] He also stated that State troops plundered and burned villages and otherwise terrified them as they extorted ivory and rubber.[65] Even so, Verner praised the Zappo Zaps:

They counted themselves the special friends and allies of the white man; were more advanced in civilization than any of the other natives, as they made every effort possible to get full suits of European clothing, to build their houses in imitation of those built by the whites; to use imported cooking utensils and dishes; to speak French and English; to carry firearms, and to trade in barter goods.

Verner had no difficulty justifying the way in which Belgian officials made use of African slavers:

The principal occupation of the Zappo Zaps . . . was trading in slaves. . . . They knew where they could buy slaves or make stealthy raids upon unsuspecting villages, and they also kept up with the best market for their human wares. The explicit policy of the Belgian-Congo government . . . was, in theory at any rate, to abate and abolish this slave trading in every form. The practical difficulties in the way, however, were numerous and often insuperable. Where, for example, the chief dealers in human beings were the strongest professed allies the government possessed, as in the case of the Zappo Zaps, the officials at Lusambo and Luluaburg experienced troubles well nigh insurmountable in putting down the trade.[66]

Apart from the "quite civilized" Zappo Zaps and the Christian Africans, Verner evaluated the rest of the Africans as deficient in some distinctively human qualities. They are, he opined, "very apt to learn things requiring the sharp eye, quick hand and steady foot. . . . They rather lack the higher reasoning and introspective faculties."[67] Again, he declared:

Nowhere is our oft-derided doctrine of original sin more clearly shown than among these people. Depravity oozes from their very skins. They will lie in order to try to enter the church; will steal from the person of a dying benefactor; will trade wives for a chicken to boot; will bear false witness for the consideration of a handful of salt, and will murder a man for the brass rings on his arms. And yet, converted to Christianity, they will die rather than recant and will suffer torture rather than be forced to break a commandment.[68]

Verner thought that "savages" who became Christians should not be treated as equals, and that black missionaries should be given subordinate positions to keep them from acting "uppity."[69] Patronizingly he said of Sheppard:

He is a man of great good sense. . . . In his attitude toward the white people particularly has he shown this quality, so that the people of the South may be sure that he will conduct himself entirely in accord with their traditions and sentiments.[70]

In writing to fellow southern Presbyterians, Verner shared his notions of racial destiny: "The African race is the great coming laboring class of the world. The inferior Caucasian races—Spanish, Portuguese, etc.—will ultimately disappear. . . . The stronger Caucasians will be the directing powers of the rest of the world."[71] In a book written to promote Congo development, Verner asserted, "Africa must be made a stronghold of Caucasian power," and exclaimed, "What a magnificent field for exploitation is opened up there!" He expressed gratitude that Leopold permitted white men to rule even as they did in the United States. He hoped that in the Congo such foreigners would "become wealthy and happy colonial landlords."[72] Benedetto observes: "Verner was more interested in the exploitation of the resources of the Kasai than in the development of its people. He tried to obtain his own private lands for commercial exploitation and had hopes of developing a diamond mine."[73] Verner had found quantities of diamonds in the Tshikapa River, and fortunes are still being made there by mining companies.

After serving three years with the APCM, Verner was not reappointed because of his duplicity. When he returned to America and left mission work, he was bribed by Belgian Ambassador Baron Ludovic Moncheur to give favorable publicity for the king. In 1907 he was paid the equivalent of $240,000 in year 2000 dollars to work in the Congo for Bernard Baruch and other New York investors who were involved in Leopold's rubber business.[74] Pertaining to Verner's performance, Morrison asserted on behalf of Sheppard and other members of the APCM staff:

> We have many times, during his sojourn here, heard him most bitterly denounce the Congo State government in its atrocious treatment of the natives. . . . Since that time he has faithfully allied himself with the Leopold regime. . . . Leopold has evidently found Mr. Verner a willing tool, and one willing to sell the truth for a few royal favors.[75]

Verner was employed to obtain a group of pygmies from the Congo for the St. Louis World's Fair in 1904. He had made contact with pygmies when residing some years earlier at the temporary Ndombe APCM station in the Wissmann Falls area. Armed with permission from Leopold and his officials, he made his trip to the Kasai forest where they lived. Although the pygmies were reluctant to travel overseas, which they associated with becoming enslaved to white people, they were enticed by gifts Verner had brought. He gave them a large amount of salt, which was worth more than gold in central Africa, and instructed them in the use of guns that they had never handled before. Ten agreed to trust Verner to provide them with a safe voyage. The Sheppards, who were headed for a furlough, happened to be aboard the same steamer.[76]

In advertising his specimens for the fair, Verner claimed that pygmies were next of kin to apes and referred to the "chatter" of these "monkey-like people." Allegedly representing "the lowest degree of human development," they were characterized as having "a snout-like projection of the jaw" and as "leaping about like grasshoppers." Millions of Americans had their first sight of Africans at the Fair exhibit.

In 1906 Verner arranged to have Ota Benga, one of the pygmies that he had purchased, placed in the primate house at the Bronx Zoo. He brazenly defended his action by claiming that the creature was "absolutely free" and was placed in a cage only "to prevent him from getting away from the keepers." Throngs were attracted to see Ota wrestle with Dohong, the orangutan. "Their heads are much alike and both grin in the same way when pleased," the *New York Times* reported in a front-page lead article. Some spectators concluded that pygmies were the evolutionary "missing link" because Ota could communicate with apes in their own language and also speak some broken English. Protests by black clergy eventually resulted in the ending of the degrading popular daily show. Although Verner discouraged those who desired to provide education for Ota, he was placed in a Christian school. While Ota was there one reporter claimed that "now and then he will sing at the top of his voice in his own tongue the song his people sang while gathered around some nicely cooked missionary who had been sizzling on the fire for several hours, and who was all ready to be eaten." For the next decade Ota lived in Lynchburg, Virginia, and had difficulty conforming to the mores of racial segregation. After a period of depression, he committed suicide.[77]

The views of Verner on blacks mirrored those of many of his fellow Americans. But those views, and his later outlook on Leopold's enterprise, stood in sharp contrast to the commitments of other APCM missionaries. There is no evidence that other members of that staff were mainly interested in Caucasian and capitalistic power at the expense of the human rights of the Africans.

Many Protestant missionaries in the Congo from other denominations, however, did accept the State's policies uncritically. Even those who privately commented on injustices did not speak out for fear that the State might prohibit them from continuing to make Christian converts. "With regard to the Protestant missionaries," Morrison observed, "I may say generally that their policy seems to have been to see just as little as they could and to speak just as little as they could about what they could not help seeing."[78] The Protestant-chaired Native Protection Commission did not take action against a single case of injustice reported to them. Occasionally there were bogus investigations which gave the appearance of accountability, but no prosecutions followed.[79]

By 1902 the APCM was convinced that neither the State agents in the Congo nor the Belgian king would effect substantive changes in African labor practices without strong international pressure. Presbyterian missionary Motte Martin put the matter succinctly: "By stealthy encroachments and bold usurpations, the Congo Free State had been converted into the Congo Slave State."[80] Morrison's years of appeal to Leopold, to the Congo Governor-General, and to their Kasai subordinates had all been in vain.

On his return home from Africa in the spring of 1903, Morrison was invited to speak to the Aborigines Protection Society in London. Several members of Parliament were included in the meeting at Whitehall, where he told about the appalling cruelties that were happening in the Congo. In addition to reminding his listeners of Sheppard's encounter with a band of Zappo Zaps several years earlier, Morrison told of two incidents in which he was recently involved. He had experienced a "reign of terror" when the State was recruiting soldiers.[81] Morrison testified, "Two white State officers came to Luebo and caught by force a number of men—I saw about eighteen of them taken away with ropes around their necks in true Arab slave-raiding style." To confirm this, Vass sent out a photograph of these men tied together, but the State claimed that it showed only fugitives from justice who had been captured. Vass asserted that were it not for the strong protests of the APCM most of the Luebo people would be placed in "practical slavery."[82]

The other incident happened on Morrison's way to embark for Europe: "On March 25 last, I boarded the Congo railway train at Leopoldville, on Stanley Pool, and found three trucks [railway cars] loaded with slaves, who had been caught only a few days' march east of Luebo and were being taken they knew not where." Morrison learned that these people from Kasai had been captured for forced labor and transported a thousand miles from their home region to deter them from escaping. He evaluated Leopold's system of exploitation as "the most iniquitous since the days of the Spaniards in Mexico and Peru." In conclusion, he charged, "As a result of this forced labor system, the rubber and the ivory have been pouring into the port of Antwerp, and the blood of thousands of innocent men and women in Africa has been freely shed to satisfy the greed of the man who poses as their benefactor."[83]

The testimonies of Morrison and Sheppard were much appreciated even by those wary of missionaries. Businessman Edmund Morel, who founded the Congo Reform Association, admitted that he was generally "no lover of missionaries" but recognized that their reports of abuses by Leopold's agents were trustworthy. Morel asserted about Morrison: "There was nothing of the fanatic about him; no rhetoric; no invocations to the Deity; no prayerful entreaties. He was merely a capable, honest, strong, fearless man, and he told his story with a moral force which thrilled all who heard it."[84]

After Morrison addressed the Aborigines Protection Society, a motion was passed urging the British government to use its considerable international power to secure humane treatment for the Congolese.[85] Liberal party member Herbert Samuel then alerted fellow House of Commons legislators to the forced-labor tyranny in the Congo and to Sheppard's riveting account of "80 human hands being slowly dried over a fire." On the basis of such concrete evidence, Foreign Secretary Lord Landsdowne denounced the Congo operation as "bondage under the most barbarous and inhuman conditions, maintained for mercenary motives of the most selfish character."[86] Samuel offered a motion that was supported by Prime Minister Arthur Balfour:

> That the Government of the Congo Free State having, at its inception, guaranteed to the Powers that its native subjects should be governed with humanity, and that no trading monopoly or privilege should be permitted within its dominions, this House requests His Majesty's Government to confer with the other Powers, signatories of the Berlin General Act, by virtue of which the Congo Free State exists, in order that measures may be adopted to abate the evils prevalent in that State.[87]

According to Slade, "The motion of Congo affairs which was passed unanimously by the Commons in May 1903 marked a decisive stage in the anti-Congolese campaign. The motion had committed the British Government to action, and to the thesis that the Congo State was not a fully autonomous state."[88] The British then communicated this resolution to the thirteen other European nations who drew up the Berlin accord of 1885. Leading periodicals gave it coverage and various governments discussed it. Some German journals endorsed the House of Commons resolution and the Belgian legislature debated it heatedly.

Delegate Emile Vandervelde proposed that an impartial investigation be made to ascertain if Congolese rights were being violated. Although his proposal was initially rejected, a year later an investigation was begun by the Belgian government.[89]

Having had success in dealing with the British Parliament, Morrison went on to attempt to raise the consciousness of American legislators. He was able to have an extensive report published in the *Congressional Record* and elsewhere that included an account of a Belgian commander who bragged about killing women while searching for ivory:

> The officer who made this raid was in Luebo some days after the affair, and he jokingly remarked that he had killed many people, and had secured a fine lot of curios. He also said that while his soldiers were firing on the villagers they ran wildly about crying "Shepite! Shepite!" They were calling for one of our well-known missionaries, Rev. W. H. Sheppard, F. R. G. S., to come to their assistance. No explanation was ever made to the people of the reason for these raids.[90]

Soon after Morrison returned to America, he spoke to the PCUS General Assembly. He told of the abominations that Sheppard had reported years earlier and he pleaded for the "emancipation of the Congolese." The alarmed Assembly expressed its approval for what Morrison and Sheppard were doing in making Belgian atrocities known to the world. Also it decided to send a delegation to President Theodore Roosevelt to request United States intervention on behalf of the Congolese.[91]

The Foreign Missions Committee sent Samuel Chester, its executive secretary, and Morrison to lay before Roosevelt the need for Congo reforms. Chester had come to believe that Leopold's scheme of crushing the Congolese had become "the most cruel and brutal regime of exploitation to which any conquered people were ever subjected."[92] Morrison hoped the president would realize the United States' obligation in this situation, since it had been the first nation to recognize the Congo Free State. When Chester and Morrison met with the president on November 7, 1903, they were encouraged to see Morel's book *Red Rubber* lying open on his desk. Morel's gruesome report of mixing blood with rubber included Sheppard's account of the Zappo Zaps and photographs of a Congolese child and an adult with a severed hand or foot. The popularity of the book had assisted Morel in promoting Congo Reform Associations in Britain and America.

Roosevelt disappointingly told the Presbyterian delegation that no direct action would be taken by their government unless American citizens were personally mistreated. His inaction may have been the result of the effectiveness of Leopold's propaganda. The king responded to criticism by manipulating the media. The shrewd publicity manager set up a press bureau in 1903 for providing journalists with favorable information about his Congo operations.[93] Its effectiveness was displayed in the tardiness of protests against Leopold by most church missions. They preferred to think of him as a philanthropic person who had encountered difficulties in employing subordinates who shared his idealism. For example, Baptist missionary leader Grenfell, as late as 1904, wrote, "I cannot believe his Majesty is careless of the people so long as the rubber comes in, or I would have to join his accusers."[94]

Stanley, although he had been a Member of Parliament and had been knighted by the British, was Leopold's henchman to the end and spoke up for his former employer at an interview published in Brussels in 1903:

> I am convinced that since I left Africa, King Leopold has done his best to prevent all crime on the Congo. . . . The Congo is succeeding better than any other state of Africa. . . . The white man must remain master of the Congo. . . . I do not think there is another sovereign living who has done so much for humanity as Leopold II.[95]

Leopold also worked through Cardinal James Gibbons, the most influential Catholic in the United States. The Cardinal thanked the Congo government "for its successful efforts to introduce Christianity and civilization into Central Africa."[96] In return for his defense of Leopold's business operations, the king bestowed on Gibbons the Grand Cross of the Order of the Crown.[97]

Gibbons wrote the Congo Reform Association that its 1904 Boston Peace Conference should be informed that the few missionaries who have raised an outcry against the Congo administration have depended "largely on the untrustworthy hearsay evidence of natives." Even though Leopold sent his best agents to push for the removal of the Congo issue from the agenda of the Conference, Morrison spoke there at length about the plight of the Congolese. He ranked the Congo system of forced labor as "the most heartless and iniquitous in the history of modern colonization enterprises."[98] Morrison concluded with this contrast:

> The Congo government points to its prosperity, to its millions of dollars worth of exports, to its railways and steamboats, to its plantations and beautiful military posts and monopolistic companies which are paying fabulous dividends. I point to the lash and the chains and the repeating rifles and the 30,000 cannibal soldiers which have made all

this so-called prosperity possible; a prosperity which is felt in Brussels, but not on the Congo. Instead of the taxes going back for the benefit of the native people, they either stop in the coffers of King Leopold and the stockholders of the monopolistic companies, or they are sent back to the Congo to build more railroads and more steamboats and more state posts and to buy more rifles.[99]

After Morrison's Boston address, the Congo Reform Association passed a resolution asking the nations who signed the Berlin Act to meet again to inquire into the conduct of the Congo Free State. Also, an American Congo Reform Association was formed to attack Leopold's brand of imperialism.[100]

The British launched their own investigation of the Congolese situation by instructing their Congo consul Roger Casement to tour the hinterland and report to London. Conrad had gotten to know him while in the Congo and thought highly of his judgment. Casement visited the Equatorial rather than the Kasai district, but his findings, published in 1904, corroborated the American missionaries' claim of native mutilation and other barbarous treatment that was related to bringing in large quotas of rubber. Other ghastly details in Casement's diary tell of terrified people:

> Hunted women clutching their children and flying panic-stricken through the bush; the blood flowing from those quivering black bodies as the hippopotamus-hide whip struck again and again; the savage soldiery rushing hither and thither amid burning villages.

That widely used rawhide whip had sharp edges and was as hard as wood. A few blows brought blood and two dozen left the victim insensible. The resulting gashes and broken spirit often endured for a lifetime. Snyder noted that violent words also cut deeply into the natives: "The Belgians take great pleasure in calling them 'animals,' a name which stings to the quick. . . . They would prefer at any time a whipping to the word *nyama* (animal)."[101]

Casement's observations were especially significant because he had traveled in the same region sixteen years earlier when the impact of Leopold's agents had not been felt. He commented:

> The most striking change observed during my journey into the interior was the great reduction observable everywhere in native life. Communities I had formerly known as large and flourishing centers of population are today entirely gone, or now exist in such diminished numbers as to be no longer recognizable.

Some natives on Leopold's side of the Congo River had chosen exile from their ancestral lands and had crossed into French territory. Casement learned that the reason for this was that the State's demand for rubber was causing weakness and starvation for those remaining in the Congo Free State. Casement concluded, "Looking around on the scene of desolation, on the untended farms, . . . the unspeakable condition of the prisons at the State posts—all combined to convince me over and over again that, during the last seven years, this 'Domaine Prive' of King Leopold has been a veritable hell on earth."[102]

A year after the Morrisons came home on furlough, the Sheppards also had an extended stay in America. Sheppard joined Morrison in unleashing a barrage of criticism of Leopold's Congo policies on the podium and in the press. A newspaper scrapbook was kept by the Sheppards to document the many places where they spoke during the furlough, often to crowded auditoriums, ranging as far westward as St. Louis.[103] Sheppard wrote of being an eyewitness to "mangled bodies, severed hands, devastated villages, terrorized districts . . . done for gold."[104]

Sheppard effectively raised consciousness of the emergency situation that was affecting the Congolese. On August 21, 1904, while he was visiting with his mother and sister at Warm Springs, Virginia, the Rev. William White invited him to speak at the Presbyterian church in the village. On learning that Sheppard would be speaking there, Belgian Ambassador Moncheur and newspaper reporters, who were vacationing at the nearby Homestead mountain resort, came to hear him. When Sheppard had dined with Moncheur earlier that year in Washington, the Ambassador found him so genial that he concluded that the African-American would not have the moral courage to protest against Congo policies when separated from Morrison's promptings.[105] However, Sheppard told the congregation about the brutalities he had witnessed when with the Zappo Zaps. The next morning headlines across the nation read, "ACCOUNT OF THE ATROCITIES IN THE CONGO" and there was response in cartoon form.

The visit by Sheppard to that small Warm Springs church has been remembered by some of its elders as one of the more significant happenings in its long history. The church still possesses a machete from Congo that Sheppard gave one of the members.[106] It is interesting to note the quandary precipitated when White invited Sheppard to his manse for dinner after the church service. The white ladies withdrew from the dining room to eat elsewhere, perhaps due to the Southern obsession with the notion that contact with a black man might sully the purity of a white woman.

From the very beginning of the church, some have frowned upon extending social equality. The apostle Peter was reprimanded by leaders of the Jerusalem church who were upset over the integrated dining that Peter had condoned among Jewish and Gentile Christians. The Jerusalem Christians did not question the revelation on which his affirming the religious equality of all Christians was based, which led to his baptizing of converted Gentiles. They did, however, insist that having table fellowship with a different ethnic group would overthrow an established Jewish custom, and that was unacceptable.[107] Over the two millennia of Christian history it has continued to be diffficult for Christian groups to accept as fully equal those who are racially and culturally different.

Roosevelt received Sheppard at the White House on January 14, 1905. To display the abilities of the persecuted Congolese, Sheppard presented to the president several handsome Kuba artifacts and told of the printing press that Africans were operating to publish educational materials in the vernacular.[108] In return, as the Hampton archives display, the president wrote "To Rev. William H. Sheppard" on his autographed photo and gave it to his unofficial ambassador who was promoting "liberty and justice for all."

In June 1905 Sheppard received further notoriety when he was awarded an honorary doctoral degree at Biddle University, an institution for blacks that had been established by northern Presbyterians in Charlotte, North Carolina. Daniel Sanders, who had risen from slavery to become the university's outstanding president, had arranged for this tribute without Sheppard's knowledge because he admired the missionary's witness.[109] That African American institution has since been renamed the Johnson C. Smith University.

In 1906 the PCUS General Assembly, echoing what Sheppard had been urging, again protested against "the cruelty and atrocities which have been committed by the military authorities of the government of the Congo Independent State" and petitioned the American government to "compel the abatement of this outrage against our common humanity."[110] Secretary of State Elihu Root was exasperated by the quantity of petitions he received, and he later recalled, "The Protestant Church and many good women were wild to have us stop the atrocities in the Congo."[111]

Senator Morgan, now near the end of his many years in Congress, responded to the Congo issue because of his personal interest through-

out his career in the pioneer Presbyterian missionaries in the Congo.
At this time he recalled having been greatly impressed by the son of
James Lapsley, his former law partner. Decades earlier, when young
Sam drove Morgan to the train depot after a visit to the Lapsley coun-
try home, he was asked what he intended to be when he grew up. Sam
promptly replied, "I intend to be a minister of the gospel, sir."[112]

The irrefutable reports of Sheppard caused Morgan to feel betrayed
by the king whom he had strongly supported two decades earlier. Recognizing Roosevelt's reluctance to protest Leopold's actions in the
Congo, Morgan decided that the Senate should take up the issue. Consequently, in 1906 he submitted to his Foreign Relations Committee
the evidence that Protestant leaders had compiled of mass murder and
extortion by Leopold's agents. A resolution was introduced decrying
"capitalists" who joined with the king in the "most arbitrary and unjus-
tified usurpation . . . that has ever existed in any country or over any
people."[113] Morgan still believed that ten million blacks could be persuaded to leave America and settle in the Congo if Leopold made his
estate more attractive.[114] At that time Senator Henry Cabot Lodge
received unanimous support for a resolution he introduced in the Senate calling for Roosevelt to take all necessary measures to ameliorate
the situation in the Congo. However, no action was taken by the government because its imperialistic president sympathized with the Belgian imperialist.

Unable to stop the crescendo of international criticisms by the public
relations approach, Leopold gave more attention to curtailing the mission activity of his critics. Even though the Treaty of Berlin declared
that mission societies would have free access to the Congo, Leopold
recognized that preferential approval or closing of stations would dis-
courage opposition to his regime. The APCM temporary station at
Ndombi near Wissmann Falls was ordered closed, probably pursuant
to the king's decree that no petition of missions with "hostility toward
the State" should be approved.[115] The Secretary of State for the Congo
informed the American Presbyterians that henceforth no concessions
would be granted them.[116] Leopold succeeded in enlisting Vatican support against Protestants "who imagine crimes by agents of the State."
In 1906 he signed a concordat with the pope that provided state subsi-
dies for Belgian Catholic missions. Both parties hoped that this
arrangement would diminish the influence of Protestant missions in
the Congo.[117] In response, the Congo Reform Association sent Guinness on an American tour to attack the Catholic support of Leopold.[118]

Mark Twain became interested in the testimonies that Sheppard and Morrison were giving against Leopold's exploitations in the Congo. Twain had an outstanding record of advocacy for the black race, and his special concern over this matter may have been due to the involvement of an African American as well as Africans. Also, he was a liberal Presbyterian who detested the way in which imperialists were trampling on human rights.[119] He viewed the king as one who cloaked his insatiable greed in religious piety. Even though aged and ailing, Twain devoted some of his final literary effort to writing *King Leopold's Soliloquy*, which portrays the king's futile efforts to hide the grim truth. This withering satire contains extended quotations and gruesome illustrations taken from what Sheppard had recorded after visiting one of Leopold's mutilation and extermination camps. Twain let Leopold incriminate himself:

> In these twenty years I have spent millions to keep the press of the two hemispheres quiet, and still these leaks keep on occurring. . . . The natives consider them [American missionaries] their only friends; they go to them with their sorrows; they show them their scars and their wounds, inflicted by my soldier police; they hold up the stumps of their arms and lament because their hands have been chopped off, as punishment for not bringing in enough rubber, and as proof to be laid before my officers that the required punishment was well and truly carried out. One of these missionaries saw eighty-one of these hands drying over a fire for transmission to my officials—and of course he must go and set it down and print it. . . .
>
> Meddlesome missionary spying around—Rev. W. H. Sheppard. Talks with a black raider of mine after a raid; cozens him into giving away some particulars. The raider remarks: . . . [The quotation that follows is from Sheppard's record:] "I sent for all their chiefs, sub-chiefs, men and women. . . . They refused to pay me, and I ordered the fence to be closed so they couldn't run away; then we killed them here inside the fence."
>
> The kodak has been a sore calamity to us. The most powerful enemy that has confronted us, indeed. In the early years we had no trouble in getting the press to "expose" the tales of the mutilations as slanders, lies, inventions of busy-body American missionaries. . . . Then all of a sudden came the crash! That is to say, the incorruptible kodak—and all the harmony went to hell! The only witness I have encountered in my long experience that I couldn't bribe. Every Yankee missionary and every interrupted trader sent home and got one; and now—oh well, the pictures get sneaked around everywhere, in spite of all we can do to ferret them out and suppress them.[120]

In the wake of Twain's lampooning of Leopold, the *Boston Herald* commented: "The missionaries, who go out at the risk of their lives, are much better witnesses than . . . Leopold [who] sits at home and drinks blood. The conditions of things in the Congo are atrocious, as shown by the photographs of children whose hands have been cut off."[121]

The pressure of public opinion over the scandalous conditions in the Congo virtually forced Leopold to appoint a blue ribbon Commission of Inquiry. For its membership he selected a Swiss judge, the President of the Court of Appeals in Boma, and, as chairman, the Belgian Advocate-General. He calculated that these men would probably bring back a generally positive report. But after a fact-finding tour of the Congo, even this hand-picked Commission cited instances of flagrant maladministration. Its 1906 report contained these findings:

> The exaction of a labor tax is so oppressive that the natives on whom it falls have little, if any freedom. . . . The natives are practically pris-oners within their own territory. . . . There is abuse of the natives by white representatives of officially recognized companies. . . . [There are] punitive expeditions, not for the purpose of establishing peace and order, but for the purpose of terrifying natives into paying a tax . . . [that] the commissioners regard as inhuman.[122]

The Commission of Inquiry also told Leopold some things about the Protestant missionaries that he would rather not have had reported:

> Sometimes . . . in regions where Evangelical missions are established, the black, rather than address himself to the magistrate . . . is accus-tomed, when he has a complaint against a . . . *chef de zone*, to go and confide in the missionary, who listens, assists him to the best of his ability, and becomes the recipient of all the complaints of a district. Hence the remarkable authority of the missionaries in some parts of the country. They acquire ascendancy not only over the natives sub-jected to their religious teaching, but over all the villages whose griefs they hear. The missionary becomes, for the natives of a district, the sole representative of equity and justice.[123]

Since Leopold had become highly unpopular even with his fellow Belgians, he recognized that he must at least act conciliatory on receiv-ing the Commission's findings. In a desperate effort to hold on to his source of opulence, in June 1906 he decreed some minor changes in Congo policy. He accepted the recommendations that attempts be made to settle disputes peacefully before sending in a military force and that State companies limit compulsory labor to forty hours per month.[124]

While Leopold was trying to calm public indignation by acting humane, he was exercising his imperial arrogance in a less visible manner. He reorganized his monopolistic companies so as to increase his profits. His holdings were by now so vast that it would have been impossible to calculate his riches. Some indication of his affluence is displayed in the money he spent on European palaces and swank resorts where he consorted with young women.[125] At the same time Belgian Jesuit philosopher A. Castelein asserted in his book defending Leopold:

> Some people . . . have represented Leopold II sitting on a throne of human skulls and surrounded by bags of gold, the fruit of his plunderings. These odious tales have been spread among their people by the Protestant missionaries. In reply to these calumnies, His Majesty authorized the heads of the administration of the Congo to declare in the Official Gazette "that the King has never derived from his African possessions the smallest personal benefit."[26]

While Castelein in 1907 was blaming Protestants for the troubles in the Congo, Morrison was expressing on behalf of the APCM the political philosophy under which action had been taken. Drawing on the ideas of John Locke, he stated:

> Every man has an inalienable right to his life, his liberty, and his property. This is a right which is above all government and all man-made decrees, and it is in defence of these primary rights of natives that we must raise our voice. . . . Public protest and appeal should be made when it has become clear that the settled policy of the government is such that similar wrongs are liable to recur at any time. The evil has become entrenched. Leopold is backed by his royal position, by his shrewd and disreputable diplomatic methods, by his great personal wealth and by an indomitable will. He has shrewdly brought to his aid the Vatican and the Belgian Parliament. . . . He has instituted bogus reforms, mostly on paper, and intended for European consumption. All the light, and liberty, and civilization which we enjoy today have been won at the expense of agitation, battling against sin, and wrong, and tyranny.[127]

Back in Africa the supply of latex was becoming depleted, but the Kasai Company continued to demand the same amount from the Congolese. That company, in which Leopold held half of the stock, included all the APCM area and much more. Bedinger told what was happening in the Kuba country, beginning in 1906, and the dilemma the missionaries confronted:

> The people were forced to do nothing else but make rubber. A famine threatened them, who were once a prosperous and thrifty people.

What was the Mission to do? Sad experience had taught the useless-
ness of appealing either to the State or the Company. On the other
hand, to keep silence, when no one else could or would speak for the
natives, was both unjust and inexpedient.[128]

The forests were suffering as well as the people. In the past the vines
had not been damaged when they were tapped at several months inter-
vals. But now, in order to respond to the ever rising world market in
the new vehicular era that ran on rubber tires, all thought of conserva-
tion was abandoned. Sheppard expressed his distress over the ecologi-
cal destruction that resulted from the State's obsession to make quick
profits:

> The vines were [previously] never cut off, for it takes from forty to fifty
> years for a vine to produce rubber. But this manner was too slow for
> those who wanted money at once, at any cost. Three hundred thou-
> sand Bakuba people had whips and guns at their backs and were forced
> to leave their homes and their other industries and begin this work of
> destruction.[129]

VINDICATION AT LAST

After returning to the Congo in 1906, the Sheppards and Morrisons
found no real improvement in the forced labor conditions. The State
officials were only more subtle and less blatant. Morrison made this
assessment, "We are not now suffering from the old forms of outrage
so much—handcutting, slave-raiding, murdering, etc.—but . . . I believe the sum total of suffering is much more than it was formerly."[130]
He protested to the Director of the Kasai Company, "Your company
is ruthlessly stripping the country of its natural wealth, and you are
adding to the crime by forcing the natives to destroy their own
country."[131]

By returning to Ibanche to reside, Sheppard could see firsthand what
was occurring among the Kubas. He was shocked to discover that they
were even worse off than before he went on furlough in 1904. Previously they could pay their small tax in goats but now a large quantity of
rubber was required. Moreover, they were receiving only one-sixth the
compensation per pound that they previously received when trading
companies were competing. The Lukengu was forced to deliver to the
Kasai Company thousands of rubber balls every twenty days.[132]

The change from self-determination to wretchedness is the theme of a brief article the now Doctor of Divinity Sheppard wrote in 1907 for the *Kassai Herald*, a journal published in Luebo mainly for the American constituency of the APCM. In this article, titled "From the Bakuba Country," Sheppard reflected on his fourteen years of experience among people dear to him:

> These great stalwart men and women, who have from time immemorial been free, cultivating large farms of Indian corn, peas, tobacco, potatoes, trapping elephants for their ivory tusks and leopards for their skins, who have always had their own king and a government not to be despised, officers of the law established in every town of the kingdom; these magnificent people, perhaps about 400,000 in number, have entered a new chapter in the history of their tribe. Only a few years ago, travelers through this country found them living in large homes, having from one to four rooms in each house, loving and living happily with their wives and children, one of the most prosperous and intelligent of all the African tribes, though living in one of the most remote spots on the planet. . . . But within these last three years how changed they are! Their farms are growing up in weeds and jungle, their king is practically a slave, their houses now are mostly only half-built single rooms and are much neglected. The streets of their towns are not clean and well-swept as they once were. Even their children cry for bread. Why this change? You have it in a few words. There are armed sentries of chartered trading companies who force the men and women to spend most of their days and nights in the forests making rubber, and the price they receive is so meager that they cannot live upon it. In the majority of the villages these people have not time to listen to the gospel story, or give an answer concerning their soul's salvation. Looking upon the changed scene now, one can only join with them in their groans as they must say: "Our burdens are greater than we can bear."[33]

The Kasai Company immediately attacked Sheppard's article because it gave bad publicity to the company's operations. Recognizing that it had a monopoly in the Kasai basin, the most lucrative region for extracting rubber, the company acknowledged that Sheppard's criticism of "chartered trading companies" must be exclusively directed to the Kasai Company—even though the identification was not explicitly made. Victorien Lacourt, an officer in the company, indignantly denied Sheppard's charges, calling them "defamatory allegations."[134] He demanded an apology from Sheppard and a retraction from editor Morrison for having published the article in the *Kassai Herald*.

Morrison rose to the occasion and challenged Director Dreypondt of the Kasai Company to first establish that the charges were inaccurate:

Dr. Sheppard asserts that he is prepared to prove the assertions he makes before an impartial tribunal which is not itself personally interested in the collection of rubber and has not been appointed by any one so interested. . . . It is undoubtedly true that impositions are made on the villages and, through fear of the state, the natives make the rubber, for which they are paid only a pittance. . . . If you are pained and astonished that Dr. Sheppard should write such things, I must say that I am equally astonished and pained that you should so hastily conclude that a man of Dr. Sheppard's long residence in Congo, and his well-known integrity, should write a serious article of this kind without knowing what he was doing. It might, at least, have raised a question in your mind, and caused you to institute an impartial investigation, in which your Company and Dr. Sheppard would participate. . . . Finally, I will say that we do not blame personally the individual agents and officials of your Company, except in so far as they may purposely misrepresent the facts; but we do and must condemn this whole monopolistic system by which the country is being ruthlessly stripped of its natural products, with the natives getting but little in return. Your company in the meanwhile is paying to its stockholders enormous dividends, if the available figures are correct.[135]

In the wake of Sheppard's article and Morrison's response, the British ordered their Congo consul Wilfred Thesiger to conduct a fact-finding tour in the Kasai province. They realized that the world learned much from the investigation conducted five years earlier by former consul Casement in another Congo region. The APCM did not know of Thesiger until he arrived and was in search of a translator. Since no European agents of the Kasai Company could speak the native languages, Sheppard agreed to accompany him to many villages. Thesiger was an able investigator, for he was not content to visit only the State stations where native soldiers were adequately compensated and where workmen loading the steamers were decently housed and fed. He compared the general situation with the sweatshops of London:

When he [the chance traveller] judges of the condition of the country by what he actually sees at these stations, his opinions may be perfectly honest, but they are absolutely worthless. It is as though some well-meaning person, who had heard that a certain fashionable firm was making a fortune by sweated labour, were to venture to deny the facts because a cursory visit to the West End establishment showed that the salesmen behind the counter were well dressed and well nourished, ignoring altogether the festering misery of the sweaters' dens in which every article sold over that counter was made up.[136]

What Leopold's policies had done to the Congolese can be discerned from Thesiger's on-site report. He combined description with reflection:

> For some distance around the mission station of Ibanj, as is also the case at Luebo, the people are not compelled to make rubber, and thus lead a comparatively untroubled existence. In this zone are several Bakuba villages which I visited frequently. The houses were all in good repair and carefully constructed. . . . The villages were always far above the average in cleanliness, and the men were almost always occupied either in making mats and cloth, carving, or house building; the women dyeing and embroidering cloth, or in household or field work. . . . Having seen these villages it was a real experience to compare them with those outside the pale, where the people are subjected to the rubber tax. Here the villages were dirty, the houses slowly falling into ruin, the holes in the roofs patched by a handful of palm leaves thrust into the thatch; the manioc fields overgrown; . . . the whole dominated by the monotonous thudding of mallets beating out rubber. . . . There is no doubt that the Bakuba are the most oppressed race today in the Kasai. . . . One asks oneself in vain what benefits these people have gained from the boasted civilization of the Free State. One looks in vain for any attempt to benefit them or to recompense them in any way for the enormous wealth which they are helping to pour into the Treasury of the State. Their native industries are being destroyed, their freedom has been taken from them, and their numbers are decreasing.[137]

Thesiger's report to the British government in 1908 refers to Sheppard's article, but indicates that he understated the plight of the Kubas. Thesiger documented that the Kasai Company demanded monthly quotas of rubber balls from particular villages and any shortage was punished by imprisoning, fining, or whipping. He found instances where wives were held hostage to bring pressure upon their husbands to produce more. The amount of rubber required was so high that the villagers had no time to hunt, fish, or grow food. Agents were ordering vines to be cut rather than tapped as in the past.[138]

Thesiger found the diminishing population ominous:

> There is no sleeping sickness to account for the decrease, there have been no epidemics of late years; exposure, overwork, and shortage of proper food alone are responsible for it. The Bakuba district was formerly one of the richest food-producing regions in the country. . . . In nearly all the villages I examined the lofts, which at that season of the year should have been full of corn; 50 percent were empty.

Believing that the Kasai Company was beyond reform, Thesiger called for "the entire abolition of the Company."[139]

The Kasai Company would probably have ceased to harass Morrison and Sheppard had it not been for the publication of Thesiger's report by the British government a year after Sheppard's *Kassai Herald* article was printed. The American branch of the Congo Reform Association soon publicized the Thesiger-Sheppard tour:

> Dr. Sheppard is a Negro, one of the most able and eloquent of his race. . . . In the summer of 1908 Dr. Sheppard made a journey through this [Kasai] region, visiting 59 villages. He set down the results of his investigation: . . . "Every village that we visited is forced to make rubber against their will. . . We have seen no gardens. . . There is not one ear of corn. . . We heard the cry of hunger and persecution in every one of these villages."[40]

Much public indignation followed the exposé by the Briton and the American, causing a sharp drop in the stock of the Kasai Company. The furious directors decided that dramatic action needed to be taken against their international critics in order to restore confidence in the company. However, due to diplomatic immunity, nothing could be done legally to Consul Thesiger. The critics of the Kasai rubber business thought to be vulnerable to intimidation and punishment were those who were living and publishing in the Congo. Hence, Leopold's palace aides began to scrutinize journals for articles by Sheppard and others living in the Congo who were crusading against rubber collection procedures. They were armed with Leopold's 1906 decree that imposed a mandatory five-year jail sentence or fine for "any calumny against a Congo state official."[141]

A month after the Thesiger report was published, the Kasai Company brought formal charges against Sheppard and Morrison as a means of discrediting all critics of their business practices. Since both men had years earlier become celebrities on both sides of the Atlantic from accusing Leopold's agents of involvement with atrocities, they were excellent targets for attack. Louis Chatlin, the company's new Africa director, contended that Sheppard's article contained lies that had resulted in "tarnishing the honorability" of his company. For defamation and injury to the Kasai Company, punitive damages of 30,000 francs were demanded of Sheppard—about a hundred times his annual salary—or six years in prison at Boma.[142] Morrison was also fined but he informed Chester that he and Sheppard preferred to go to prison rather than attempt to obtain funds to pay the exorbitant fines if they lost the case.[143]

The naming of a court of jurisdiction in the suit revealed that the

Belgian government had by then taken over the Congo. Pending international recognition, the Congo Free State had become the Belgian Congo on November 15, 1908, when the Belgian legislature enacted the Colonial Charter. Leopold's practices were now recognized as so immoral that his nation was unwilling to await the old king's death to gain control of the private domain he had earlier willed to his government in order to borrow capital.

Morrison and Sheppard recognized a positive feature of being legally charged by a foreign court. Its unjust contention against American citizens fulfilled the requirement for United States intervention. The defendants' immediate concern was not that there would be a trial but that it was set for an early date in Kinshasa. Both the time and place were to their disadvantage because preparing a defense and establishing international sanctions for a fair trial would take some months. Also, it would be difficult to persuade Kuba witnesses to travel a great distance beyond their kingdom to testify.

APCM friends from America and Europe were quick to assist by demanding that justice prevail. The PCUS General Assembly requested President Taft to use his influence to have the trial postponed and to see that court procedures were proper. In addition, the Assembly expressed admiration to Sheppard and Morrison for alerting the world of the Kasai Company's wrongdoings. Presbyterian congregations of the American South were asked to set aside May 23, 1909, as a time of special prayer for the accused missionaries, asking "for their deliverance from any miscarriage of justice under the forms of law, and also for the deliverance of the people of the Congo Independent State from the hand of the oppressor."[144]

On behalf of the Presbyterian Foreign Missions Committee, Chester brought to Secretary of State Philander Knox a letter requesting government intervention to protect the Americans who were charged with libel by the Kasai Company and were assigned an unreasonable time and place of trial. Knox became sympathetic after comparing Sheppard's article with the report from William Handley, who had recently been appointed as the American consul in the Congo because of Presbyterian overtures to Washington. The Secretary found that Handley was even more critical of the Kasai Company than the Presbyterians had been. Chester completed his appeal to the State Department with this appreciative comment:

> We desire, in closing, to express our profound gratification at the stand
> taken by our Government, in declining to recognize the transfer of the

sovereignty of the Congo Independent State from King Leopold to Belgium, except upon the basis of satisfactory guarantees of the abolition of forced labor and the restoration to the natives of their rights in land and in the produce of the soil.[145]

Ironically, atrocities against blacks in America at this time caused little public outcry from Southern Presbyterians, who stood by while the Ku Klux Klan and other groups engaged in violence.[146] The heyday for lynching in America was during the years Sheppard was in the Congo; mobs killed an average of ninety blacks annually from 1891 to 1910, nearly all in the South.[147] The fact that there were more lynchings in the United States than legal executions betrays some degree of breakdown of the judicial system in the United States at that time.

President Taft recognized the duty of his government in this possible infringement of its citizens' rights, and discussed the forthcoming court case against Sheppard and Morrison at a White House cabinet meeting. Taft may also have had special interest in the welfare of the noted Hampton alumnus because he was a dedicated member of the Institute's Board of Trustees and an advocate of black rights.[148] Knox was directed to warn the Belgian government that fairness of the trial proceedings would be used to measure reform intentions. He cabled the Belgian authorities to demand a trial postponement in order to stop a travesty of justice. The American government hinted that diplomatic recognition by the United States of the newly formed Belgian Congo was in jeopardy because of the mistreatment of Morrison and Sheppard. As a result of this intervention the trial was delayed several months.[149]

To defend Sheppard and Morrison, APCM's European agent Whyte, with the advice of Morel, secured the services of Vandervelde. He had never served as a defense attorney before but, as leader of the socialist party in the Belgian legislature, he had denounced the Leopold regime in the Congo, especially after his visit there in 1908. He took the case pro bono, requesting only that his travel expenses be paid. He recognized the difficulty he would have in obtaining justice because the Belgian government not only owned half of the Kasai Company, but had appointed both its director and the judge trying the case. Pertaining to the Protestant missionaries, Vandervelde wrote:

> I certainly cannot share their religious convictions . . . but from the standpoint of humanity, my heart is in unison with theirs, and I feel a sympathetic admiration for their efforts in delivering the natives from the system to which they have been subjected for so long.[150]

Morrison was ill when preparations were being made in Kasai for the trial, so Sheppard traveled without him among Kuba villages to gather witnesses to take on the steamer to Kinshasa. He stated that it would be easy to obtain 300,000 witnesses if the trial were held in the APCM region, but that the Kubas were understandably fearful of becoming enslaved by the State if they went far from home. The Kuba king, angry that the State had attempted to pressure him to testify against Sheppard, gave permission for Sheppard to take with him the twenty witnesses he requested.[151]

While recruiting witnesses, Sheppard was told of a Belgian who was critically ill in another village. The Congolese had refused to help him because he was an agent of the hated rubber company. However, Sheppard made a four-hour march and saw that "he was as yellow as a pumpkin and very weak." From his medicine case he found the proper drugs to administer and, after Sheppard had nursed him for five days, the young man's fever lowered. When his strength began to return, he expressed amazement that his life had been saved by a man whom his own company had charged with libel. The Kasai people were also much impressed by the person who could express compassion for a presumed adversary and have the skill to assist him in regaining his health.[152]

Before the trial began, Sheppard and Morrison participated in the fifth United Missionary Conference that met in Kinshasa, at which fifty representatives from seven Protestant mission societies voted for this supportive petition:

> We are compelled, once more, to record our protest against the continuance of the system of forced labour and excessive taxation which still prevails, in various forms. . . . On behalf of these suffering natives, we thank those who have used their influence in endeavouring to secure for them their guaranteed treaty rights. And we again appeal to all lovers of humanity in every land, to do everything in their power to bring about, as speedily as possible, the deliverance of these peoples from their state of practical slavery.[153]

Because the case had been postponed, the defense party had time for sightseeing in Leopoldville. Sheppard described a statue there that was intended to represent the "*liberté, egalité, fraternité*" motto of modern democracy. It depicted a native woman holding a torch, but Sheppard noted that it was extinguished. He thought the symbolic woman also needed the added touch of tears streaming down her face![154]

The trial was high drama for that colonial city. The Kasai Company

found the publicity more international, and the opposition more for-
midable, than had been anticipated. Not only were the prosecutors
confronting Vandervelde, one of the most influential and eloquent Belgian lawyers, but American Consul-General Handley was also present.
There being no court stenographer, he took detailed notes to send to
the State Department in Washington.[155] Kuba chief Niakai was awaiting to testify as one of the principal witnesses. Sheppard's album contains a photograph of him and the Kasai witnesses who came down on
the steamer with him. Twenty natives from eleven villages who had
been employed as armed sentries for the Kasai Company were on hand
to confess that they had compelled their fellow Africans to make rubber.[156] One side of the courtroom was filled with Protestant missionaries from various denominations and other APCM supporters; on the
other side were Catholic missionaries, Belgian officials, and supporters
of the Kasai Company. There was a fear that the floor might collapse
under the weight of the overcrowded courtroom.

When the trial began in September 1909, Judge Charles Gianpetri
dropped charges against Morrison because of a legal technicality, leaving Sheppard as the sole defendant. Attorney Gaston Vandermeeren,
who argued on behalf of the Kasai Company, denied that "pressure was
ever brought to bear on the natives in the production of rubber." If
there were abuses, he reasoned, why had there been silence from
Catholic missionaries who resided in the district where the alleged
wrongs had occurred? The prosecutor alleged that Sheppard's article
was motivated in part by his resentment of the State's supposed
favoritism toward the Catholics and in part from political malice.
Moreover, he contended, Sheppard's fabrication resulted from a plot in
which he and Thesiger were attempting to justify British seizure of the
colony. Vandermeeren admitted he had no documentation of his con-
spiracy charge.

Vandermeeren's argument that Catholic as well as Protestant missionaries would be voicing criticism of the means for collecting rubber,
if such were true, was farfetched. Catholic vested interests amply
explained why their missions reported no abuses. The Scheutist
Catholic order had named some of their stations after Kasai Company
directors who were generous benefactors, and one of those stations was
being used by the company as a site for operating their rubber business.

Defense attorney Vandervelde began his rebuttal by stating that the
suit was "not between the Company Kasai and Mr. Sheppard, but
between the Company Kasai and the natives who live in the territory
exploited by this company for over ten years."[157] He went on to show

the absurdity of the charge that Sheppard intended to halt Belgium from annexing the Congo. If this had been his intent, why would he have resorted to making a vague charge in an obscure journal circulated among a few Presbyterians in the southern region of the United States? Rather than Sheppard attempting to subvert the sovereignty of the State, he was making a humanitarian appeal on behalf of the Kubas. The defense attorney portrayed Sheppard as one who had so identified himself with the Congolese that he now belonged more to the Kasai than to America.[158] Vandervelde argued that his client was not intending to injure the Kasai Company but was simply describing the existing conditions, which it was his right and duty to do. He then confirmed Sheppard's charge of exploitation by the Kasai Company by showing that the price paid to the Congolese for harvesting rubber drastically declined as soon as the Company established a monopoly.

Vandervelde asked permission to receive testimony from the Kubas who had waited in Kinshasa for five months to substantiate the veracity of Sheppard's description. When the prosecution refused to give its consent to hear these witnesses, the defense interpreted this to the court as an admission of guilt. Since no proof had been offered to show that Sheppard had been spitefully motivated in writing or that the article had caused the company injury, Vandervelde asked for dismissal of the suit. The judge ruled that the charges against Sheppard be dropped and that the Kasai Company pay the costs of the trial.[159]

After the trial, Sheppard reported, Judge Gianpetri as well as the leading Catholic priest of the Kasai district congratulated Vandervelde.[160] Sheppard and Morrison wrote to their Southern constituency about how their attorney kept the courtroom spellbound for two hours:

> His speech in our defense was a masterpiece of eloquence, invincible logic, burning sarcasm, stinging rebuke of the whole iniquitous system of forced labor and a pathetic appeal for justice to be done in this case not only for the sake of the missionaries who had dared to speak out in behalf of the oppressed but especially for the native people in whose behalf he had primarily come.[161]

In a letter Sheppard wrote on October 4, 1909, the day of the acquittal, he expressed gratitude to all who banded together to break the Congolese "fetters." In particular he singled out those in the American government who "have fought for justice," those in various Christian denominations who have taken the "deepest interest in us possible," and those in the PCUS whose "holy and high mission has always been to feed the hungry, clothe the naked and to succor the distressed." Sheppard added the postscript that he had just "been taken down with a severe attack of fever."[162]

When Morrison wrote to Conan Doyle about the trial, the Sherlock Holmes creator responded by commending Sheppard and Morrison "for telling the truth about the scoundrels." In his little book, *The Crime of the Congo*, Doyle suggested even before the trial began that it would display a finer representation of liberty than the recently erected statue by Bartholdi in the New York harbor.[163] Doyle also wrote at this time that what Leopold's agents had done to the Congo ranked as "the greatest crime in all history, the greater for having been carried out under an odious pretence of philanthropy." He compared it to what had been considered in Britain as the most horrible crime: "In the slave trade the victim was of market value, and to that extent was protected from death or mutilation. In this case the State is the owner of all, so that if one be dismembered or shot, another is always available."[164]

The trial's outcome was confirming to people in widely scattered places. An article in the *Boston Herald* following Sheppard's trial displays the wide attention the case had attracted. "AMERICAN NEGRO HERO OF CONGO" and "FIRST TO INFORM WORLD OF CONGO ABUSES" were the headlines. This tribute was given: "Dr. Sheppard has not only stood before kings, but he has also stood against them. In pursuit of his mission of serving his race in its native land, this son of a slave . . . has dared to withstand all the power of Leopold."[165]

In Britain, Thesiger remarked that it was "impossible to overestimate the importance of the trial" because it was "an attempt on the part of the state to destroy . . . the power of the missionary societies to criticize the maladministration of the state and the companies in which it holds a majority of the shares."[166] During the month after Sheppard's acquittal, Albert Hall, the largest meeting place in London, was filled with those concerned about injustices in the Congo. The Archbishop of Canterbury chaired the meeting and gave a speech that the *Times* published, in which complete reform in the Congo was demanded.[167]

Back at Luebo, after the triumphant missionaries returned, Lucy Sheppard wrote, "Mrs. Morrison and I waited almost breathlessly for the return of our loved ones. As the *Lapsley* came steaming in, hundreds of Christians began singing hymns and waving their hands and shouting for joy. It was a glorious time—a time for thanksgiving."[168] The Kinshasa trial came a decade after Sheppard's initial testimony to massacres, so half of his years as a missionary had been dominated by concern to rectify the gross human rights violations.

Bedinger commented that the results of Sheppard's trial went far beyond the legal victory:

> It proved to the natives that the missionaries were willing, if necessary, to suffer for them. It proved, also, to the world that our [APCM] missionaries were not prompted by any merely religious or political motives, with which they had been so persistently charged, but had been compelled to oppose the existing regime from purely unselfish and humanitarian reasons.[169]

In Brussels, Jules Renkin, the colonial minister for the new Belgian Congo, stated that a judicial inquiry had been ordered into the APCM charge of brutalities and that the Belgian government would tolerate no abuses in the Congo.[170] Belgian officials promptly went to Kasai to examine conditions there. As an outcome of the investigation, the power of the Kasai Company was diminished. Benedetto notes that the "failure of the lawsuit and continued pressure from home and abroad forced the Belgian government to enact a free trade law."[171] The use of compulsory labor by trading companies in the Congo was outlawed. In effect this meant that a milder form of the practice was discreetly continued for another generation. The United States gave diplomatic recognition to the Belgian Congo in 1911 after being assured that Africans were no longer oppressed and that trade was more competitive. The Kasai Company continued to thrive and to have a virtual monopoly. As the supply of rubber became exhausted, the company turned to copper and diamond mining, with palm oil becoming the main organic export.[172]

The Congo Reform Association was soon dissolved after the Sheppard court case because its Anglo-American members were convinced that the Belgian government was instituting policies that would make the Congo a place where human rights abuses would be no worse than those found in colonial governments. Rubber from plantations of cultivated trees began to take the place of rubber from wild vines, and this resulted in more humane practices.

In 1911 Morrison wrote Belgian colonial leader Renkin, "It is with greatest pleasure and profound satisfaction that we are able to say that we find much improvement over the conditions which prevailed under the old Congo Free State."[173] Historian Shaloff pays tribute to Sheppard and his fellow missionaries for the amelioration of harsh labor conditions:

> Efforts by government officials to intimidate the Presbyterian clerics and to frighten them into silence failed. Such attempts only stiffened

them in their resolve to persevere in their criticism. . . . If it had not been for the APCM, few people anywhere would have given any thought to the plight of the Congolese in the Kasai. . . . They were courageous, resourceful, and unrelenting crusaders for justice and decency in the Congo. . . . The libel trial was a tempest of more than ordinary significance. It galvanized the reformers and gave them something to focus on at a critical moment. More than that, it induced the United States to take a more direct hand in the effort to root out the last vestiges of the "Leopoldian system."[74]

Chester viewed the role of the American government as crucial to the outcome of the lawsuit. He wrote to the Presbyterian missionaries in Kinshasa:

> Undoubtedly, when the [Belgian] state began this prosecution it had fully made up its mind to go through it regardless of any right or justice in the case, with the view of getting rid of us altogether in Africa, and I believe they only failed to carry out that program because our own government had asserted your rights in such a way that they felt it would not be safe for them to do so.[175]

After more than four decades as a cunning and ruthless despot, Leopold at last received some retribution. Many in the international community detested him because of his African policies. He had finally become such an embarrassment to his own people that they took his Congo possession away from him a year before he died. Bauer, in *Leopold the Unloved*, tells how the Belgians were also fed up with his hedonistic excesses. The aged lecher's teenage mistresses and illegitimate sons were causing a national scandal.[176]

Several weeks after Leopold learned of the outcome of Sheppard's trial, he died following surgery, but not before he was refused extreme unction because of his sexual liaisons. Mark Twain thought an appropriate memorial for him would be a pyramid composed of millions of skulls. Lachlan Vass quipped that if the scoundrel does not fry he would have to believe in universal salvation! Vachel Lindsay also expressed a longing for retributive justice in his poem about Leopold:

> Hear how the demons chuckle and yell
> Cutting his hands off, down in Hell.[177]

Most social history deals in shades of gray with regard to morality, but the clash of good with evil is clearly displayed by the opposing parties in issues pertaining to Congo's political economy during this era. As Conrad put it, Leopold was involved in "the vilest scramble for loot that ever disfigured the history of human conscience."[178] He belonged to the era of robber barons who prospered by curtailing free trade. He owned the Congo just as the slightly younger John Rockefeller owned Standard Oil. Each monopolistic capitalist had a voracious appetite for becoming the wealthiest man in the world. The Belgian despot succeeded in obtaining more real estate filled with industrial raw materials while Rockefeller turned more immediate profits by cornering the world's oil market. In return for the vast wealth he drained from the Congo, Leopold did little to improve its economy other than building the rail line to export rubber. He had no interest in providing schools and hospitals for the Congolese. Most of his profits went for such things as adding palace wings, constructing a golf course, developing a racetrack, and purchasing a resort in France where he could keep his yacht.[179]

Both tycoons presumed that the white elite were divinely commissioned to suppress whoever got in their way. Speaking to a Sunday school class at the turn of the century, Rockefeller declared: "The growth of a large business is merely a survival of the fittest. . . . The American Beauty rose can be produced . . . only by sacrificing the early buds which grow up around it. This is not an evil tendency in business. It is merely the working out of a law of nature and a law of God."[180] The inevitable demise of the unfit in this alleged evolutionary scheme of economics tended to remove moral accountability. By perverting the theory of organic evolution into a system by which ruthless humans exploited Third World peoples, the exploiters appeared to be in line with the latest in biological theories.

The practices of the Belgian king eventually killed the goose that laid the golden rubber egg. In a craze for immediate profits, the wild latex-producing vines were slashed ruthlessly and bled to death. Efforts to replant vines and cultivate trees in the Congo resulted in little success. After a few years of fabulous harvests there was no latex sap left to exploit. It is difficult for those now living in the Kasai to believe that once their region was a main source of that most valuable product.

Sheppard's two decades in the Congo were a period of rapid transformation. When he arrived, Leopold's rubber realm was just beginning to develop. His years there coincided with the era of the worst atrocities in central African history. The depopulation of the Congo during the twenty-five years of Leopold's rule by approximately 50 percent was similar to what had happened earlier when slavers were kidnapping along the African coast. More people were killed by the village raids of state agents than there were slaves sold in the New World.

In *King Leopold's Ghost*, Adam Hochschild contrasts Sheppard's sincere heroism with Leopold's duplicitous villainy. Sheppard was the victor in the first international human rights contest of the twentieth century, and he significantly hastened the demise of Leopold's so-called Congo Free State.

6

After Leaving the Congo

PROBATION BY PRESBYTERIANS

Sheppard spent the most significant years of his life in the Congo. He was not associated with Belgian Congo developments, and the independent Congo nation was formed many years after his death. Two months after the libel trial victory, he and Lucy suddenly decided to leave Africa permanently. In a letter to the APCM annual meeting in December 1909, Sheppard requested that he be allowed to retire. The first reason he gave was his ill health: "For more than two months I have not had a real well day. I have had a continuous dull headache, attended with a little fever; I have taken all kinds of medicine at Leopoldville and on the steamer coming up the river. There is no change in my condition." Another reason was "some family matters which I believe need my attention."[1] Although he did not elaborate on the second reason, it must have been in part the anguish that he and his wife had over years of separation from their daughter, who had remained in Virginia for educational and health reasons. Sheppard wrote Dr. Henkel: "I have been examined by two doctors, and they say I must get out of the country and have proper treatment from a good doctor or my trouble would be serious. We shall be glad too, to get our little one [Max] home in a more healthy climate." One of those physicians was probably Dr. Sims, who had advised Lapsley that his life was imperiled unless he left the Congo for treatment elsewhere.[2] Sheppard planned to receive special treatment in London on the way home.[3]

Recognizing that the Sheppards had devoted themselves to the Congolese and to the mission personnel in an extraordinary way, their

APCM colleagues expressed deep regret over their resignation. They adopted, and published in a church journal, this resolution:

> We . . . express our sincerest and deepest regret at Dr. Sheppard's prospective retirement from this mission. This is felt by us all the more keenly because of his being one of the founders of the Mission, because of his close personal friendship with us, because of his remarkable hold on the native people, and especially because we feel that our work among the Bakuba will be much crippled, for he had been an apostle among them for so long. . . . We must also express equal regret at losing from the mission his noble wife, whose long service, sincere devotion to duty, and beautiful Christian character have endeared her to us and to all the native people. . . . It is our belief that their united labors of love during these years will be for time to come a blessing to these peoples of the Congo.[4]

In addition, the next issue of the *Kassai Herald* expressed this tribute: "Dr. Sheppard's genial personality and jovial companionship will be missed by everyone on the field. Mrs. Sheppard, by innumerable acts of kindness, has endeared herself to everyone, and it is with infinite regret that we lose such a consecrated and successful missionary, as well as fond friend."[5]

An unstated factor in Sheppard's resignation was the liaisons he had had with Congolese women. At the same time, bachelor Henry Hawkins resigned for similar misconduct.[6] Sheppard's adulterous conduct, like that of King David, was exposed when he was at the pinnacle of his career. A son resulting from one of the affairs proudly bore his father's Congolese name, Shepete. He was quick-witted and eventually became the foreman of the Leighton Wilson Press. Former APCM missionaries David Miller and John Coffin recalled having seen more than one offspring of Sheppard in Kasai and having thought that they resembled him in appearance. Sheppard's only grandchildren and great-grandchildren may now be living in the Congo.

A decade after Sheppard's initial moral lapse, Lachlan Vass of the APCM made an issue of his adultery. After Sheppard consulted with his good friend Morrison about his predicament, Morrison wrote a friend, "I have told him that it is impossible for me to say what he ought to do, for it is a question which he alone can settle."[7] Sheppard soon realized that he could no longer continue with the Mission and informed Chester that he planned to retire. The Mission Committee initially refused to accept his letter of resignation but instructed him to return to America to repair his broken health.[8] Once back in the United States he met with Chester and James Reavis at Montreat to make a personal confession. The Mission Committee secretaries then wrote Morrison:

> We were all in tears. . . . The confession will bring peace, I believe. "He that covereth his sin shall not prosper, but he that confesseth his sin shall find mercy." [Proverbs 28:13] . . . In a short time, with these confessions, the wound will heal. Sheppard can then go to work for the Lord here at home. Only a few need know about the trouble at all. My heart goes out to him.[9]

Later in 1910 Sheppard submitted this statement to the Atlanta Presbytery:

> Some time in the years 1898-1899, while my wife was at home and I was left alone in my work, I fell, under the temptation to which I was subjected in my relations with one of the native women at Ibanj Station and was guilty of the sin of adultery. My wife was away from me for about two years, and during this time the action was repeated twice with the same person. . . . For the sin which I do confess I have asked God's forgiveness, and have written to the native church at Ibanj, asking its forgiveness. I ask my brethren of the Presbytery of Atlanta also to forgive me for the reproach I have thus brought upon the presbytery as one of its members, and then to impose upon me such ecclesiastical censure as, in its judgment, the honor of Christ and the good of His cause may require.[10]

The presbytery resolved that no publicity would be given the matter apart from the official record and that Sheppard would be suspended from exercising his ministerial office for a year.

Sheppard returned to Staunton to be with his extended family while recuperating from his physical illness and emotional stress. During that time Eva Anderson, his only sibling, died there after an overturned lamp threw burning oil on her during Christmas preparations.[11] She had raised Wilhelmina Sheppard from infancy along with her own daughters.

In a few months Sheppard regained his strength and began to address nonchurch audiences. President Frissell of Hampton Institute, recognizing Sheppard as one of the most prominent alumni of his school, sought him out as a speaker for important occasions. He wrote Sheppard to express gratitude for the Congo curios he received from him and to involve him in some forthcoming events at the Institute if his health permitted. Accordingly, Sheppard attended the 1911 Founder's Day commemoration and met President Taft, who was the main speaker.[12] Taft was deeply concerned about racial prejudice and hoped that blacks would be recognized as having "that equality that the Declaration of Independence assured them."[13] In pursuing that ideal, he became a member of the Hampton Board of Trustees and, when in attendance, slept on campus at the Mansion House in a bed made for his portly frame. Inspired by the Kuba geometric designs on household objects that Sheppard had brought to Hampton, students in the woodworking class had hand-carved similar ones on the bed frame. It remains in that house, which is now the residence of the university's president.[14]

After participating in the Founder's Day celebration at Hampton, Sheppard traveled to northern states with Booker T. Washington, president of Tuskegee Institute, and Hollis Frissell to promote African American higher education. Although Dr. Washington was the most noted black alive, he was upstaged by Sheppard on the tour. After a New York meeting where both spoke, a newspaper headline reported, "CONGO MISSIONARY ADDRESSES WHITE AND BLACK AUDIENCE." Washington was reported to have remarked that "the influence of Hampton, as shown by Dr. Sheppard's address, already has been felt in the heart of Africa." Harvard's President Charles Eliot presided at a Boston meeting where both of these Hampton alumni spoke.[15]

In 1912 Sheppard spoke about his twenty years in the Congo at the First International Congress on the Negro that Washington convened in Tuskegee, Alabama.[16] During that year the administrators of the Young Men's Christian Association sent Sheppard to speak at colleges in Arkansas, Mississippi, Louisiana, and Texas "to quicken the interest of the young men in Y. M. C. A. work."[17]

In 1914 Sheppard accepted an invitation from the president of Hampton to be the principal Founder's Day speaker and to share his experiences at other campus gatherings. Frissell reminded Sheppard that previous Founder's Day keynote speakers included Dr. Washington and President Woodrow Wilson.[18] On that occasion he said:

> I am glad to return to Hampton, the place of my birth—not natural birth, but the place where I was born in instruction and inspiration and vision. It was here I learned to do the impossible. It was here that I learned that there were no barriers, no mountains, that with God all things are possible. It was here I did my first missionary work.

The alumnus acknowledged that he had put into practice the "spiritual, mental, and industrial" lessons learned at Hampton.[19]

In a second address on that Founder's Day, entitled "Give Me Thine Hand," Sheppard recalled how President Armstrong's appreciation of both Native Americans and African Americans had been coupled with his interest in exhibiting artifacts from their cultures at Hampton. As a student, Sheppard had perceived that Hampton's founder "was a great and powerful dynamo, and into those lives gathered about him he sent life, light, and a holy inspiration."[20]

Armstrong's personal encouragement to Sheppard had continued for years after his student years at Hampton. He had been given new zeal by a letter from Armstrong that arrived in Luebo when he was brokenhearted by Lapsley's death. Armstrong wrote, "We are praying for you, and we expect the story of Hampton to be told in the Congo valley." Sheppard attempted to transmit Armstrong's spirit to the twentieth-century campus:

> Will you not, my fellow students, follow and emulate the splendid example of your great Founder? Will you not be moral and intelligent dynamos? Will you not stretch forth your hands to those who are bearing a great burden? Will you not be lighthouses in your communities? Will you not keep in view man's chief end? Now is your opportunity. Apply faithfully your hand, your heart, and your brain to all that is offered you.[21]

Sheppard wrote a series of "True African Stories" that Hampton published as illustrated pamphlets.[22] One of them, entitled *An African Daniel,* is about a village chief named Katembua who worked for "the Belgian soldiers who were cruel and hard-hearted." He became a Christian and decided "to give up pillage and killing to teach his people the arts of peace." The Belgians called Katembua crazy and imprisoned him far from his home area until some missionaries obtained his release. Another story, *A Little Robber Who Found a Great Treasure,* told of a chicken-stealing boy who became so responsible after becoming a Christian that he was put in charge of the chickens. Eventually he became the head instructor of the industrial school at Ibanche and a picture is shown of him in the carpentry shop.[23] Soon Sheppard became known as "The Children's Friend."

W. E. B. Du Bois, the cofounder of the National Association for the Advancement of Colored People, was suspicious of Christian missions but he had great respect for Sheppard. In one of the "Men of the Month" columns Du Bois wrote for his NAACP journal in 1915, he featured Sheppard, commending him for his courageous leadership in the Congo and in America.[24] Du Bois recognized Sheppard as an effective advocate for Africans and invited him in 1919 to participate in a NAACP symposium.[25]

At a time when the police as well as the Ku Klux Klan were intimidating blacks, the editors of *Southern Workman* hailed Sheppard as "a fearless fighter for human rights."[26] While blacks were generally marginalized in the United States, Sheppard could proudly claim to have been a mover and shaker of people on three continents. What other black American who lived most of his years in the nineteenth century can claim to have been received in the White House by two presidents and to have been discussed at a cabinet meeting by a third president? No other African American during that period did more to stir up forces of liberation in the Congo, in Europe, and in the United States.

HOTEL MACEO

213 West Fifty-third Street, Corner of Broadway
BENJ. F. THOMAS, Proprietor
REGULAR DINNER 6 TO 8 P.M., 35 CTS.   SUNDAYS 1 TO 3 AND 6 TO 10 P.M., 45 CTS.
**ROOMS, $5.00 PER WEEK AND UP.   BY NIGHT $1.00 AND UP
TWO IN ONE ROOM, 75 CENTS UP**
First Class Accommodations only.   Steam Heat.   Elegant Restaurant for Ladies and
Gentlemen.   Salads, Oysters and Chops, a Specialty.   General Caterer.
Orchestra Every Evening 8.30 to 12 O'clock, also Sunday Afternoons

Temporarily at NEW YORK, _February 7th,_ 1911.

Dear Miss Sherman:-

President Frissell and Major Moton had a splendid meeting Sunday morning at one of the Presbyterian churches. I am to speak tonight at the Ethical Culture Hall. I hope much good will be done for Hampton.

I am more grateful to you than I can express for your goodness to me both in Africa and in America. You are really too good.

Your obedient servant,

Sheppard

On returning from the Congo, Sheppard traveled widely to tell about his work. He enjoyed staying at racially integrated lodges when outside the American South. This letter to a staff member of Hampton Institute illustrates his graciousness and his single-word signature.

After the year of suspension by the Atlanta Presbytery was over, approval was given for him to again "exercise his gifts as a minister of the gospel." But Sheppard's conscience continued to bother him because he had not given a full account of his adulterous conduct, probably because of the even greater embarrassment it would have given his wife to acknowledge openly that he had engaged in sexual intercourse with other women when she was in Kasai with him. On December 8, 1911, Sheppard submitted this statement at a meeting he attended in Atlanta:

> I desire as a servant of God and a member of Atlanta Presbytery to make additional confession of three errors which happened during my last stay in Africa. When I was before Presbytery in 1910 I made a statement to the effect that I had committed this gross sin twice. I did not give a full and exhaustive statement of the facts in the case. . . . I do now, in the fear of God (from whom no sins can be hidden), make to my Presbytery a full and exhaustive statement of my conduct. During the last four years spent in Africa I fell into sin with three different women. These sins occurred only once and at different periods. I do now, brethren, make a clean breast of the whole matter. I have been influenced by the Holy Spirit to make this full and final statement to my Presbytery. I have fully repented of my sins. God has pardoned me freely. . . . And allow me to say, that those sins shall never occur again, God being my helper.

On receiving this new testimony, Atlanta Presbytery withdrew his reinstatement and continued the previous suspension until the committee that was given oversight of this matter could make a recommendation at the next regular meeting of the church judiciary. Then, on April 18, 1912, Sheppard was examined and his functions as a minister were restored.[27] About this time he had a card printed for distribution on which he had written, "Do not grope among the shadows of old sins, . . . but turn the leaf and smile . . . to see the fair white pages that remain."[28]

CHURCH WORK IN AMERICA

After completing the fifteen-month period of probation, Sheppard returned to church work. While residing in Staunton, the Sheppards had participated in the activities of the First Presbyterian Church. With that church's sponsorship, Sheppard organized the Stafford Street Colored Sunday School. In the few months that he was its superintendent, the enrollment increased to seventy. His parents were members of the fashionable First Church and attended there with their grandson; in 1912 "Maxamalinge Sheppard" was received as a communicant member.[29] Max recalled watching the "bluestocking" students marching into the church from Mary Baldwin Seminary, which was located across the street.

Aware of Dr. Sheppard's charisma, Dr. John Little invited him to engage in home mission work among blacks in Kentucky. His admiration for Sheppard began in 1904 when Sheppard spoke to an overflow meeting at the Second Presbyterian Church, the largest in Louisville. A large offering was collected then to support black schools that Little supervised in the segregated city.[30] Little, like Lapsley, was an Alabama slave owner's son and a graduate of the University of Alabama. He found it ironical that his fellow Presbyterians were more interested in providing education, medicine, and salvation for blacks in the Congo than in supporting the less romantic work among the deprived blacks in the American South. At that time the PCUS contributed twenty-five times as much to the former work as to the latter.[31] After enrolling in the recently opened Louisville Presbyterian Theological Seminary, Little found that Presbyterians had made no effort to minister to the 40,000 African Americans who lived in that city. In 1896 he helped form the Student Missionary Society, which organized a Sunday school at a former lottery office in a slum near the seminary. From this came the Hope Mission and then the Grace Mission in Smoketown, the area containing the poorest community in Kentucky's largest city. Shacks built of rough wood were cramped together along dusty alleys amid saloons and brothels. Some who lived there were employed at the large tobacco market or at one of the many bourbon distilleries in the city.

Recognizing the enormity of the challenge in Louisville, Little changed his plans to become a missionary to Africa and remained with the work in Smoketown until his death fifty years later. Scornful of "Sunday religion administered in one-hour doses," he supplemented it with a weekday program that provided job training, health care, and recreation for youth. In 1902 he led volunteers in renovating an abandoned organ factory in order to establish a Presbyterian center.[32]

For the Sheppards and other blacks, early twentieth-century America was an exceptionally difficult time for career development or rebuilding. E. T. Thompson writes that by 1910 in the South, "the triumph of racism, enforced by law, sanctioned by religion, supported by custom, and, if need, by social ostracism was complete."[33] African Americans were being increasingly disfranchised politically, and racial separation was becoming more rigid. In Louisville, previously integrated recreational facilities were segregated. Before 1911, blacks had ridden the majority of winning horses in the Kentucky Derby, but afterward there were only white jockeys. Blacks were excluded from juries and forbidden to live in areas where whites predominated. The Ku Klux Klan, thirty thousand strong in Kentucky, called for "pure blooded 100 percent American" rule.[34] During the years that Sheppard was a minister in Louisville, fourteen blacks were killed by lynch mobs in Kentucky, while whites charged with raping black women in Louisville were not even imprisoned.[35] During that period *The Leader*, an African American newspaper in Louisville, frequently carried articles about rampant violence, often sponsored by the KKK, and efforts to deny blacks their fundamental rights.

Even physical survival must have been a struggle for Sheppard and his family in Louisville, since his initial annual salary was $120, one-tenth that of a pastor of one of the smaller white Presbyterian churches there.[36] Over the years of his pastorate, his salary increased sixfold, but it never rose to half that of white ministers with mediocre performance. Sheppard was the token black member of Louisville Presbytery.

Soon after the Sheppards settled in Louisville, an article about them in the city's leading newspaper conveyed the outlook on blacks in the place where they had come to work. Entitled "From Darkest Africa to Darkest Louisville," it expresses amazement that Queen Victoria conferred a high honor on one who once was "a little pickaninny playing about the streets of Waynesboro, Va."[37] However, he and his wife rose above that prejudice and were able to make an abiding mark in the city.

During 1912, Sheppard's first year as pastor of Grace Church in Louisville, sixty new members were added—a 50 percent increase in the congregation's size. In 1913 he worked with a group of boys to renew his church building at Hancock and Roselane.[38] Two years later Sheppard had 970 enrolled in Sunday school, making it by far the largest Presbyterian Sunday school in Jefferson County. More growth was limited by the size of the classrooms; overcrowding resulted in as many as 200 in a room measuring twenty by forty feet.[39]

At the nearby neighborhood center, Lucy helped organize cooking, sewing, and choral clubs. Her husband gave oversight to the carpentry and shoe repairing schools and to the recreational facilities. The Presbyterians had "the best gym in the city, black or white."[40] In addition, there was a free medical clinic, a school for religious education, and a room with many baths that provided hundreds of children with their only opportunity to use a tub.[41] The all-encompassing youth program that the Sheppards helped develop was similar both to what they had effectively begun in the Congo and to Jane Addams's Hull House in Chicago. Little evaluated Sheppard's efforts in this way:

> He has given himself to this work in the same earnest and self-denying spirit that characterized his service in the Congo and has won the love and confidence of his associates and of the people among whom he labors. He has not only done much to build up the membership and train it properly, but he has also cultivated a friendly co-operative spirit with the other previously hostile denominations.[42]

The flourishing "Presbyterian Colored Mission" provided not only the best educational and recreational program for blacks in Louisville, but in surveys of black settlement houses in America it was rated as one of the best. One reason for this accomplishment was the financial backing and the support from the white community.[43] In 1921 the Mission served 60,000 people, and more than one hundred white men and women volunteered their assistance. In writing about American Presbyterians, Thompson called it "the most successful mission for Negroes in the country."[44]

The Sheppards often crossed the Ohio River at Louisville to visit the Indiana Reformatory. Lucien Rule, the chaplain there, had fond memories of Lucy singing to the men. He recalled the eloquent description Sheppard gave of the forgotten prisoners: "Locked in steel cages, they heard no news or tidings of the great throbbing life of mankind—and when they went forth at last with the mark of crime and Cain still upon them—oh, how they needed a friend!"[45] To guide African American boys so that they would not become inmates in the penal system, Sheppard was active for years in the Louisville Council of the Boy Scouts of America and provided entertainment at the summer scout camp.

In 1916 Sheppard wrote memoirs of his earlier years in the Congo that supplemented many articles he had previously written about various activities there. Much has been recorded about the colony by white traders, missionaries, explorers, and state officers who were there at the turn of the twentieth century, but Sheppard's record is virtually all that is available written by someone of African descent. Nothing is said in his book about his decade of conflict with Leopold's rubber business, perhaps because white Americans did not wish to read about his successful efforts in restraining a capitalist who exploited black workers. Publishers of missionary books found more market for stories about converting people than for stories about defects in Christendom.

In a 1917 publication, Chester ranked Sheppard as "perhaps the most distinguished and certainly the most widely known minister of our Southern Presbyterian Church." That Foreign Missions official had obviously forgiven him of his adulterous behavior many years earlier. In support of his use of superlatives, Chester stated:

> He is the only minister on our roll holding a fellowship in the Royal Geographical Society of London. On behalf of the Executive Committee of Foreign Missions, I wish to say that there is no missionary on our roll more beloved or more highly esteemed by the Committee under which he serves. During the time of his missionary service he has been called to represent us on many important occasions. He has stood before kings, both white kings and black kings, as our representative. He has never represented us anywhere that we have not had reason to be proud of the manner in which he has done it. He is now recognized both in London and Brussels as one of the greatest of African missionaries. That for which the Committee of Foreign Missions esteems him most is not the fact that he has achieved this prominence and recognition, but that, having achieved it, he has come back to us the same simple-hearted, humble, earnest Christian man that he was when we first sent him out.[46]

Lucy Sheppard's comments on her family's move to the Smoketown neighborhood of Louisville reflects the plight of blacks in the segregated South:

> We first had a little home in a crowded neighborhood. This was a trying experience, for I had been accustomed to open spaces and to beautiful country. The noises and unkept condition of the streets and the poorly lighted and inadequately ventilated rooms were hard to accept. It was with a thankful heart that a few years later we acquired our present home in a good neighborhood. I had always longed to be able to make a home for my mother to repay her, in some measure, for her many sacrifices for me, and here she came to spend her last years. Mr. Sheppard's aged mother also lived with us for many years.[47]

Lucy directed the choir at Grace Church for as long as her husband was pastor there. Rule comments that her years as a superb soloist of "spirituals and the whole range of hymns and songs . . . wonderfully embodies" qualities of Marian Anderson, whom Lucy had heard perform in Louisville.[48] Also, from 1918 to 1935 she was employed as a public social worker in Louisville with responsibilities for improving the employment and health conditions of those in need. In her retirement Lucy taught a women's Sunday school class, sharing with the members her stories of personal struggle and success. She spoke widely to schools and churches of both races about missions, and in 1938 she was honored as the first black to receive life membership in the Ken-

tucky Synodical, the state level of the Presbyterian women's organization.[49] At that time she was featured in an article that was part of a series
entitled "Sons and Daughters of the Morning." The purpose of the
series was to recognize African Americans in Kentucky who had arisen
to achievement after the Civil War. Lucy was called "one of the greatest women missionaries of the whole Presbyterian Church in America."[50] She shared the steady vision of other black notables that
tomorrow would be a brighter day for their race.

Lucy lived to the age of eighty-eight, but had no grandchildren to
dote on even though her daughter and son had married. Wilhelmina
became a kindergarten teacher and moved to California. Max obtained
a government job in Washington, D.C., and remained there for the rest
of his life. Lucy and her husband enjoyed their younger relatives in Virginia and occasionally returned to the Staunton area to visit. Grand-
nephew Arthur Ware became a high school principal in Staunton and
later had a school there named for him. He informed me that his Aunt
Lucy was quite demanding of his attention when she visited the family
of her niece, Rheba Anderson Ware. Grandniece Eva Barnes, the
daughter of Dr. Eugene and Leona Dickinson, told me about Uncle
Willie's visits in her home in Harrisonburg. She was most impressed by
the python skin he brought that stretched across two rooms.

G. Caliman Coxe, recipient of Kentucky's 1987 Governor's Award in
the Arts, remembered knowing the Sheppard family in Louisville.
From his teenage years he recalled that Sheppard had "an outgoing and
absorbing personality." In an interview at his Louisville home in 1990,
Coxe shared with me vivid memories of Sheppard as a big man who
laughed with gusto and spoke in an awesome style. Coxe was introduced to some types of African American art by Max Sheppard, who
had studied at the Chicago Art Institute and had returned to Louisville
in the 1920s to develop a business for the silver jewelry he designed.

Because of his ability to articulate so clearly the aspirations of
African Americans, Sheppard was much sought after to address gatherings beyond his own parish. William Rule recalled the impact Sheppard made while visiting a Knoxville church in 1920. This is what the
eight-year-old Rule remembered:

> As a backdrop for his missionary message he decorated the pulpit and
> all of the wall behind it with an extravaganza of African artifacts, curios
> and impedimenta. There were warriors' knives and spears, and leop-
> ard skins and python hides. An elephant tusk was on prominent dis-
> play. There were ceremonial dance drums, cowry shell head dresses,
> and carved figures in wood and ivory.[51]

Rule showed me a hippo tooth that Sheppard gave him on that occasion, which had a hole bored in it for wearing around the neck. When he became a medical missionary two decades later, he took it back to the Kasai and told people how he had received it. There Rule found that "'Shepede's' memory was now a hallowed legend."

Dr. Sheppard's labors were ended by a paralyzing stroke in 1926, when there were 270 members of the Grace Church and 393 pupils in its Sunday School.[52] A year later, November 27, 1927, his funeral was held at the Second Presbyterian Church, an appropriate place because of the steadfast support he had received from that white congregation.[53] It was "attended by a gathering of white and colored persons that crowded the building, while several hundred were unable to find even standing room in the church."[54] This crowd of more than one thousand mourners included his ninety-one-year-old mother. In *Kentucky Presbyterians*, Louis Weeks claims that Sheppard's funeral "afforded the first auspicious occasion for integrated worship among Louisville's Reformed Christians."[55]

A memorial tribute to Sheppard by the Presbytery of Louisville affirmed, "He was, in the language of the Apostle, 'clothed with humility,' perhaps the rarest of Christian virtues and along with it manliness, and self respect, and high courtesy."[56] Another tribute to Sheppard at this time stated:

> The Executive Committee of Foreign Missions would record its deep appreciation of his invaluable service in the founding and establishing of our African Mission, and in representing us on many important occasions before the authorities of several foreign countries. . . . He was one of the most eloquent advocates of the missionary cause who ever represented us before the churches and church courts of our own land.[57]

Sheppard's body was interred on top of a hill in Louisville Cemetery, and subsequently the bodies of his mother-in-law, a former slave, and his wife, in 1955, were placed in the lot beside him. In 1921 his mother's remains were buried beside those of her husband in Fairview Cemetery in Staunton. Both cemeteries were for black patrons. Did Southern whites fancy that they could force racial separation everlastingly and stifle the "free at last" song of African Americans?

On Sheppard's memorial stone is this inscription:

Rev. William H. Sheppard, D. D., F. R. G. S.

1865–1927

Missionary to the Congo 1890–1910

Pastor, Grace Presbyterian Church 1912–1927

HE LIVED FOR OTHERS

The simple tribute placed over Sheppard's grave may have been selected by his son Max. When interviewed in 1980, he stressed his father's generosity: "He always took bags of fruit with him to visit the sick at the hospital. . . . He probably didn't have a quarter when he died."

Shortly after the Louisville funeral, an interracial memorial service was held in Waynesboro, Virginia, at the First Presbyterian Church, to honor the most renowned person to have been born in that town. The first eulogy was by Dr. John Calvin Scarborough, an African American minister whom Sheppard had selected for best man at his wedding. Church educator Robert Lapsley spoke on behalf of his deceased brother Samuel. Dr. Lapsley acknowledged that the work of either pioneer missionary would have been impossible without the other, and he trusted that their beautiful earthly relationship was now being joyously renewed. He paid glowing tribute to Sheppard's ability as an orator and worker, recalling also his deep humility and sacrificial spirit. Sheppard "had one ambition and that was to be of service in the neediest places in the world," Lapsley concluded.[58]

7

Abiding Influences

DIVERSE LEGACIES

Over the past century, Sheppard's legacies to the Congolese and American cultures have been many and overlapping. Among the more notable are his witness to the importance to Christians of social justice in government, his emphasis on the indigenization of the church in Congo, his stress on a well-educated laity, his interest in transmitting to others the rich qualities of the Kuba culture, and his humanitarian accomplishments in Louisville.

Thompson, in his monumental history of southern Presbyterians, points to factors that gave the APCM more success than other Congo missions. Sheppard's participation was basic to all of them:

> the choice of a site in the midst of a numerous people, all speaking the same language and open, as others were not, to the gospel; the determination, dedication, and resourcefulness of the Southern missionaries of both races working together for the common good; the wide use of well-trained native evangelists left in charge of outpost stations (a method in which the Congo mission pioneered), and, last, but certainly not least, the struggle of the mission for an overhaul of the Congo administration, looking toward a fuller measure of justice for the overly exploited Congolese.[1]

Interest in Christianity increased among the Congolese as they learned that the APCM was dedicated to their humane treatment. Hank Crane, a missionary who served the APCM long after Sheppard, believes that "there is no doubt that the missionaries' espousal of the cause of human rights during this [King Leopold] period did more than

190

anything else to open the door to the Gospel in the years that followed."[2] Jewish scholar Shaloff is also of the opinion that "nothing was more important in winning the respect and loyalty of the people of the Kasai than the active role of the Presbyterians in the struggle to bring about an end to the abuses of the colonial administration." He discerns that the APCM viewed Christianity as "a revolutionary force" for transforming secular as well as spiritual life.[3]

When Sheppard arrived in Luebo, there were only a few Christians in the vast Kasai basin. The annual reports of the PCUS Foreign Missions Committee show that for the first several years at Luebo there were no communicant members. In 1896, forty-eight were reported, most of whom were young ex-slaves who had been ransomed by the missionaries with the payment of seashells, cloth, or salt. Victims of injustice in Kasai tribes continued to be the ones most open to the gospel promise of a new community of liberty. For these converts, the Sheppards and other African American members of the APCM provided a powerful witness to Christianity as a force of cultural reintegration. Having been cut off from fulfillment in their native tribes, both the blacks from America and the redeemed slaves in the Congo had found, in effect, a new tribe led by Jesus. Crane points out that many Lubas viewed the church as "a way of emancipation from their age-old status as a slave people, and readily welcomed the missionaries throughout the whole territory that they occupy."[4]

What transpired in Luebo has happened many times in Christian history, beginning in Corinth. The best known of the early churches was planted by the apostle Paul among people who were alienated from the traditional Greek community. Even as the underclass in ancient Corinth became the main responders to Paul's appeal, and as the untouchables have been the ones more attracted to the gospel in India, the ransomed Luba slaves provided the seed of the church in the Luebo area.

Looking at the APCM as an outsider from South Africa, missiologist Johannes DuPlessis rated it "one of the most successful missionary enterprises in Africa." A decade after the Sheppards left, he stated that its rapid growth

> is due in great measure to the sympathetic attitude of the Mission towards the slaves. . . . Slave-raiding, though tacitly encouraged by the State in the early days, was strongly opposed and denounced by the missionaries, who thereby earned the gratitude and confidence of the oppressed natives. . . . Concurrently with the swift extension of the Mission there was an intensification of the work at Luebo.[5]

Although the Sheppards gave due emphasis to working with the low-caste Lubas, they did not overlook those in the high strata of society who were generally content with their tribal values. Sheppard dreamed of converting the Kuba nobility so that their enslaving practices would cease. He was especially incensed at their custom of killing slaves to accompany members of the royal family into the next life and their custom of allegedly proving one's innocence or guilt by drinking poison.

In 1915 Sheppard's hope pertaining to the Kuba people moved toward fulfillment when Hezekiah Washburn was invited to choose a site for a new station in their heartland. It was named Bulape for two reasons: it was the name of the first member of Kuba royalty to become a Christian, and it was the African name of Annie Taylor Rochester, who died in 1914 after devoting much of her adult life to working with the Kubas. The station was fifteen miles from Mushenge, less than half the distance of the Ibanche station that it replaced. When the station came closer to the capital, several members of the Kuba royal family became Christian converts.

Sheppard's work with the Kuba royalty has continued to have an effect in that kingdom. The *Lukengu*'s approval of the Bulape station was influenced by the medical care it rendered. Subsequently, a hospital was established there that for more than seventy years has served a population of more than 100,000. Its medical staff was trained at the Christian Medical Institute of Kasai located at the Good Shepherd Hospital in Tshikaji. Along with the hospital in the Mushenge area, there are now several churches, primary and secondary schools, a seminary, and a nursing school, all staffed by Congolese teachers, pastors, and physicians.

Lukengu Kot aPe did not become a Christian, but as he lay dying of dysentery during an epidemic in 1916, he gave this injunction to his successor:

> I myself and my predecessors have all showed unrelenting hostility to all the foreigners; I want you to change that policy in so far as it affects the people of the Mission. I am able clearly to see now that in all the years they have never done anything to harm us or our people; in my degradation and imprisonment they helped me; when I am gone and you wear the eagle-feather, send messengers of friendship to the Mission.[6]

For the next two decades, the *Lukengu* was Kot Mabiinc. He placed Washburn on his tribal council out of gratitude for the heroic measures he took to save many lives during the global influenza epidemic at the end of World War I. The new Kuba king insisted that, while the body of Kot aPe lay in state, the missionary stay in Mushenge so that he could witness that the human sacrifices previously associated with such occasions had been terminated. Washburn reported that no longer was the former *Lukengu's* favorite wife required to kill herself or be killed and buried with her spouse. During the nine-day royal funeral, he also saw that similar treatment was no longer given the spokesman and cooks that had belonged to the deceased king, because the assumption was no longer made that servants would be needed in the life after death. Washburn told of another change from the traditional *Lukengu* burial custom:

> When the coffin was lowered into the grave it must not touch the earth. They took slaves, broke their legs and arms and laid them alive down in the grave to form a carpet of cushion upon which the coffin was to rest. These slaves were supposed to go along to do any work that the king might need. The new king said, "Instead of putting down slaves, we will put down sticks of camwood."[7]

Kot Mabiinc, who was a polio victim and overweight, used a wheelchair given him by the APCM as his throne. On receiving his eagle feather he turned to Washburn and Wharton, whom he had invited to the inauguration, and proclaimed:

> The elephants roam the jungles in herds; the monkeys pass through the tree-tops in bands; the driver ants travel in columns; . . . but the leopard hunts alone! I am the leopard, I hunt alone! Following my own will and judgment, I now pledge you in my authority as King of the Bakuba, to friendship with the mission! Let them come and build their village at my capital![8]

The king proved his interest in having a presence of the APCM in Mushenge by building a house for the Edmistons, who opened there an auxiliary station of Bulape. The Sheppards must have been gratified to learn that the eminent Kuba linguist and her husband, both whom they had trained, had gone to live in the capital, and that trial by poisoning and slave slaughter at burials were long gone.

Late in life Kot Mabiinc professed his Christian faith, and that resulted in several hundred prominent Kuba men and women following his lead. Before his death he requested that Washburn preach the gospel at Mushenge during the days when thousands of Kubas would come there for his funeral rites. At that time, in addition to the traditional dirges, Christian hymns were sung by a large choir that included some from his harem.[9]

This consideration of the more recent Kuba culture brings to mind a personal experience with the *Lukengu*. With my wife, mother, and brother-in-law, the Rev. Bill Metzel, I traveled through Kuba country in 1956. Like Sheppard, we also became aware of Kuba cultural richness in musical instruments, metal weapons, and traditional clothing. We had an audience with the aged Kuba king, Mbope Mabintshi, who had many wives. Reputedly, the number in his harem was about the same as his weight in pounds. His obese figure was covered with a raffia skirt, and he wore a conical cap. Although he was the last king to continue much of the traditional style, he had replaced the hammocks of earlier centuries with a fleet of cars, and porters with chauffeurs.

In his classic book *Christ and Culture*, Richard Niebuhr discusses how missionaries have generally tended to expect converts to abandon wholly their "heathen" customs. He describes another approach, set forth by John Calvin, that views the gospel as a transformer of culture.[10] Sheppard's ministry was like that. There is little in his writings about the unconverted Congolese being totally corrupt and destined for hell. He was sensitive to perversions in all human culture and viewed the gospel message as able to restore what had been corrupted. Sheppard's outlook on native culture was more accepting than that of most missionaries of his time. For example, he did not attempt to cut out certain notions of ancestral spirits, he condoned much of traditional dancing, and he did not demand that a polygamist become a monogamist before he became a Christian.

The accomplishments of the APCM came in spite of the Belgian colonial government. After that nation assumed sovereignty over the Congo, the Catholic religion continued to enjoy a privileged status. David Barrett states that Leopold's "trinity of power"—colonialism, Catholicism, and commercialism—remained in control.[11] Largely because of State funding and concessions, Catholic missionaries increased one hundred fold between 1891 and 1931, while the Protestants increased tenfold.[12]

The APCM was hindered by the racial attitude as well as the religious favoritism of the Belgian administration. William Seraile recognizes Sheppard as the most outstanding black American missionary of his era in Africa, but states that colonialists preferred not to have more like him on the continent. They recognized that new black missionaries who shared his outlook would promote political rights among the Africans and thereby jeopardize the colonial system.[13] Shaloff writes, "The Belgian Government came to view Negro missionaries as potential subversives and troublemakers."[14] The newly established Belgian Congo permitted blacks who were already on the mission field to continue, but new blacks were not welcomed.[15] After the Sheppards left, Edna Atkinson was the only new African American to join the APCM, allowed as a second wife for Adolphus Rochester after his first wife died. Alonzo Edmiston, who had been appointed while Sheppard was in the Kasai, was the last American black missionary with the APCM, and he retired in 1941. However, since Congo received its independence in 1960 a number of African Americans have served in partnership with the Congolese.[16]

Maria Fearing was recognized as one of the more effective missionaries to serve in Africa, so she was disappointed when the Mission Committee eventually required her to retire from working at the place she considered to be her real home. Actually she would have been permitted to return to the Congo in 1915 when she was eighty years old had her companion for the return trip not become ill. The girls' home that Fearing began was so successful that similar homes were created on other APCM stations. She was honored at the age of ninety-three when funds were raised in her name to build five permanent homes, each housing one hundred girls.

During the era of the Belgian Congo, the racial mores of the Southern United States were also reflected in missionary employment in Africa. Sylvia Jacobs writes: "With Jim Crow disfranchisement in the early twentieth century, white mission boards became distrustful toward black missionaries. . . . By 1920, the idea of using black missionaries in Africa was all but dead in the white religious community."[17] The Congolese were disturbed by the white superiority complex displayed at APCM church services. They noted that missionaries sat apart from others in the "chief seats," that is, chairs or benches with back supports.[18] When I visited the APCM in 1956, the missionary force was the largest ever, and an exclusively Caucasian operation. Few there could remember when the racial composition was significantly different, and none of the missionaries seemed concerned about the matter.

As the Christian church in Congo has grown in maturity of faith, the role of Western missionaries has changed. I recall visiting with a missionary who assumed that blacks belonged to a backward race and could not be trusted with much responsibility, but during the past generation it has been the APCM policy to withdraw from church leadership and to work as consultants with Congolese pastors, educators, health care workers, and administrators. In 1970 an autonomous Presbyterian church in Congo was established to assume the authority formerly exercised by the Presbyterian Mission Board in America. This news item was reported from Luluaburg:

> In formal ceremonies here today the Presbyterian Church in the United States recognized the coming of age of the Presbyterian Church of the Congo. The mission of the American Church was dissolved and henceforth the missionaries of the denomination will work within the structure of the Congolese Church. The ceremonies mark the fulfillment of the dream of the founding missionaries, the Rev. William Sheppard, a black man, and the Rev. Samuel N. Lapsley, a white man.[19]

Since colonialism was ever a festering thorn in the ecclesiastical body of Christ, its exit has resulted in more Christian vigor in spite of the lessening of funds from abroad. Christianity in Africa is now indigenous and no longer under Euro-American control, and as a consequence it may now be the most powerful force in sub-Saharan Africa. Barrett extrapolates on the massive statistical data he has accumulated that shows 23,000 new Christians in Africa every day in recent years. Presbyterians in the Democratic Republic of Congo have increased from 320,000 in 1970 to 1,280,000 in 1995, making it by far the largest component of the Protestant church in the nation.[20] Largely due to church growth in parts of Africa and Asia, world Christianity is no longer predominantly Caucasian.

Sheppard's legacy has had some impact on the Congolese government. Even before he left the Congo, the Belgians took away the sovereignty over the colony of their disgraced king. The policies of subsequent Belgian Congo administrators became somewhat more humane. Whereas Leopold never set foot in the Congo and never saw the mayhem he was effecting, his nephew Albert traveled extensively through the land in 1909 before becoming king. He could not have failed to witness the dire results of Leopold's policies. Due in no small part to Sheppard's efforts, the new regime did not practice human enslavement. But the Africans were given no voice in the colonial government nor training for eventual political freedom. At the same time, the British in India began to include elected Indians in legislative councils, and other African colonial powers acted similarly. Near the end of the colonial era, Ako Adjei remarked that while the British aim at eventual independence of their subjects, the French aim at making French citizens out of Africans in their domain, and the Belgians "aim at a permanent possession and exploitation of African territories as sources of raw material."[21]

At the end of the Belgian Congo era, Basil Davidson observed from extensive African travel that "much of the Congo is as woefully poor as the rest of the colonial continent, because most of the wealth produced in the Congo is carried away and spent elsewhere."[22] The Congo is still potentially one of the wealthier countries in the world. Found there are immense reserves of copper, cobalt, tantalum, and diamonds. Even so, the per capita annual income is among the world's lowest. Unlike the situation a generation ago, the Congo is no longer a net exporter of food and many of the people are poorly fed. Transportation, communication, and health systems have broken down while leaders of factions squander large economic resources in massive power struggles. Life expectancy in the Congo is about thirty years less than that of Americans.

Congo's tragedy since independence from the Belgians has deep roots that can be understood in fictional form through the tales of Conrad or in factual form by Sheppard's reports. Leopold's exploitation of his royal domain ominously laid groundwork for the social injustices a century later. Most postcolonial African rulers have tended to imitate the vices of former European conquerors. Leopold set the pattern of sucking his possession dry; ships from the Congo laden with rubber and ivory returned with little other than armed soldiers. The one-man rule of Congo presidents Mobutu Sese Seko and Laurent Kabila resembled in some ways the kleptocracy of the first colonial ruler of the country. From the export of the rich Congo basin resources, each kept for himself most of the profits he was skimming off. Mobutu, for example, built three luxurious palaces in the remote village of his nativity. In spite of their claim to have religious and moral principles, they only talked about democratic rights and generated fear among their subjects by the exercise of autocratic power.

Peter Davies, a recent Kasai mission coworker, noted uncanny parallels between Sheppard's atrocities report and the situation a century later:

> People continue to live unsheltered in the bush. Barbarities continue. In the name of unregulated free-market economics where profit margins reign, the terrible pillage continues. Sadly, one can no longer say that pillaging is masterminded by a colonial King Leopold. Surely, Kabila and his cronies have been touched by his ghost. [Yet] Kabila certainly did not invite Rwanda and Uganda to invade, nor has he authorized them to extract massive mineral and timber resources from

> Congolese soil. . . . One thing is clear: we are all blinded by profits of
> free-market capitalism. Instead of human realities of tragic suffering,
> we see but $$$.[23]

Now as then, corporate stockholders, with the aid of negligent Western political policies, act to increase the economic subjugation and misery of the Congolese people. "The heart of darkness" is as dark as ever.

A significant political legacy to the American church has resulted from the exposure by Sheppard and Morrison of State-condoned atrocities in the Congo. Indignant over Leopold's irresponsibility in colonial affairs, the Presbyterians of the South began to move away from their founding principle of noninterference with government policies. The first General Assembly, meeting in 1861, had been composed mainly of slaveholders who wished to protect their economic interests by keeping blacks disfranchised. They claimed that their church had "planted itself upon the Word of God and utterly refused to make slaveholding a sin. . . . It will be our aim to resist the real tyrants which oppress the soul—Sin and Satan."[24] In effect, this meant that human rights issues were the domain of Caesar and not of Christ. Social issues that the church deemed Satanic focused on Sunday recreation, alcohol drinking, card playing, theatergoing, and ballroom dancing. It was presumed that the founder of Christianity was most grieved by such issues.

A different notion of spirituality developed in the Congo mission. As Shaloff puts it, "The APCM was just as competent a pressure group as it was a Christian mission."[25] In particular, the pleas of Morrison and Sheppard caused several General Assemblies to break out of their decades of silence on public affairs and repeatedly petition the federal government to intervene internationally for liberation of the Congolese. By becoming involved with economic and political matters, the southern Presbyterians affirmed that Leopold's suppression of blacks was of profound concern to the church. Louis Weeks credits Sheppard and Morrison for helping to produce a "metamorphosis" among many Presbyterians who had previously been staunchly opposed to church involvement in political issues. They flooded the State Department with letters urging their government to take a stand against abuses of human rights in the Congo.[26] Beginning with the publication of Sheppard's discovery of atrocities in 1900, and progressing slowly through the century, there has been a growing interest among many Presbyterians in returning to the traditional Calvinist concern for issues involving the freedom and dignity of all peoples.

In the Congo and elsewhere in the world, Presbyterians have probably made their most lasting contributions in the field of education. Calvin, their French founder, stood as much for an informed faith as for a reformed religion. Fearful of the fanaticism that is sometimes associated with evangelism, he established the Geneva Academy to forge links between faith and reason. That Academy became the forerunner of Harvard, Princeton, Hampton, Stillman, Talladega, Mary Baldwin, and hundreds of other institutions of higher education formed by Calvinists. Their legacy is emphasized in the report of the African Education Commission, composed of African and Euro-American representatives who visited various African countries in 1921. "The splendid accomplishments in education" of the APCM are commended as being among "the most notable mission achievements in Belgian Congo."[27] In that same decade, DuPlessis wrote about the APCM:

> Careful attention was given to education and to the preparation and issue of educational literature. . . . The various schools on stations and out-stations count more than 20,000 pupils. At Luebo stand the Carson Industrial School, an agricultural school on a 250-acre farm, and the well-equipped McKowen Hospital.[28]

Until 1954, Congolese education was entirely in missionary hands and it was within the church schools that consciousness of national independence arose among future political leaders.[29]

The life of Kasonga Paul, known, as were many converts, by the combination of indigenous and biblical names, illustrates the effectiveness of the APCM's educational program. A Zappo Zap raiding party had seized the boy from his Luba village in the late-nineteenth century. After being redeemed from slavery by the APCM when Sheppard was at Luebo, he was placed in a mission school. Following his conversion, he first became a training school teacher and then was sent as an evangelist to the village of his captors. In 1924 this church leader was called on to help establish a new APCM station at Lubondai.[30] When visiting that station in 1956, I heard that senior pastor speak on his favorite text, John 3:16. From his personal experiences, he related God's love to human freedom. Later, when Lubas were being threatened with death during a tribal conflict at Lubondai, Kasonga Paul and his wife remained with their congregation and gave them encouragement.

The Sheppards' educational work in the Congo continues to be honored a century after they worked there. In Mbujimayi, the largest city of Kasai, the William Sheppard College now operates. IMPROKA continues the work of publishing in Tshiluba materials needed for

Christian worship and nurture by operating a press in Kananga. Also at that Kasai city, the Sheppards and Lapsley Presbyterian University opened both law and theological schools in 1998. In a conversation with Wakuteka Hany, the dean, I learned that this institution, which developed out of the Reformed Seminary located there, is recognized by the government. The law school, he said, continues the liberation emphasis of Sheppard and Morrison. The university hopes next to develop an agriculture school when the political situation stabilizes in the Kasai.

Sheppard left an educational legacy in America as well as in Africa. The educational institutions that he attended honor him as one of their preeminent alumni. "William H. Sheppard: Fighter for African Rights" is the title of a chapter by Larryetta Schall in a book that highlights the heritage of Hampton University.[31] In 1968 Hampton also honored the outstanding alumnus by publishing a special lecture about his life. Stanley Shaloff's Sheppard lecture concludes:

> He always exhibited calm courage and steadfast resolve in the pursuit of his objectives. That is one reason why he succeeded in reaching Mushenge when others before him had failed. It was this same inner fortitude that enabled him to overcome his fear and enter the camp of the Zappo Zaps when they were curing the remains of the Pianga. . . . He could be proud of his role in helping to bury the rubber regime in the Kasai.[32]

A 1946 book entitled *A Study of Stillman Institute* contains a photograph of Sheppard with this inscription beneath it: "Dr. Sheppard is the most distinguished alumnus of Stillman Institute."[33] To honor the place where he completed his higher education, the Sheppard Memorial Library was erected at Stillman College in 1956. That columnated structure sits at the center of the campus, with Mary Blakely's portrait of Sheppard dominating its entrance hall. The words of Dr. Cordell Wynn inscribed near the library show that Sheppard's aim continues to be alive and well. When inaugurated president in 1982, he said, "Stillman's prime focus is to lift up the truth so that it will be advanced and made manifest among all peoples to the extent of having lasting freedom for everyone." Wynn made it clear that he had in mind not only intellectual truth but the manifesto attributed to Jesus, "The truth shall make you free."

In 1972 the Sheppard Lecture Series was inaugurated at Stillman by Kasai native Remy Tshihamba. He reported: "To the Africans, Dr. William H. Sheppard was and still is a hero—a legend and also pretty much a reality."[34] Oral history continues to be strong in Sheppard's culture and the Kuba speak fondly of the American black who identified with their plight. Picking up the Sheppard mantle, Dr. Tshihamba has served as an educator and as the secretary general of the church in West Kasai. Dr. John Mbiti, a theologian from East Africa, became the next Sheppard lecturer. He may have been selected because of the point of view he expressed in one of his books:

> Mission Christianity is officially and consciously attempting to respond and contribute in form of service to human needs in . . . schools and hospitals, areas of racial, political, and religious tensions. . . . Only religion is fully sensitive to the dignity of man as an individual, person, and creature who has both physical and spiritual dimensions. . . . It provides a common denominator for all in origin, experience and destiny.[35]

The William Sheppard Memorial Scholarship Fund was established in 1964 by Ruth and Bill Metzel, to honor the distinguished missionary from Waynesboro's First Presbyterian Church. The church administers the fund to assist black students in their educational pursuits. I had the privilege of instructing the first of the Sheppard scholars, François Muyumba, who came from Zaire to be a student at Davis and Elkins College. Dr. Muyumba has long taught on the faculty of Indiana State University and is a consultant for Presbyterian projects in Africa.

Another abiding Sheppard legacy has resulted from his role as the earliest black American to collect African art. In 1911 Sheppard offered the best of his collection to the museum at Hampton, enabling his alma mater to establish the first extensive collection of African art in America and to exhibit the finest selection of Kuba art in the world. Hampton purchased several hundred pieces, paying Sheppard a nominal sum of about one dollar per item.[36] Frissell reported that Sheppard "devoted considerable time to helping in the cataloguing of the interesting African exhibit,"[37] and his explanations of some individual pieces are now posted beside them. For the Hampton Museum to have objects from tropical Africa that date back more than a century is rare because most are made of perishable materials such as wood and fiber.

In 1921 an editor of the *Southern Workman* noted the significance of the Sheppard artifacts:

> That he and his able wife could have made such an exhaustive collection is nothing short of miraculous, for it meets not only the requirements

of the ethnologists, but those of the artist as well. Already it has been used by scientists to establish the origin of the culture of the Bakuba tribe.[38]

Harold Cureau also comments on why Sheppard's collection of artifacts is special:

> A substantial number of these works of art found an early, safe, and welcome repository in a historically black institution of higher learning, Hampton Institute. . . . The collection is extant, visible, and physically available for students, scholars, and others to see, study, and enjoy. The presence of this collection, through the years, has stimulated donors to contribute art objects, and money. Such funds have been used to purchase works of art, and to help provide for some adequate conservation and maintenance. Through this collection of African art, Sheppard emerges as a person who contributed a major resource to a vital aspect of black higher education in America, the visual arts. This is significant because, historically, this class of institutions has been deficient in such resources, particularly facilities for housing and display.[39]

In 1997 the Hampton Museum was moved from its 1881 housing to a state-of-the-art building that is spacious enough to do justice to its Congo objects, more than half of which were collected by Sheppard. Also located there are the most complete archives pertaining to the Sheppards. Among the items displayed in the gallery are the unique ceremonial knives already described, musical instruments, carved drinking cups and pipes, exquisite raffia and bark cloth, and highly decorated costumes.

Sheppard's collection of textile embroidery shows much originality in design. The fabric has impressed Patricia Darish, who studies aesthetics in the history of clothing. "Kuba raffia textiles are recognized as one of the great decorative art traditions of sub-Saharan Africa," she writes.[40] The Hampton Museum's curator, Mary Lou Hultgren, comments on some items Sheppard preserved: "Patterned cloths reached a height of elaboration and importance among the Kuba unparalleled in other African groups. The governing aesthetic called for an accumulation of pattern on pattern. . . . Kuba royalty wore patterned, beaded gloves, foot coverings with separate toes, and held beaded regalia."[41]

The distinctive weapon of the Songas was the battle axe. A Zappo Zap warrior gave Sheppard one, which is featured in one of his Congo photographs. Eventually, it was lodged in the Hampton Museum.[42]

Norman Hurst gives this description: "The heavy wrought-iron blades of their axes are frequently composed of radiating spokes, which are often twisted and knotted in fanciful designs and chisel-cut with human heads."[43]

The Hampton Museum contains numerous belts profusely decorated with cowrie shells, then the principal form of currency in Kasai. A striking piece in the Museum is a beaded mask that was used at initiation ceremonies. Sheppard explained that strength is signified by the leopard skin face and by the elephant's trunk representation at the top. According to Sheppard, a mask of that type was worn for initiating new members into a kind of secret police force founded by an early Kuba ruler.[44]

Selections from the Sheppards' collection have been featured in scholarly publications and are frequently loaned out for museum

The knife of iron, copper, brass, and wood from the seventeenth century that had been handed down by Kuba royalty across seven generations. This treasure given to Sheppard is now in the Hampton Museum.

exhibitions. For example, the *Encyclopaedia Britannica* describes and illustrates some of the pieces.[45] At the Smithsonian Institute, David Binkley, curator of the National Museum of African Art, is planning a large traveling exhibition of Kuba art and it will feature contributions by the Sheppards.

In 1988, when the Center for African Art in New York prepared an exhibition for six states, only one piece was selected from any one individual collector. Amazingly, seventeen pieces of Sheppard's collection were exhibited at the Center, and half of the entire selection was from the Hampton Museum. *Art/Artifact*, the book featuring that exhibit, contains a grandly illustrated chapter accompanying the text by Mary Lou Hultgren and the Museum's director, Jeanne Zeidler. They have shared with the world the favorites of visitors to Hampton University for nearly a century. Also in the book is a photograph of a scene from a pageant presented by Hampton students. Objects that Sheppard brought to the campus were used to develop a dramatic simulation of African cultural events. Hultgren notes that "as a collector, Sheppard possessed two valuable characteristics: he enjoyed unique acceptance by Africans, and in return he genuinely admired and respected them."[46]

More recently, Hultgren and Zeidler have published a book exclusively on Congo art from the Hampton Museum. Its title, *A Taste for the Beautiful*, is appropriately a phrase from Sheppard, whose contributions make up most of the sixty pages of illustrations. The authors provide this description of Hampton's holdings:

> The collection Sheppard assembled to illustrate Kuba culture was large, diverse and of consistently high quality. The nearly four hundred objects included the rare or unique, as well as the common and mundane. . . . Moreover, since Sheppard's collection was to be educational, he recorded in great detail the use, meaning, and provenance of the pieces. This collection, therefore, can serve as a standard against which other Kuba material can be evaluated or identified.[47]

The artistic legacy of the Sheppards is also in evidence in Alabama. The Lucy Sheppard Art Club of Tuscaloosa, organized in 1911, was active throughout the past century. It was named to honor an outstanding native of the city, whose interests were not only home and church but also involvement in the broader community. The second oldest federated club in the city aims to enhance art and promote cultural interests among black women, as well as to stimulate involvement in service projects.

The Speed Art Museum in Louisville displays several Kuba artifacts that Lucy Sheppard contributed, and Museum spokespersons have gone to various sites to give an illustrated lecture to "celebrate an American hero, William H. Sheppard." The script accompanying the slide program affirms that the museum is proud of having a share of Sheppard's collection and gives tribute to Sheppard as "one of the very first Americans to foster an appreciation of the beauty of African art."

The Kubas have continued to be among the most prolific decorative artists in Africa. Dr. James Lankton, an anesthesiologist in North Carolina, became fascinated with Kuba art and culture in 1989 while visiting Presbyterian clinics in Zaire. Entertained by Lukengu Kot aMbweeky III, who succeeded Mbope in 1969, Lankton listened to some of the king's 300 wives chant the names of 125 royal predecessors. He heard stories of Sheppard and was shown Lana N'gana, the parcel of land near the royal court where "Shepete" lived on his visit to

Mushenge. In order to finance current needs at his capital, the king took the initiative to arrange with Lankton to sell in American shops in Hampton and elsewhere hundreds of the fabrics and masks from the royal storehouse.[48]

Although the Sheppards' legacy can best be found in the Congo, their impact can also be found in the city where they lived for the last fifteen years of Sheppard's life. Two generations after his Louisville ministry, he continues to be remembered there. The Grace Presbyterian and Hope Presbyterian churches of Smoketown combined in 1964 to form the Grace-Hope Presbyterian Church, which is located on Breckinridge Street—the same street where the Sheppards lived. Those entering the sanctuary are reminded of their preeminent pastor by his prominently displayed portrait above a commemorative bronze tablet. The Rev. Terrance Davis, a recent pastor, told me stories of Sheppard that were passed on to him—such as of his riding a bicycle to make parish visits. (A photograph of Sheppard at Ibanche indicates that he had earlier used a bicycle for similar purposes on the Kasai plateau.)[49] His son Max recalled that the family also possessed a Model T Ford.

Dr. Lawrence Bottoms, the first African American moderator of the PCUS General Assembly, commends the way both Sheppard and Martin Luther King Jr. combined love with humanitarian reform and thereby witnessed to the Christian message in an authentic and relevant manner. By contrast, Bottoms finds little evidence that many of the missionaries during the era of the Belgian Congo displayed the commitments of those modern prophets. Also, he perceived that Sheppard, while serving in the Congo, "opened the eyes of the world through his witness of evangelism with justice." But in Louisville, Bottoms reports, "I have heard much about his evangelistic efforts but have heard nothing about his evangelism with justice in domestic mission activity." Bottoms was pastor of the Grace-Hope Church twenty years after Sheppard served there. He thinks Sheppard wished to continue to witness to that dual theme but the forces of oppression were too powerful to permit him to speak out against the dehumanizing segregation there.[50] Dr. Blaine Hudson, Chairman of the Pan-African Studies Department at the University of Louisville, said regarding the international hero who came to live in Kentucky: "Sheppard enjoyed freedom in Africa that he couldn't here. He tried to carry on his work in a different setting . . . and speak for the interests of African Americans."[51]

Even so, different places in Louisville do show signs of Sheppard's public achievements. Probably no African American in Kentucky was given more honor in the first half of the twentieth century than Sheppard. His efforts as a community leader led in 1925 to the construction of a city playground with a swimming pool on the western side of Louisville.[52] It was regarded as the finest recreational accomodation for blacks in the region. The Board of Park Commissioners honored Sheppard after his death by naming it the William Sheppard Park, and it is still a recreational area for youth.

Also, the Louisville Municipal Housing Commission, acting on the recommendation of black leaders, named an inner-city project "Sheppard Square" when it was constructed in 1942.[53] Six blocks are filled with several hundred units of public housing in the area where the Sheppards' work centered. Credit for the development ultimately belongs to Eleanor and Franklin Roosevelt, who persuaded the federal government to establish decent residences for low-income blacks. In its midst is the Presbyterian Community Center, which still offers a range of social services, thereby continuing youth clubs and adult educational and welfare services that the Sheppards developed. A grand new facility that fills a nearby block has now replaced the worn-out building. Conditions have so improved in the former slum that "Sheppardtown" would now be a more apt name for the area than "Smoketown."

There are some indications that American interest in Sheppard is reviving in the present generation. He has been featured in Hochschild's widely heralded book on Leopold, now also in French translation, and by National Public Radio in 1999. NPR reporter Alex Chadwick, after interviewing Hochschild and myself, gave a dramatic treatment of Sheppard's accomplishments as one of a series on great explorers, which the National Geographic Society sponsored.

Sheppard is also being more remembered in the states where he was born and educated. On returning recently to his and my home church in Waynesboro, I found illustrated articles about the Sheppards displayed on the bulletin board. Included there was a photo of a new highway marker erected at Warm Springs in 1998 by the State of Virginia to commemorate the Sheppards' association there. In Louisville, a historical marker was dedicated to Sheppard during Black History Month in 2000, and efforts are being made to establish an African American history museum at Sheppard's former Louisville residence.[54]

In an introduction to a text about archival material on Sheppard, William Aery of Hampton University wrote in 1991, "Romance has not entirely gone from the world, when a barefooted Negro boy in Virginia can stand, in time, before a powerful Colonial court in Africa and win his case for the human treatment of natives, . . . and can win for his race a 'new place in the sun.'"[55] Sheppard is now ranked high by Hultgren, also of Hampton, for more than the artifacts he accumulated:

> He was important not only for his advocacy of African rights but also for his educational work among Americans. Sheppard had an admiration for Africans and a respect for their culture which were unique in his time. . . . After his 1910 return to the United States he . . . worked to break down the prevailing stereotypical notion of Africans as savages.[56]

One auspicious result of the reunion in 1983 of the northern and southern Presbyterians, after a rupture for more than a century, has been a new name for a presbytery in central Alabama. Patrick Willson, pastor of the Shades Valley Church in Birmingham, suggested the name "Sheppards and Lapsley" for that presbytery in the Synod of Living Waters. The name symbolized for him a racial, gender, and economic unity that was present among some Presbyterians of the deep South a century earlier. African American pastor William Jones of the Westminster Church in Birmingham enthusiastically endorsed Willson's suggestion and soon the governing body members agreed on a name that is unique among presbytery names in being inclusive of gender and race. Appropriately, the Sheppards are given priority in the name of the new presbytery composed of more than one hundred churches. Lapsley had but two years in the Congo, while William and Lucy Sheppard worked as global missionaries for a combined total of thirty-five years, and as home missionaries even longer. In a letter to me, Willson indicated that he likes the name because it provides an opportunity for churches to tell again the remarkable story of the Sheppards and Lapsley. Hopefully, their mission witness will stimulate similar joint interracial activity in the future.

The first meeting of the Sheppards and Lapsley Presbytery was held at the First Presbyterian Church of Selma—Samuel Lapsley's boyhood church. Dr. Harvey Jenkins, an executive of the Presbytery, explained its new name: "It celebrates a partnership in mission between black and white, male and female, in the Presbyterian Church that predates the twentieth century. Sheppard and Lapsley worked in a genuine partnership, as did William and Lucy Sheppard, without overtones of benevolence or paternalism."

The story of Sheppard working with Lapsley shows that persons from both ends of the caste system of the South have worked together as close friends to accomplish wonders. Among Southerners even today, the often unstated residual racism is that all good blacks know their "place" and follow the lead of whites. However, among the two male pioneer missionaries, as well as between the two Sheppards, there was an extraordinary mutual subordination—each cherishing and relying on the special gifts of the other.

Sheppard not only left lasting influences in Congo and America, but he may also have inspired prominent leaders elsewhere. Mahatma Gandhi probably learned from his older contemporary some strategies for making effective social protests. Sheppard realized the importance of the print media to inform Euro-Americans of the need for radical reform. Gandhi was a "colored" lawyer in South Africa during the same period that Sheppard was in Kasai. He probably read some of the frequent articles in the *Times* of London about the Congo Reform Association that was formed in response to the reports of Sheppard and his colleagues. Neither reformer could have accomplished much in their colonies had it not been for their savvy in working through international journals and advocacy organizations to publicize their struggle for human rights.

Albert Schweitzer, another younger contemporary of Sheppard, was aware of his testimony about the atrocities. In his hometown of Colmar on the border between France and Germany, Schweitzer frequently gazed at a troubling statue by Bartholdi (who also created the Statue of Liberty) that depicted a colonial military hero towering over a strong but subjected African.[57] He also found disturbing Jesus' parable of the rich man and Lazarus. "Out there in the colonies," Schweitzer said, "sits wretched Lazarus" lorded over by the European imperialist who lives in luxury.[58] In 1905, when the outcry against Leopold was intense, Schweitzer read a recently published article entitled "The Needs of the Congo Mission" that convinced him to devote his life to alleviate the suffering of natives in central Africa.[59] Expressing his sense of guilt over what Europeans have done to Africans, Schweitzer asked, "Who can describe the injustices and atrocities committed?"[60] He was especially aware of the forced-labor abuses in Belgian and French colonies.[61] Schweitzer felt impelled to turn aside from a life of acclaim as musician, philosopher, pastor, and historian in Europe to prepare to be a medical missionary. He, like Sheppard, served Africans who lived a few degrees south of the equator.

THE CONGO LIVINGSTONE

There were significant personal similarities between Sheppard (born in 1865) and David Livingstone, who was born a half century earlier (1813). Both came from lowly beginnings. In a highly industrial area of Scotland, I visited the tenement that had been occupied by the Livingstone family. Livingstone spent his early years in an overcrowded slum outside Glasgow, where the living conditions were more squalid than what Sheppard confronted as a child. Livingstone lived with his parents and four siblings in a single-room apartment, fourteen by ten feet in area, owned by Blantyre Mills. Sunlight was infrequently seen from that grimy cotton mill where the boy worked seventy-five hours a week. A survey of British cotton mills at that time concluded that the working conditions for children were generally as miserable as for slaves across the Atlantic.[62]

The Scotsman and the Virginian shared a strong determination to seize any opportunity to become educated. Only 10 percent of British children then working in factories learned to read, a proportion similar to that of literate black children in the postbellum American South. While in school the two boys saw God's faithfulness in the events they experienced and began to think seriously about becoming missionaries. Both accepted the basic Calvinist beliefs in which they were reared and became ordained as Protestant ministers.

The overall purpose of both Livingstone and Sheppard was to bring Christianity to new regions of Africa. They wanted the gospel to permeate African cultures, enhancing the sacredness of human life. Both had strong faith in the capabilities of Africans and did not fault them for lack of wisdom, religion, and morality—although they believed that improvement was needed in all those areas. Each wanted to do good for the Africans and had as much appreciation of them as of people on their own continent. Livingstone rejected notions of black racial inferiority.[63] Sheppard expressed his identification with Africans in a national journal for American blacks. In "my central African home," he wrote, "we have found the natives kind and obliging with a few exceptions."[64] Neither man resorted to condemnation of African cultures.

Livingstone and Sheppard were not otherworldly mystics. Both had practical outlooks and wanted to ameliorate conditions that would enhance human dignity. They observed that traditional African ways were in transition because of the encroachment of Muslims and Europeans, and they approved of some cultural modifications. Although

Livingstone was more accepting of tribal customs than most missionaries or colonialists, he advocated changes derived from democratic and Christian values. Sheppard also realized that the gospel could not be spread until basic infringements on individual rights to life and liberty were removed. On the other hand, he encouraged native crafts that celebrated individual and tribal achievements.

The two missionaries developed undefeatable spirits and bravely surmounted daunting circumstances that would have caused others to despair. Sufferings abounded for both, some of their own making. Frequent health problems were accepted by both as routine occupational hazards for living in the tropics. When debilitated by malarial attacks, they doctored themselves with quinine. Both men attempted to use the limited medicine at their disposal to heal others, but their primary interests were directed elsewhere. Africans appreciated the medical benefits they brought and their desire to learn from Africans.

Livingstone had more success in his second role as explorer than in his first role as evangelist, for he had but one convert, who subsequently apostatized. The mission he helped establish in Malawi ended in disaster, for a large proportion of the missionaries died who had been sent there. Both Livingstone and Sheppard focused on moving into unmapped areas. Livingstone explored the southern part of the Kwango and Kasai region on one trip, but did not enter the areas where Sheppard traveled. On returning to England he was awarded the Royal Geographical Society's gold medal. Sheppard penetrated as deep into the center of Africa as Livingstone had done and was similarly recognized by the Royal Geographical Society. He adopted Livingstone's practice of taking along beads, cloth, and wire as trading goods. Their treks were mainly by canoe or on foot, but both occasionally used steamer assistance. Both were confronted with the possibility of desertion when their porters perceived danger from fierce tribes. Both men had shooting skills but were not always protected by such. Livingstone once shot a lion but only wounded it, resulting in the ferocious beast mauling his arm. Sheppard made an elephant more dangerous by irritating it with a bullet, and he scampered up a tree to protect himself. Livingstone, unlike Sheppard, shot some Africans defensively.[65]

Livingstone and Sheppard made ethnological and geographical discoveries, even though neither had specialized training in those areas. Livingstone's observations focused more on physical description—geographical, botanical, and zoological. His main interest was in exploring the terrain and waterways of central Africa. As geographical pioneers, Livingstone and Stanley did more than any other persons to open up central Africa to European colonialization. Sheppard was more interested in exploring the internal life of the Congolese, understanding their cultures, both their noble and their base qualities.

Above Victoria Falls there is a statue of Livingstone looking out over the spectacular drop in the Zambezi River, which he was the first white man to discover. "Liberator," the one word that I read at its base, summarizes his third role. Livingstone wanted to enlighten Anglo-Americans about the twenty thousand slaves that were being shipped out of Zanzibar annually and the brutality by which that cargo was produced.[66] He became angered by Arab slavers who left their victims to die if they became too weak to keep up with others who were being marched toward the coast. "Groups of corpses were found [by Livingstone] with remorseless regularity. Some had been stabbed to death, others shot, and many had simply been left tied together to die slowly of starvation."[67] He pleaded with the British Foreign Office to send warships to halt this practice. Livingstone selected the biblical term "broken-hearted" to diagnose the devastating slave illness. He said, "The strangest disease I have seen in this country seems really to be broken-heartedness, and it attacks free men who have been captured and made slaves."[68] In Livingstone's day, slave trading was still legal in some countries bordering on the Indian Ocean. Also, he found in Mozambique that slavery was condoned even though the Portuguese ruler of the colony claimed that it was unlawful.[69]

By Sheppard's time, on the western side of Africa, de jure slavery had been widely outlawed, but the more subtle de facto slavery was prevalent. He became aware of thousands of rubber slaves who were dying from overwork and other forms of cruelty. Like Livingstone, Sheppard had seen the inhumanity of man to man that included the cannibalization of slaves. They were chagrined to find slave operations still present in the inner regions of central Africa, and both exposed the ugly entrails of the brutal system that powers outside of Africa were using for economic exploitation.

Both men thought they could diminish evil by persuasion. This involved not only their manner of speaking to illiterates but their attention to writing in an attractive style to inform educated people about the oppression of some Africans. As a result of their publicizing the abounding evil they witnessed, some governments took notice and acted to protect human rights.

The aims of Livingstone have been encapsulated in the slogan, "Christianity, civilization, and commerce." Those three "C's" appear to be similar to the Catholic, colonial, and commercial triple thrust of

Leopold. But Livingstone, as well as Sheppard, thought of Christianity as the gospel of liberation for the oppressed and did not equate civilization with colonialism.

These nineteenth-century liberators faithfully transmitted a heritage as old as the Hebrew prophets. Like Moses, they identified with those who were being downtrodden by inhumane taskmasters. Like Amos, they called for justice that would have precipitated practices diametrically opposed to those of the current rulers. Lucy Sheppard sang the protest song, "Go down Moses . . . ; tell ole Pharoah to let my people go!" They all sang in harmony the gospel song of Jesus' mother:

> My spirit rejoices in God my Savior . . .
> Who has brought down the arrogant from their thrones
> And lifted up the lowly.[70]

Sheppard and Livingstone shared a brand of Protestantism that for centuries has spoken out against government tyranny. "Resistance to tyrants is obedience to God" was the banner under which intrepid Calvinists marched. Believing in the right to revolt against oppressive colonialism, Scottish Presbyterian John Witherspoon was the only clergyman who risked his life by signing the Declaration of Independence. In that same eighteenth century, Presbyterian minister David Rice published *Slavery Inconsistent with Justice and Good Policy*. That Virginia native, who was evicted from his home state, designated slaveowners as "licensed robbers."[71] In 1818 abolitionist George Bourne, the Presbyterian pastor of a church along the same South fork of the Shenandoah River where Sheppard was born, was ousted from Virginia. He wrote *The Bible and Slavery Irreconcilable*, which advocated immediate emancipation.[72]

When Sheppard and Lapsley were in London, their greatest inspiration was a visit to Livingstone's tomb.[73] His heart had been buried in Africa, but the rest of his sun-dried corpse was interred in Westminster Abbey. The Africa-bound missionaries appreciated the poet who at the time of his funeral said "Here lies Living Stone," punning on a biblical figure for Jesus.[74] They pondered the epitaph that stated Livingstone's three objectives:

> For thirty years his life was spent in an unwearied effort to evangelize the native races, to explore the undiscovered secrets, to abolish the desolating slave trade of Central Africa, where with his last words he wrote, "All I can add in my solitude is, May heaven's rich blessing come down on every one, American, English, or Turk, who will help to heal this open sore of the world."

In his dying prayer Livingstone may have been thinking especially of other missionaries who would perceive the need to deliver Africans from threats by outsiders who were ravishing some of the areas of central Africa. Sheppard fulfilled Livingstone's hope by spending two decades of his life tirelessly pursuing his predecessor's three roles as evangelist, explorer, and abolitionist of forced labor.

A balanced comparison of Livingstone and Sheppard needs to include differences as well as similarities. The former was brusque, distant, and uninterested in bonding with peers; the latter was gregarious and a pleasant travel companion. Livingstone was such a loner that he was reluctant to accept assistance even when ill.

Sheppard was more of a partner with his spouse than Livingstone, who left his wife and children in poverty during his years of absence. Tim Jeal, the best Livingstone biographer, observes that "he saw his wife's position as that of an inferior, rather than an equal partner."[75] Livingstone envied celibate Catholic missionaries and longed for the greater independence that he could have were he unmarried. He commented on the "frightful nudity" of African women,[76] but Sheppard photographed unclothed African men and women whom he found attractive.

There were not only differences between the lifestyles of Sheppard and Livingstone, but also some of their goals can be distinguished. Like many Europeans and Americans, Livingstone was heavily influenced by Adam Smith, a fellow Scotsman who had taught at his University of Glasgow a century earlier. Livingstone naively presumed that the maximizing of free trade would in itself improve human life. Even though he knew from personal experience in a cotton mill some cruel consequences of the industrial revolution, he did not question the capitalist dogma. Livingstone thought that African improvement was dependent upon "contact with superior races by commerce."[77] He sought to replace slave trade with free trade between Africa and Europe. He wrote that he was "extremely desirous to promote the preparation of the raw materials of European manufactures in Africa."[78] Cotton was the export commodity that interested him, but rubber would have served as well. Sheppard also approved of free trade and showed the way in which the Kasai Company monopoly had diminished the quality of life. Yet he did not have confidence that free trade bereft of concern for the welfare of the individuals involved could be a force for liberation. While recognizing the benefits in the Congo from European technology in the areas of transportation and communication, promoting Western commercialization was not his concern.

Livingstone left his mission society to work for the British Foreign Office, but Sheppard never held a government office. Livingstone was an advocate for the establishment of British colonies in Africa, but Sheppard had no interest in such imperialism by the United States. Both made a lasting impact on colonial politics, but Livingstone increased imperial power by influencing Britain to add areas of Africa to its empire while Sheppard helped to diminish colonial power. Livingstone was the forerunner of businessman Cecil Rhodes, who extended British control over much of Africa by opening up many trading posts.

Sheppard did not share Livingstone's hope that primal cultures would evolve toward Victorian excellence. Being aware of the ruthless exploitation by Leopold, he did not associate progress with colonial domination. Livingstone wanted to Europeanize natives, but Sheppard strove to develop and improve the indigenous culture. He was fascinated by the traditional skills of the Africans with whom he lived, and he recognized that the Kubas possessed a civilization before they had been influenced by foreigners.

Livingstone towers in Anglo-American history, and much of his fame has been posthumous. Most of the notoriety Sheppard received was at the peak of his life, from the age of twenty-five to forty-five. For most of the past century he has been virtually unknown in America and is rarely mentioned even during the month when black history is commemorated. As Schall observes, "Sheppard has fallen into oblivion, his personal courage and his active participation in the struggle for African rights remembered by only a few historians and theologians."[79] Actually, most historians of African Americans, as Phillips Bradford and Harvey Blume point out, have neglected him: "Sheppard led a life that has, perhaps, been inadequately explored by historians. First visitor to the Forbidden Land of the Kuba people and first American witness of Free State atrocities, Sheppard's effect on the development of the Presbyterian Mission to the Congo is hard to overstate."[80] In a large volume titled *Dictionary of American Negro Biography*, which includes only deceased persons, Sheppard is omitted.[81] Also, *Great Negroes Past and Present* has chapters on many leaders in various careers, but nothing on Sheppard.[82] In addition, there is no reference to Sheppard in the two-volume *History of Blacks in Kentucky*.[83] Nor does Lucy Sheppard's name appear in the biographical dictionary of African-American women.[84]

Sheppard, but not Morrison, was listed in each edition of *Who's Who in America* from 1906 to 1911. Yet Morrison, but not Sheppard, is treated in the *Dictionary of American Biography*, published in 1934, and in *American National Biography*, published in 1999. Morrison was certainly significant enough to deserve the columns devoted to him in those volumes, but can any objective person claim that Sheppard had less breadth of influence? Sheppard, unlike Morrison, had considerable impact as a pioneer missionary, as a Kuba ethnographer, and as a pastor in America.

There is also a misplaced focus on Morrison's role in two recent books. In his book on African colonialism, Thomas Pakenham calls Morrison "the Mr-Valiant-for-Truths of the Congo for exposing atrocities," but Sheppard's name does not appear. Elsewhere, in a chapter entitled "The Severed Hands," Pakenham discusses Morrison's "testimony" even though he was not the one who risked his life to see and report on bodies butchered by soldiers working for Leopold.[85] The relative significance of Sheppard as compared with Morrison has also been distorted by an otherwise excellent recent source book entitled *Presbyterian Reformers in Central Africa*. Robert Benedetto, its editor, provides this subtitle, "A Documentary Account of the American Presbyterian Congo Mission and the Human Rights Struggle in the Congo." His selection of documents from the reformers is unbalanced, there being seventy by Morrison but only two by Sheppard. Benedetto states that Sheppard's focus upon the Kubas rather than the Lubas was "misdirected," and gives the wrong impression that Morrison was the head of the APCM and "allowed" Sheppard to continue Kuba work that was unpromising. Actually, as has been shown, missionary work among both the Kubas and the Lubas was immensely successful. Morrison usually served as the APCM legal representative but Sheppard also was elected by his missionary colleagues to serve a term in that office. The interracial APCM was not reluctant to select Sheppard for positions of leadership. The Mission's minutes state the 1903 annual meeting was "called to order by the president, Rev. W. H. Sheppard;" also Edmiston was the elected chairman of the APCM for 1907 and Sheppard for 1909.[86] It was not the case, as Benedetto affirms, that PCUS policy during Sheppard's tenure with the APCM was that "the work would be done by African-Americans, with white managers." That was the hope of DeWitt Snyder and Phillips Verner, members of the APCM for several years. They were atypical and Verner was not reappointed because of his arrogant attitude. Benedetto also gratuitously questions "Sheppard's art collecting activities which seem to run counter to his primary purpose for being in the Congo."[87] Sheppard's appreciation of Congolese art illustrates one way by which he established an extraordinary rapport with the people he was sent to serve. By contrast, those missionaries who had an antipathy to weapons, masks, and musical instruments, which they classified as "heathen," were less effective in ministering to the Congolese.

Walter Williams, a specialist on Christianity in black Africa, credits Sheppard for doing more than other missionaries of his era to rise above ethnocentrism and protest imperialism.[88] Williams writes:

> Sheppard rejected the view that soul-saving excluded earthly consider-ations, and he worked hard to aid those Congolese in material ways. Whether giving medical aid, ransoming slaves, or protesting colonial exploitation, Sheppard tried to improve African standards of living. . . . Sheppard, because of his influence on black Americans and his efforts on behalf of Africans, deserves to be ranked among the most important of early Afro-American missionaries.[89]

Toward the end of Sheppard's years in Africa, the leading newspaper of Virginia proudly noted his ties with his native state and ranked the "pioneer missionary and explorer in Africa" as "second only to Livingstone and Stanley in the opening of Central Africa."[90] The comparison is apt, but from the perspective of the twenty-first century Sheppard can be seen as more influential than Stanley and at least on a par with Livingstone. Both Livingstone and Sheppard left their hearts in Africa.

The legacy of William Sheppard marches on, even as an ancestral spirit in the culture of Kasai. His and his wife Lucy's enormous contributions to education, religion, humanitarian reform, and Kuba artifact preservation have insured their social immortality on both sides of the Atlantic.

Notes

Foreword

1. *William H. Sheppard: Pioneer Missionary to the Congo* (Nashville: Executive Committee of Foreign Missions, PCUS, 1942), 4.
2. *Presbyterian Standard*, 8/10/1899, 9.

Chapter 1: Preparation

1. *Sheppard: Pioneer Missionary*, 4.
2. Nelson County Register of Free Negroes, entry 9/27/1858, on microfilm; Katherine Bushman, *A Register of Free Negroes for Augusta County* (Staunton, Va., 1989), 92.
3. June Guild, *Black Laws of Virginia* (Richmond: Whittet, 1936), 50.
4. Herbert Klein, *Slavery in the Americas* (Chicago: University of Chicago Press, 1967), 241.
5. From research by John Thornton reported in *Richmond Times-Dispatch*, 6/27/99, C5.
6. Hugh Thomas, *The Slave Trade* (New York: Simon & Schuster, 1997), 805; Michael Davis and Hunter Clark, *Thurgood Marshall* (New York: Citadel, 1994), 30.
7. Joseph Waddell, *Annals of Augusta County, Virginia* (Staunton, Va.: Caldwell, 1903), 498.
8. George Hawke, *A History of Waynesboro to 1900* (Waynesboro, Va.: Historical Commission, 1997), 114–23.
9. Waddell, *Annals*, 414.
10. William Sheppard, *Presbyterian Pioneers in Congo* (Richmond: Presbyterian Committee of Publication, 1917), 15; henceforth PPC.
11. Comer Woodward, *The Strange Career of Jim Crow* (New York: Oxford University Press, 1974), 31–57.
12. Charles Wynes, *Race Relations in Virginia 1870–1902* (Charlottesville: University of Virginia Press, 1961), 150.
13. Hawke, *History of Waynesboro*, 135.
14. W. E. B. Du Bois, *The Souls of Black Folk* (New York: Washington Square, 1970 [1903]), 149.
15. PPC, 15–16.
16. *Staunton Vindicator*, 4/3/1874.
17. *Union Primer* (Philadelphia: Sunday School Union, 1875); Sheppard papers, Presbyterian archives, Montreat, N.C.
18. *Sheppard: Pioneer Missionary*, 4–5.
19. PPC, 16. He and my mother seem to have received similar Bible instruction, for she cited the reference to "gnashing of teeth" (Matthew 8:12) by some persons in the life after death as evidence of a full physical resurrection.

20. PPC, 16.

21. Robert Engs, *Freedom's First Generation* (Philadelphia: University of Pennsylvania Press, 1979), 144.

22. PPC, 16–17.

23. *Southern Workman*, 3/1915, 167.

24. Mary Hultgren and Jeanne Zeidler, *A Taste for the Beautiful* (Hampton, Va.: Stinehour, 1993), 16–17.

25. PPC, 17.

26. Booker T. Washington, *Up from Slavery* (Williamstown, Mass.: Corner House, 1971), 104–6; James Anderson, *The Education of Blacks in the South 1865–1935* (Chapel Hill: University of North Carolina Press, 1988), 54–57.

27. Booker T. Washington, "Cruelty in the Congo Country," *The Outlook*, 10/8/1904, 377; *The Tuskegee Student*, 4/4/1905.

28. Anderson, *Education of Blacks*, 36–53.

29. *Southern Workman*, 1/1883, 9.

30. Edward Blyden, *Christianity, Islam and the Negro Race* (London: Whittingham, 1887), 46, 124, 170, 277.

31. Records of the Synod of Virginia, microfilm reel VL, 109, 4/16/1884.

32. *Minutes of the General Assembly of the PCUS* (Augusta, Ga.: Steam Power Press, 1861), 56, 58.

33. *Minutes of the General Assembly* (Augusta, Ga.: Constitutionist Office, 1865), 370.

34. *Minutes of the General Assembly* (1861), 17.

35. *Minutes of the General Assembly* (1865), 372.

36. Isaiah 18:1.

37. *Harvard Library Bulletin*, spring 1998, 11.

38. *United States' Consular Reports*, no. 55, 8/1885, 551.

39. J. Leighton Wilson, *Western Africa* (New York: Harper, 1856), 506.

40. David Livingstone, *Missionary Travels* (New York: Harper, 1858), 464, 483.

41. J. Leighton Wilson, *The Catholic Presbyterian* 1/1879, 262–64.

42. Wilson, *Western Africa*, 313.

43. Ernest T. Thompson, *Presbyterians in the South* (Richmond: John Knox, 1973), 3:123.

44. *Christian Observer*, 11/28/1894, 16.

45. Sheppard, *Pioneer Missionary*, 7–9.

46. PPC, 18.

47. Franklin Talmage, *The Story of the Presbytery of Atlanta* (Atlanta: Foote & Davies, 1960), 106–7.

48. Du Bois, *Souls of Black Folk*, 68–69.

49. Walter Williams, *Black Americans and the Evangelization of Africa 1877–1900* (Madison: University of Wisconsin Press, 1982), 23, 94.

50. *Minutes of the General Assembly* (Richmond: Presbyterian Committee on Publication, 1888), 611; Isaiah 6:8.

51. *PCUS Annual Report of the Executive Committee of Foreign Missions of the PCUS* (Baltimore: Sun Press, 1889), 83–84.

52. Minutes of the Executive Committee of Foreign Missions, PCUS (Montreat archives), 10/15/1889, 168.

53. *Presbyterian Survey*, 6/1978, 24.

54. *Christian Observer*, 2/21/1894, 14.

55. James Lapsley, ed., *Life and Letters of Samuel Norvell Lapsley* (Richmond: Whittet & Shepperson, 1893), 13.

56. Lapsley, *Life*, 14–15.
57. *The Century*, 1/1885, 410–18.
58. Lapsley, *Life*, 16–17, 26.
59. Winifred and Lachlan Vass, *The Lapsley Saga* (Franklin, Tenn.: Providence House, 1997), 7; Winifred Vass, an authority on Presbyterian missions in Congo, claims that "coequals" comes from a document in the Montreat archives.
60. Robert Benedetto, *Presbyterian Reformers in Central Africa* (Leiden: Brill, 1996), 56.
61. Thompson, *Presbyterians in the South*, 3:124.
62. Minutes of the Executive Committee, 6/8/1901.
63. "Presbyterian Church (South), USA," Edwin Bliss, ed., *The Encyclopaedia of Missions* (New York: Funk & Wagnalls, 1891). Lapsley has long been given more prominence than Sheppard, but now, more than a century later, exaggerated prominence is given to Sheppard. Ken Ross and Nancy Taylor of the Presbyterian Historical Society say of him, "In 1890, he led the first contingent of PCUS missionaries to the Belgian Congo." Lapsley is not named in this comment on pioneer Congo missionaries. *Mission Yearbook* (Louisville, Ky.: PCUSA, 2000), 141.
64. *Minutes of the General Assembly* (Richmond: Presbyterian Committee on Publication, 1890), 69.
65. Lapsley, *Life*, 21.
66. Quoted in Joseph Fry, *John Tyler Morgan and the Search for Southern Autonomy* (Knoxville: University of Tennessee Press, 1992), 56, 77–78.
67. *The Missionary*, 9/1890, 352.
68. PPC, 19.
69. Lapsley, *Life*, 25.
70. Ibid., 27, 34.
71. PPC, 20.
72. Lapsley, *Life*, 37.
73. PPC, 20.
74. Fanny Guinness, *Congo Recollections* (London: Hodder & Stoughton, 1890), 109.
75. Lapsley, *Life*, 68.
76. Quoted in Robert Smith, *Zaire Perception and Perspective* (Valley Forge, Pa.: International Ministries, 1982), 62–63.
77. Lapsley, *Life*, 23, 45.
78. Ibid., 44–45.
79. Quoted in *The Missionary*, 9/1890, 353.
80. Joseph Fry, *Henry S. Sanford* (Reno: University of Nevada Press, 1982), 144–45.
81. David Lagergren, *Mission and State in the Congo* (Uppsala: Gleerup, 1970), 74.
82. Kenneth Latourette, *A History of the Expansion of Christianity* (New York: Harper, 1943), 5:421.
83. C. G. Baeta, ed. *Christianity in Tropical Africa* (London: Oxford University Press, 1968), 86.
84. PPC, 85.
85. PPC, 20–21.
86. PPC, 19.
87. *The Missionary* 9/1890, 355.
88. Lapsley, *Life*, 163.
89. Adam Hochschild, *King Leopold's Ghost* (New York: Houghton Mifflin, 1998), 13–14.

90. Robert Rotberg, *A Political History of Tropical Africa* (New York: Harcourt, 1965), 78.
91. Harry Johnston, *History of the Colonisation of Africa* (Cambridge: Cambridge University Press, 1913), 158.
92. *The Missionary*, 2/1900, 62.
93. Quoted in Colin Legum, *Congo Disaster* (New York: Penguin, 1961), 14–15.
94. Neal Ascherson, *The King Incorporated* (Garden City, N.Y.: Doubleday, 1964), 29.
95. Quoted in Hochschild, *Ghost*, 58.
96. Edward Glave, *Six Years of Adventure in Congo-land* (London: Low, 1893), 209, 233.
97. Peter Forbath, *The River Congo* (New York: Harper, 1977), 357.
98. Ibid., 349.
99. Ascherson, *The King Incorporated*, 106, 129–30.
100. Ibid., 132–33.
101. William Phipps, "Cartographic Ethnocentricity," *Social Studies*, 11/1987, 262.
102. John Reader, *Africa* (New York: Knopf, 1998), 525.
103. Maurice Hennessy, *The Congo* (New York: Praeger, 1961), 18.
104. Quoted in Henry Fox Bourne, *Civilisation in Congoland* (London: King, 1903), 114.

Chapter 2: Beginnings in Africa

1. Lapsley, *Life*, 52.
2. PPC, 21–22.
3. Lapsley, *Life*, 54.
4. *The Missionary*, 9/1890, 355.
5. Lapsley, *Life*, 55.
6. Henry Stanley, *The Congo* (New York: Harper, 1885), 1:148.
7. Richard Stanley and Alan Neame, eds., *The Exploration Diaries of H. M. Stanley* (New York: Vanguard, 1961), 141, 199.
8. Ludwig Bauer, *Leopold the Unloved* (Boston: Little, Brown, 1935), 274.
9. Stanley, *The Congo*, 1:96.
10. PPC, 22.
11. PPC, 25.
12. PPC, 26.
13. John Crawford, *Protestant Mission in Congo 1878–1969* (Kinshasa: Librairie Évangélique du Congo, n.d.), 4.
14. "Congo Free State," *The Encyclopaedia of Missions.*
15. PPC, 23.
16. PPC, 24.
17. Lapsley, *Life*, 99.
18. *Southern Workman*, 12/1893, 182.
19. PPC, 25.
20. Lapsley, *Life*, 63; Guinness, 16.
21. Lapsley, *Life*, 192.
22. Robert Rotberg, *A Political History of Tropical Africa* (New York: Harcourt, 1965), 260.
23. Lapsley, *Life*, 58.
24. *The Missionary*, 3/1897, 115.
25. Lapsley, *Life*, 59.
26. *Southern Workman*, 12/1893, 182.

27. Lapsley, *Life*, 65.
28. Conway Wharton, *The Leopard Hunts Alone* (New York: Revell, 1927), 17.
29. Lapsley, *Life*, 67.
30. *Southern Workman*, 12/1893, 182.
31. PPC, 27.
32. *Southern Workman*, 12/1893, 182.
33. *Southern Workman*, 12/1893, 182.
34. Lapsley, *Life*, 68.
35. Guinness, *Congo Recollections*, 94–95.
36. Lapsley, *Life*, 72.
37. PPC, 28–29.
38. PPC, 30–31.
39. Lapsley, *Life*, 168.
40. PPC, 31, 98.
41. PPC, 32–33.
42. PPC, 32.
43. Ruth Slade, *English-Speaking Missions in the Congo Independent State* (Brussels: Royal Academy of Colonial Sciences, 1959), 87.
44. Lapsley, *Life*, 83.
45. Joseph Conrad, *Congo Diary* (New York: Doubleday, 1978), 7–15.
46. Stanley, *The Congo*, 1:496.
47. Quoted in Hochschild, *Ghost*, 110.
48. Lapsley, *Life*, 82–83, 108.
49. Ibid., 94.
50. *The Missionary*, 1/1891, 34.
51. PPC, 39.
52. PPC, 37.
53. PPC, 38.
54. *The Missionary*, 1/1891, 34.
55. *The Missionary*, 1/1891, 33.
56. *Southern Workman*, 12/1893, 182.
57. PPC, 43–44.
58. Lapsley, *Life*, 97.
59. Lapsley, *Life*, 117.
60. *The Missionary*, 12/1898, 554.
61. Stanley, *The Congo*, 1:424.
62. *The Missionary*, 7/1891, 255–56.
63. PPC, 45.
64. Lapsley, *Life*, 101.
65. Ibid., 108.
66. Ibid., 93, 108.
67. PPC, 46.
68. Lapsley, *Life*, 124.
69. Ibid., 134.
70. Ibid., 120.
71. Ibid., 137.
72. Ibid., 117.
73. *Kassai Herald*, 7/1/1902, 28.
74. *The Missionary*, 7/1891, 256.
75. PPC, 47–48.

76. Lapsley, *Life*, 124, 127.
77. Thomas Pakenham, *The Scramble for Africa* (New York: Random House, 1991), 403, 436.
78. Lapsley, *Life*, 126.
79. Ibid., 88, 123–24, 127, 143.
80. Ibid., 132–33.
81. *The Missionary*, 7/1891, 259.
82. Fox Bourne, *Civilization*, 121.
83. G. Jean-Aubry, *Joseph Conrad in the Congo* (New York: Haskell, 1973), 71.
84. Lapsley, *Life*, 135.
85. "East London Institute," *Encyclopaedia of Missions*.
86. Lapsley, *Life*, 134.
87. Ethel Wharton, *Led in Triumph* (Nashville: PCUS Board of World Missions, 1952), 43.
88. *The Missionary*, 2/1893, 70.
89. PPC, 51.
90. Lapsley, *Life*, 138–39.
91. Joseph Conrad, *Heart of Darkness* (London: Dent, 1946), 92–93.
92. Lapsley, *Life*, 139.
93. PPC, 52.
94. PPC, 52–53.
95. PPC, 59.
96. PPC, 54, 56.
97. PPC, 55.
98. 2 Corinthians 11:23–27.
99. PPC, 59.
100. Acts 27:10, 31.
101. PPC, 58–59.
102. PPC, 57–60.
103. Hermann Wissmann, *My Second Journey through Equatorial Africa* (London: Chatto & Windus, 1891), 38.
104. PPC, 81.
105. *Annual Report* (Nashville: Foreign Missions Committee, PCUS, 1891), 41.
106. Lapsley, *Life*, 163.
107. PPC, 153.
108. PPC, 127.
109. PPC, 142.
110. Robert Bedinger, *Triumphs of the Gospel in the Belgian Congo* (Richmond: Presbyterian Committee of Publication, 1920), 34, 70.
111. PPC, 75.
112. *The Missionary*, 2/1905, 60.
113. PPC, 61; Matthew 28:20.
114. PPC, 62.
115. *Southern Workman*, 12/1893, 182.
116. PPC, 98–99.
117. PPC, 67.
118. PPC, 72.
119. PPC, 73.
120. PPC, 60.
121. PPC, 77.

122. PPC, 76.
123. PPC, 66.
124. PPC, 67.
125. PPC, 71.
126. Sheppard's address "The Land of Perpetual Summer." Courtesy of Hampton University Archives.
127. Lapsley, *Life*, 165–66, 170–71.
128. PPC, 68.
129. DeWitt Snyder papers, Montreat archives, 4/17/1895.
130. *Missionary Review*, 10/1905, 743.
131. Lapsley, *Life*, 168.
132. PPC, 62; *Southern Workman*, 7/1909, 416.
133. Lapsley, *Life*, 167, 201–2.
134. Ibid., 228.
135. Ibid., 199.
136. *Missionary Review*, 10/1905, 742.
137. PPC, 63.
138. PPC, 76.
139. PPC, 63.
140. Lapsley, *Life*, 163.
141. Bedinger, *Triumphs*, 46.
142. PPC, 65–66.
143. PPC, 64.
144. PPC, 31.
145. John Mbiti, *African Religions and Philosophy* (New York: Doubleday, 1970), 49.
146. PPC, 64–65; *Missionary Review*, 10/1905, 743.
147. PPC, 70, 78.
148. PPC, 88; cf. 67.
149. Lapsley, *Life*, 187–88.
150. Margaret Fisk Taylor, *A Time to Dance* (Philadelphia: United Church Press, 1967), 117.
151. William Phipps, *Recovering Biblical Sensuousness* (Philadelphia: Westminster, 1975), 18–28.
152. Lapsley, *Life*, 88.
153. PPC, 88, 131.
154. PPC, 64.
155. PPC, 67–71.
156. Lapsley, *Life*, 218.
157. Ibid., 206–7. The "Balm of Gilead" refers to a song about the healing qualities of Christ.
158. *The Missionary*, 12/1898, 553–54.
159. *Kassai Herald*, 7/1/1902, 30.
160. PPC, 69.
161. PPC, 74; according to *Southern Workman*, 3/1915, 183, the lake Sheppard discovered is located at longitude E 21, latitude S 5.
162. *The Missionary*, 6/1909, 307.
163. Letter to Mr. Morton of Hampton, 1/21/1909, Montreat archives.
164. *The Missionary*, 12/1898, 554.
165. Lapsley, *Life*, 211–13.
166. PPC, 79–80.

167. *Christian Observer,* 1/10/1898, 15.
168. PPC, 80.
169. Lapsley, *Life,* 217.
170. *Southern Workman,* 12/1893, 183.
171. *Southern Workman,* 12/1893, 183.
172. Stanley Shaloff, *Reform in Leopold's Congo* (Richmond: John Knox, 1970), 29.
173. Williams, *Evangelization,* 24.
174. Benedetto, *Presbyterian Reformers,* 83.
175. Lapsley, *Life,* 217, 239.
176. Ibid., 232.
177. *The Missionary,* 3/1892, 85.
178. Lapsley, *Life,* 225.
179. Ibid., 60.
180. Ibid., 234.
181. PPC, 65.
182. PPC, 85–86.
183. *Southern Workman,* 3/1915, 168–69.
184. *The Missionary,* 4/1892, 151.
185. *Annual Report* (1893), 53; (1897), 13.
186. PPC, 86; Mark 14:36.

Chapter 3: The Kuba People

1. *Christian Observer,* 3/4/1896, 10.
2. *Southern Workman,* 12/1893, 183.
3. *Missionary Review of the World,* 5/1895, 328.
4. PPC, 82, 87, 93.
5. *Southern Workman,* 12/1893, 183.
6. *Southern Workman,* 12/1893, 184; Psalm 27:1, 3.
7. *Missionary Review of the World,* 5/1885, 329–31.
8. PPC, 94.
9. PPC, 96–97, 99.
10. *Southern Workman,* 12/1893, 185.
11. PPC, 100.
12. *Southern Workman,* 12/1893, 185.
13. PPC, 102.
14. *The Missionary,* 9/1895, 411.
15. *Southern Workman,* 12/1893, 185.
16. PPC, 105.
17. PPC, 107–8.
18. *Southern Workman,* 12/1893, 185; Conway Wharton, *Leopard,* 43.
19. Jan Vansina, *The Children of Woot: A History of the Kuba Peoples* (Madison: University of Wisconsin Press, 1978), 3.
20. PPC, 106–7.
21. PPC, 110.
22. Hezekiah Washburn, *A Knight in the Congo* (Bassett, Va.: Bassett Printing, 1972), 185.
23. Vansina, *Woot,* 213.
24. *African Arts,* Spring 1974, 26.
25. PPC, 112.
26. Vansina, *Woot,* 215.

27. *Southern Workman*, 12/1893, 185.
28. Geoffrey Parrinder, *African Traditional Religion* (London: SPCK, 1962), 138–40.
29. Vansina, *Woot*, 7.
30. *Southern Workman*, 12/1893, 185.
31. PPC, 117.
32. *Southern Workman*, 12/1893, 186.
33. PPC, 116.
34. PPC, 133–34.
35. PPC, 111; *Southern Workman*, 12/1893, 185.
36. PPC, 113–14.
37. PPC, 138.
38. *Southern Workman*, 12/1893, 186.
39. PPC, 140.
40. Vansina, *Woot*, 79.
41. Jan Vansina, *Paths in the Rainforests* (Madison: University of Wisconsin Press, 1990), 22.
42. PPC, 114.
43. Shaloff, *Reform*, 32.
44. Vansina, *Rainforests*, 230.
45. PPC, 97, 129.
46. PPC, 89–90.
47. PPC, 121.
48. *Southern Workman*, 9/1921, 406.
49. PPC, 125–26.
50. Quoted in Hochschild, *Ghost*, 157.
51. *Southern Workman*, 12/1893, 185, 187.
52. PPC, 113.
53. Emil Torday, *On the Trail of the Bushongo* (London: Seeley, 1925), 236–37.
54. M. W. Hilton-Simpson, *Land and Peoples of the Kasai* (London: Constable, 1911), 217.
55. PPC, 124.
56. PPC, 120; *Southern Workman*, 12/1893, 185–86.
57. Torday, *Geography Journal*, 7/1910, 41–42.
58. Hochschild, *Ghost*, 156–57.
59. *Missionary Review of the World*, 11/1905, 805.
60. PPC, 114.
61. *Southern Workman*, 12/1893, 187.
62. Vansina, *Woot*, 207.
63. John Mack, *Emil Torday and the Art of the Congo 1900–1909* (Seattle: University of Washington Press, 1990), 77, 87.
64. Emil Torday, *Geography Journal*, 7/1910, 41–42.
65. Vansina, *Woot*, 245–47.
66. Conway Wharton, *Leopard*, 30–31.
67. Washburn, *Knight*, 165.
68. René Lemarchand, *Political Awakening in the Belgian Congo* (Berkeley: University of California Press, 1964), 11.
69. PPC, 132–33.
70. *Kassai Herald*, 4/1906, 21; PPC, 112.
71. S. Phillips Verner, *Pioneering in Central Africa* (Richmond: Presbyterian Committee of Publication, 1903), 297.
72. PPC, 134.

73. *The Missionary*, 6/1896, 272.
74. PPC, 132–33; *Southern Workman*, 9/1921, 408.
75. *Christian Observer*, 3/4/1896, 10.
76. Hultgren and Zeidler, *Beautiful*, 83.
77. *Southern Workman*, 12/1893, 182.
78. *Southern Workman*, 7/1928, 266.
79. Harold Cureau, *Journal of Negro History*, winter 1982, 343.
80. Vansina, *Woot*, 237.
81. *Southern Workman*, 9/1921, 401–2.
82. *Christian Observer*, 3/4/1896, 10.
83. Vansina, *Woot*, 223–24.
84. PPC, 97.
85. Torday, *Geography Journal*, 7/1910, 40.
86. Vansina, *Woot*, 211.
87. *Southern Workman*, 8/1929, 355.
88. Norman Hurst, *Ngola* (Cambridge, Mass.: Hurst Gallery, 1977), 36.
89. *Southern Workman*, 8/1929, 355.
90. *Southern Workman*, 12/1893, 184.
91. *Southern Workman*, 8/1929, 357.
92. *Southern Workman*, 8/1929, 357–58.
93. PPC, 78.
94. *Southern Workman*, 9/1921, 404.
95. Lapsley, *Life*, 161.
96. *Southern Workman*, 9/1921, 404–6.
97. PPC, 116.
98. *Southern Workman*, 12/1893, 187.
99. PPC, 137.
100. Torday, *On the Trail of the Bushongo*, 203.
101. Vansina, *Woot*, 242.
102. PPC, 132.
103. PPC, 123.
104. Washburn, *Knight*, 165.
105. *Southern Workman*, 12/1893, 187.
106. PPC, 122–23.
107. PPC, 93, 113.
108. PPC, 146–47.
109. Hultgren and Zeidler, *Beautiful*, 69.
110. PPC, 121.
111. PPC, 127.
112. PPC, 72, 120.
113. PPC, 135–37.
114. PPC, 120–21.
115. PPC, 130.
116. PPC, 121–22.
117. PPC, 92, 122; *Southern Workman*, 12/1893, 186; *Christian Observer*, 5/1895, 80.
118. Conflation of PPC, 112, and *Southern Workman*, 9/1921, 406–7.
119. *Christian Observer*, 2/27/1895, 10; PPC, 131.
120. Conway Wharton, *Leopard*, 26.
121. *Christian Observer*, 2/27/1895, 10.
122. *Southern Workman*, 12/1893, 186.

123. PPC, 129–30.
124. PPC, 131.
125. Annual Report (1892), 52.
126. *Southern Workman*, 12/1893, 186.
127. PPC, 131.
128. *Missionary Review of the World*, 5/1895, 331.
129. A letter in the Hampton archives from Arthur Hinks, Secretary of the Royal Geographical Society, confirms that Sheppard received the F.R.G.S. honor.
130. *The Missionary*, 10/1896, 436.
131. Arista Hoge, ed., *The First Presbyterian Church, Staunton, Virginia* (Staunton, Va.: Caldwell, 1908), 67, 129.
132. *Christian Observer*, 3/4/1896, 10.
133. *Southern Workman*, 3/1891, 168.
134. Harold Cureau, *Journal of Negro History*, winter 1982, 343.
135. Diedrich Westermann, *Africa and Christianity* (London, 1937), 48–49.

Chapter 4: Mission Developments

1. Annual Report (1891), 41.
2. *The Missionary*, 6/1894, 242.
3. *The Missionary*, 6/1893, 231–32.
4. *The Missionary*, 7/1893, 276.
5. Stanley, *The Congo*, 1:327.
6. *The Missionary*, 7/1893, 277.
7. Du Bois, *Souls of Black Folk*, 82.
8. Julia Kellersberger, *Lucy Gantt Sheppard* (Atlanta: PCUS, Committee on Woman's Work, n.d.), 5–8.
9. Interview by Lucien Rule, Sheppard papers, Montreat archives.
10. Du Bois, *Souls of Black Folk*, 52–55.
11. Ibid., 206–7.
12. Kellersberger, *Sheppard*, 8–10.
13. *Missionary Review of the World*, 5/1895, 327, 331.
14. Minutes of the Executive Committee, 12/11/1893.
15. *Minutes of the Synod of Kentucky* (Owensboro, Ky.: Messenger, 1928), 46.
16. Ernest T. Thompson, *Presbyterian Survey*, 6/1978, 25.
17. Minutes of the Executive Committee, 1/8/94.
18. *The Missionary*, 8/1874, 319.
19. Althea Edmiston, *Maria Fearing* (Atlanta: Committee on Woman's Work, 1938), 5–8.
20. Ibid., 10–11, 27.
21. *Christian Observer*, 2/27/1895, 10.
22. Quoted in Kellersberger, *Sheppard*, 11.
23. *Christian Observer*, 11/14/1894, 6.
24. *Kassai Herald*, 7/1901, 1.
25. Kellersberger, *Sheppard*, 12–15.
26. *Regions Beyond*, 1893, 216.
27. Kellersberger, *Sheppard*, 15.
28. *Christian Observer*, 2/27/1895, 10.
29. Kellersberger, *Sheppard*, 16.
30. Benedetto, *Presbyterian Reformers*, 7.
31. *The Missionary*, 6/1895, 265.

32. Letter in Snyder papers, Montreat archives, 12/27/1894.
33. Kellersberger, *Sheppard*, 15–16.
34. Letter in Snyder papers, Montreat archives, 11/9/1894.
35. Essay in Snyder papers, 2/22/1895.
36. *The Missionary*, 6/1895, 264–65.
37. Letters in Snyder papers, 12/27/1894, 1/24/1895, 5/8/1895, 11/9/1894.
38. Kellersberger, *Sheppard*, 17–18.
39. Verner, *Pioneering*, 301.
40. Torday, *On the Trail of the Bushongo*, 31.
41. *Southern Workman*, 12/1893, 187.
42. *Christian Observer*, 3/25/1896, 10.
43. *Christian Observer*, 4/8/1896, 10.
44. *Christian Observer*, 3/25/1896, 10.
45. *Christian Observer*, 4/8/1896, 10.
46. *Christian Observer*, 4/15/1896, 10.
47. *The Missionary*, 6/1896, 271–73.
48. PPC, 131.
49. *Kassai Herald*, 3/1901, 11.
50. *The Missionary*, 6/1896, 272–75.
51. *Talledega College Record*, 3/1897, 4.
52. Lucy Sheppard, *From Talladega College to Africa* (New York: American Mission-
    ary Association, n.d.), 5; Bedinger, *Triumphs*, 127.
53. *Christian Observer*, 6/2/1897, 13.
54. *The Missionary*, 4/1897, 173.
55. Annual Report (1897), 15.
56. Williams, *Evangelization*, 27.
57. Annual Report (1897), 15.
58. Kellersberger, *Sheppard*, 19.
59. Verner, *Pioneering*, 118.
60. Deuteronomy 23:15–16.
61. *The Missionary*, 11/1894, 483–85.
62. Kellersberger, *Sheppard*, 20, 24.
63. PPC, 152; *The Missionary*, 10/1895, 465; 6/1899, 275.
64. *The Missionary*, 3/1898, 125.
65. Lucy Sheppard, *From Talladega*, 6.
66. Pantops was named for a school in Charlottesville, Virginia, because its principal
    sponsored that APCM work with children.
67. Edmiston, *Maria Fearing*, 15–22.
68. *Southern Workman*, 12/1893, 182.
69. Thomas Vinson, *William McCutchan Morrison* (Richmond: Presbyterian Com-
    mittee of Publication, 1921), 10–11.
70. Ibid., 135–37.
71. *Christian Observer*, 9/8/1897, 6.
72. *The Missionary*, 4/1897, 172, 217; 9/1898, 362.
73. *The Missionary*, 10/1897, 458.
74. Exodus 1:8; *Southern Workman*, 4/1905, 218.
75. Torday, *On the Trail of the Bushongo*, 179.
76. *The Missionary*, 4/1898, 172.
77. *Southern Workman*, 4/1905, 219–20.
78. *The Missionary*, 4/1898, 172–73.

79. *The Missionary*, 12/1898, 552.
80. Verner, *Pioneering*, 393.
81. *The Missionary*, 1/1899, 30.
82. Morrison's Diary, 4/9/1899, Montreat archives.
83. Quoted in *Christian Observer*, 9/28/1898, 5.
84. *Staunton Vindicator*, 12/16/1887.
85. Frank Pancake, *A Historical Sketch of the First Presbyterian Church, Staunton, Virginia* (Richmond: Whittet, 1954), 63.
86. "Minutes of the Foreign Missions Committee of the Society for Women's Work, First Presbyterian Church, Staunton," 10/13/1898, unpublished.
87. *Kassai Herald*, 7/1902, 34.
88. *The Missionary*, 12/1899, 547–48.
89. *The Missionary*, 9/1899, 408.
90. *The Missionary*, 12/1900, 552; 5/1901, 212.
91. Torday, *On the Trail of the Bushongo*, 176.
92. *Kassai Herald*, 10/1901, 32.
93. Benedetto, *Presbyterian Reformers*, 131.
94. *The Missionary*, 7/1903, 309–10.
95. Proverbs 21:1.
96. *Presbyterian Standard*, 2/24/1904, 14.
97. *The Missionary*, 11/1903, 501.
98. *Kassai Herald*, 1/1902, 3
99. *Kassai Herald*, 7/1902, 35.
100. *Kassai Herald*, 10/1902, 47.
101. *Kassai Herald*, 4/1902, 15.
102. *Kassai Herald*, 10/1903, 42; Kellersberger, *Sheppard*, 24–25.
103. *Southern Workman*, 4/1905, 226.
104. *Kassai Herald*, 7/1902, 32.
105. *Kassai Herald*, 4/1903, 21.
106. *The Missionary*, 7/1904, 340–41.
107. *The Missionary*, 5/1901, 212.
108. Letter to Mary Smith, 9/5/1903. Courtesy of Hampton University Archives.
109. *The Missionary*, 6/1901, 278–79.
110. *The Missionary*, 4/1904, 162.
111. *Kassai Herald*, 10/1902, 40.
112. Vansina, *Woot*, 184.
113. *Christian Observer*, 3/30/1898, 6.
114. *Christian Observer*, 4/21/1897, 5.
115. *Christian Observer*, 3/4/1896, 10.
116. *Kassai Herald*, 1/1904, 8, 11.
117. *Christian Observer*, 9/2/1903, 17.
118. *Christian Observer*, 9/25/1895, 6.
119. Phillips Verner Bradford and Harvey Blume, *Ota* (New York: St. Martin's Press, 1992), 73; Verner, *Pioneering*, 345; *The Missionary*, 11/1896, 483.
120. *The Missionary*, 3/1897, 114.
121. *The Missionary*, 9/1893, 355.
122. *The Missionary*, 3/1897, 115.
123. Tim Jeal, *Livingstone* (New York: Putnam, 1973), 355.
124. Julia Kellersberger, *A Life for the Congo: The Story of Althea Brown Edmiston* (New York: Revell, 1947), 57, 59.

125. *The Missionary*, 10/1903, 455.
126. Sylvia Jacobs, ed., *Black Americans and the Missionary Movement in Africa* (Westport, Conn.: Greenwood, 1982), 167.
127. Shaloff, *Reform*, 47, 51.
128. *The Missionary*, 1/1905, 12.
129. Ethel Wharton, *Led in Triumph*, 70.
130. *The Missionary*, 5/1905, 213.
131. *Kassai Herald*, 4/1906, 18.
132. *Staunton Daily Leader*, 1/7/1905.
133. *Christian Observer*, 9/7/1904, 10.
134. *Staunton Daily Leader*, 8/28/1912.
135. *Louisville Courier-Journal*, 10/4/1904; *Nashville American*, 3/29/1905; *Staunton Daily Leader*, 1/9/1905.
136. *Daily Evening Advance*, 1/30/1905.
137. *Southern Workman*, 4/1905, 227.
138. Article by D. C. Rankin. Courtesy of Hampton University Archives.
139. *Charleston Daily Mail*, 2/13/1906.
140. Letter to Miss Davis, written in Louisville, 11/8/1904, Montreat archives.
141. *Boston Herald*, 10/17/1909.
142. *Atlanta News*, 3/4/1905.
143. *Tuskegee Student*, 4/8/1905.
144. Sheppard papers, 7/5/1905, Montreat archives.
145. From a 11/3/1904 letter and a handbill. Courtesy of Hampton University Archives.
146. Mary Dabney, *Light in Darkness* (Asheville, N.C.: Daniels, 1971), 10–11.
147. *The Missionary*, 8/1894, 319.
148. James Chisholm, *Mutoto* (Richmond: Presbyterian Committee, 1914), 38, 84.
149. *Kassai Herald*, 4/1904, 14.
150. Letter to Mr. Morton, 1/21/1909, Montreat archives.
151. Sheppard's address, "The Land of Perpetual Summer." Courtesy of Hampton University Archives.
152. *The Missionary*, 4/1908, 156.
153. William Sheppard manuscript in the Hampton archives.
154. Kellersberger, *Sheppard*, 25.
155. *Kassai Herald*, 1/1907, 11.
156. Titled *Mukanda wa Misambu and Nkana mu Neema*, copies of these books are in the Sheppard papers, Montreat archives.
157. Kellersberger, *Sheppard*, 21.
158. *Kassai Herald*, 1/1909, 5.
159. *The Missionary*, 10/1910, 513.
160. *The Missionary*, 5/1910, 249; Mavumi-sa Kiantandu, "A Study of the Contribution of American Presbyterians to the Formation of the Church of Christ in Zaire" (dissertation, Union Theological Seminary in Virginia, 1978), 175–77.
161. Stephen T. Neill, *A History of Christian Missions* (London: Penguin, 1987), 321.
162. Slade, *English-Speaking Missions*, 190.
163. *Minutes of the General Assembly* (Richmond: Whittet, 1876), 300, 303.
164. Chester, *Behind the Scenes*, 134.
165. *Kassai Herald*, 1/1908.
166. *Southern Workman*, 4/1905, 226; *The Missionary*, 3/1909, 122.

167. *Southern Workman*, 3/1915, 183.
168. Calence Clendenen, Robert Collins, and Peter Duignan, *Americans in Africa 1865–1900* (Stanford, Calif.: Hoover Institution, 1966), 63.

Chapter 5: Atrocities Protest

1. Qur'an 5:38.
2. Lagergren, *Mission and State*, 227.
3. Henry Stanley, *The Congo and the Founding of Its Free State* (New York: Harper, 1885), 2:146–51.
4. Lagergren, *Mission and State*, 26.
5. *Century Magazine*, 9/1897, 796–97.
6. Lagergren, *Mission and State*, 84, 104.
7. Ibid., 127–28, 288.
8. Forbath, *River Congo*, 368, 374.
9. Verner, *Pioneering*, 470.
10. Ibid., 471–72.
11. Samuel H. Chester, *Behind the Scenes* (Austin, Tex.: Von Boeckmann-Jones, 1928), 80.
12. Ascherson, *The King Incorporated*, 241.
13. Forbath, *River Congo*, 372.
14. Bauer, *Leopold the Unloved*, 273.
15. Hochschild, *Ghost*, 227.
16. Lagergren, *Mission and State*, 157, 229.
17. Benedetto, *Presbyterian Reformers*, 9.
18. Lagergren, *Mission and State*, 227.
19. Bauer, *Leopold the Unloved*, 270.
20. Lagergren, *Mission and State*, 230–31.
21. PPC, 57.
22. Bedinger, *Triumphs*, 90.
23. Wissmann, *Second Journey*, 45–47.
24. Lapsley, *Life*, 215–16.
25. Hilton-Simpson, *Kasai*, 148–49.
26. Emil Torday, *Camping and Tramping in African Wilds* (London: Seeley, 1913), 55.
27. Alan Merriam, *An African World: The Basongye Village* (Bloomington: Indiana University Press, 1974), 86.
28. *The Missionary*, 10/1893, 391.
29. Lapsley, *Life*, 227.
30. Letter to Dr. Henkel, 1/5/1892. Courtesy of Hampton University Archives.
31. Lapsley, *Life*, 197.
32. Ibid., 104–5.
33. Legum, *Congo Disaster*, 29.
34. *Presbyterian Standard*, 1/4/1900, 8.
35. *The Missionary*, 2/1900, 62.
36. *Southern Workman*, 12/1893, 182.
37. *Southern Workman*, 4/1905, 220.
38. *Southern Workman*, 4/1905, 220, 223; Rankin, 305; *Louisville Courier-Journal*, 10/4/1904. A copy of Sheppard's journal of 9/13–14/1899, which was the basis for his report, can be found in the Hampton archives, and it contains more details than his public comments.

39. *Southern Workman*, 4/1905, 224–25; Rankin, 305; *The Missionary*, 2/1900, 62.
40. *Southern Workman*, 4/1905, 224–25.
41. Hochschild, *Ghost*, 4.
42. *The Missionary*, 2/1900, 62.
43. Quoted in Hochschild, *Ghost*, 224.
44. Benedetto, *Presbyterian Reformers*, 146–47.
45. Shaloff, *Reform*, 78.
46. Edmund Morel, *King Leopold's Rule in Africa* (London: Heinemann, 1904), 198–99.
47. *The Independent*, 2/1900, 304.
48. *The Missionary*, 2/1900, 66.
49. *The American Monthly Review of Reviews*, 7/1903, 39.
50. Benedetto, *Presbyterian Reformers*, 141.
51. Fox Bourne, *Civilisation*, 259–61.
52. *The Missionary*, 6/1902, 274.
53. Hochschild, *Ghost*, 259.
54. *The Times [London]*, 2/23/1900, 6.
55. Hochschild, *Ghost*, 228–29, 253–55.
56. Charles Lemaire, *Belgique et Congo* (Gand: Vandeweghe, 1908), 64.
57. Quoted in Forbath, *River Congo*, 382.
58. Conrad, *Heart of Darkness*, 118.
59. Henry Wellington, *The Story of the Congo Free State* (New York: Putnam, 1905), 385.
60. *The Outlook*, 10/8/1904, 375–77.
61. Lagergren, *Mission and State*, 247, 295.
62. Slade, *English-Speaking Missions*, 255.
63. Benedetto, *Presbyterian Reformers*, 236–37.
64. Verner, *Pioneering*, 351, 314.
65. Ibid., 371, 392, 400.
66. Ibid., 360–61.
67. *Christian Observer*, 4/21/1897, 5.
68. Verner, *Pioneering*, 351, 458.
69. Shaloff, *Reform*, 50.
70. *Christian Observer*, 7/20/1904, 10.
71. *The Missionary*, 8/1899, 377.
72. Verner, *Pioneering*, 4, 478–79.
73. Benedetto, *Presbyterian Reformers*, 28.
74. Ibid., 196, 244.
75. Ibid., 245, 247.
76. Phillips Verner, "The Adventure of an Explorer in Africa," *Harper's Weekly*, 10/22/1904, 1618–20.
77. *New York Times*, 9/10/1906, 1; 9/11/1906, 2; Bradford and Blume, 240–76.
78. Benedetto, *Presbyterian Reformers*, 159.
79. *American Monthly Review of Reviews*, 7/1903, 41.
80. *Christian Observer*, 12/9/1903, 15.
81. Edmund Morel, *Red Rubber* (New York: Nassau, 1906), 71–72.
82. *Christian Observer*, 5/13/1908, 7.
83. *American Monthly Review of Reviews*, 7/1903, 40.
84. Edmund Morel, *History of the Congo Reform Movement* (Oxford: Clarendon Press, 1968), 125–26.
85. Benedetto, *Presbyterian Reformers*, 165.

86. Bedinger, *Triumphs*, 202; Shaloff, *Reform*, 86.

87. *Parliament Debates*, 4:122, col. 1307.

88. Slade, *English-Speaking Missions*, 373.

89. Lagergren, *Mission and State in the Congo*, 304.

90. *American Monthly Review of Reviews*, 7/1903, 40; *Christian Observer*, 1/14/1903, 8; the full statement of this report of Morrison was printed in the Congressional Record, 58th Congress, 2nd Session, 5071.

91. *Minutes* (Richmond: Presbyterian Committee, 1903), 43, 483, 504.

92. Chester, *Behind the Scenes*, 79.

93. Ascherson, *The King Incorporated*, 255.

94. Slade, *English-Speaking Missions*, 275.

95. Henry Wack, *The Story of the Congo Free State* (New York: Sentry, 1905), 397–400.

96. Wack, *Congo Free State*, 440.

97. Hochschild, *Ghost*, 244.

98. Vinson, *Morrison*, 186.

99. Ibid., 190–91.

100. Shaloff, *Reform*, 95–96.

101. *Christian Observer*, 1/14/1903, 8.

102. Peter Singleton-Gates, ed., *The Black Diaries* (New York: Grove, 1959), 118–20.

103. Hampton Museum recently obtained that scrapbook from the estate of Sheppard's daughter.

104. *Central Presbyterian*, 1/4/1905, 2.

105. Benedetto, *Presbyterian Reformers*, 196–97.

106. Synod of Virginia Records, microfilm reel VL 108; interview with Hugh Givin, Session Clerk of Assembly (Richmond: Presbyterian Committee, 1906), 50.

107. Acts 10:34, 47–11:3.

108. *Southern Workman*, 2/1905, 127.

109. *Southern Workman*, 10/1905, 573; a letter from President Sanders in the Hampton archives tells of this award.

110. *Minutes of the General Assembly* (Richmond: Presbyterian Committee, 1906), 50.

111. Philip Jessup, *Elihu Root* (New York: Dodd, 1938), 2:62.

112. *The Missionary*, 10/1906, 476.

113. *Congressional Record*, 59th Congress, 2nd Session, 4320.

114. Joseph Baylen, *Alabama Review*, 4/1962, 128.

115. Lagergren, *Mission and State*, 338–39.

116. Shaloff, *Reform*, 86.

117. Lemarchand, *Political Awakening*, 123.

118. Slade, *English-Speaking Missions*, 313.

119. William Phipps, "Mark Twain, the Calvinist," *Theology Today*, 10/1994, 416–18.

120. Mark Twain, *King Leopold's Soliloquy* (Boston: Warren, 1905), 5, 7, 12, 39, 40.

121. *Boston Herald*, 11/6/1905, 4.

122. Vinson, *Morrison*, 54–55.

123. Slade, *English-Speaking Missions*, 155.

124. Angelo Rapport, *Leopold the Second* (New York: Sturgis & Walton, 1910), 227.

125. Forbath, *River Congo*, 372, 383.

126. A. Castelein, *The Congo State* (London: Nutt, 1907), 230–31.

127. Benedetto, *Presbyterian Reformers*, 268–73.

128. Bedinger, *Triumphs*, 205.

129. *Christian Observer*, 10/13/1909, 6.

130. Vinson, *Morrison*, 107.

131. Benedetto, *Presbyterian Reformers*, 294.

132. Ibid., 283.

133. *Kassai Herald*, 1/1908, 12, 15.

134. Official Organ of the Congo Reform Association, 6/1908, 23.

135. Benedetto, *Presbyterian Reformers*, 286–87.

136. Wilfred Thesiger, *Taxation of Natives, and Other Questions, in the Congo State* (London: Harrison, 1909), 28.

137. Ibid., 34–35.

138. Ibid., 26–27.

139. Ibid., 28, 30.

140. *Congo News Letter* (Boston), 10/1909, 2.

141. Quoted in Hochschild, *Ghost*, 260.

142. Vinson, *Morrison*, 87–90; the possibility of a prison term is given in a manuscript of Sheppard in the Hampton archives.

143. Benedetto, *Presbyterian Reformers*, 383.

144. *Minutes of the General Assembly* (Richmond: Presbyterian Committee, 1909), 14.

145. Chester, *Behind the Scenes*, 142.

146. Thompson, *Presbyterians in the South*, 3:255.

147. NAACP, *Thirty Years of Lynching in the United States, 1889–1918* (New York: National Association for the Advancement of Colored People, 1919), 29.

148. Keith Schall, ed., *Stony the Road* (Charlottesville: University of Virginia Press, 1977), 125–58.

149. Shaloff, *Reform*, 117–19.

150. Slade, *English-Speaking Missions*, 365.

151. *Christian Observer*, 10/13/1909, 6.

152. *Christian Observer*, 10/13/1909, 7.

153. Quoted in Kiantandu, *Contribution of American Presbyterians*, 156.

154. *Christian Observer*, 10/13/1909, 6.

155. A copy of Handley's record can be found in the Hampton archives.

156. *Southern Workman*, 1/1910, 11.

157. Benedetto, *Presbyterian Reformers*, 388.

158. Slade, *English-Speaking Missions*, 359.

159. Benedetto, *Presbyterian Reformers*, 411–16.

160. *Christian Observer*, 11/10/1909, 7.

161. *Christian Observer*, 11/10/1909, 11.

162. *Christian Observer*, 11/24/1909, 2.

163. Arthur Conan Doyle, *The Crime of the Congo* (New York: Doubleday, 1909), iv.

164. *The Times* [London], 8/18/1909, 10.

165. *Boston Herald*, 10/17/1909.

166. Benedetto, *Presbyterian Reformers*, 24.

167. *The Times* [London], 11/20/1909, 8.

168. Kellersberger, *Sheppard*, 26.

169. Bedinger, *Triumphs*, 207.

170. *The Times* [London], 12/16/1909, 5.

171. Benedetto, *Presbyterian Reformers*, 432.

172. Shaloff, *Reform*, 103, 138.

173. Benedetto, *Presbyterian Reformers*, 426.

174. Shaloff, *Reform*, 80, 126–27.

175. Benedetto, *Presbyterian Reformers*, 419–20.

176. Bauer, *Leopold the Unloved*, 322–34.

177. Vachel Lindsay, "The Congo" in *The Congo and Other Poems* (New York: Macmillan, 1916).
178. Joseph Conrad, *Last Essays* (London: Dent, 1926), 25.
179. Hochschild, *Ghost*, 168, 224.
180. Quoted in Richard Hofstadter, *Social Darwinism in American Thought* (Boston: Beacon, 1955), 45.

Chapter 6: After Leaving the Congo

1. Minutes of the APCM, 12/2/1909, 55–56.
2. Letter to Dr. S. H. Henkel, 2/4/1910. Courtesy of Hampton University Archives.
3. *The Missionary*, 5/1910, 204.
4. Minutes of the APCM, 12/2/1909; *The Missionary*, 5/1910, 204–5.
5. *Kassai Herald*, 1/1911, 19.
6. Minutes of the APCM, 12/3/1909, 60; Minutes of the Executive Committee, 1/28/1910.
7. Letter 11/4/1909, Montreat archives.
8. Minutes of the Executive Committee, 1/4/1910.
9. Benedetto, *Presbyterian Reformers*, 424.
10. Minutes of the Presbytery of Atlanta (1910), 16.
11. *Staunton Dispatch and News*, 1/6/1911.
12. Letters in the Hampton archives from Frissell to Sheppard on 10/10/1910 and 1/4/1911; *Southern Workman*, 3/1911.
13. Schall, *Stony the Road*, 127–28.
14. *Art/Artifact* (New York: Center for African Art, 1988), 106.
15. *New York Post*, 2/9/1911.
16. *Missionary Review of the World*, 6/1912, 442.
17. *National Educator*, 4/25/1913.
18. Letter from Frissell to Sheppard, 11/17/1914.
19. Schall, *Stony the Road*, 120.
20. *Southern Workman*, 3/1915, 167.
21. *Southern Workman*, 3/1915, 168, 169.
22. *Southern Workman*, 2/1915, 125.
23. Copies of the "True African Stories" are in the Hampton archives.
24. *Crisis*, 5/1915, 15.
25. Jacobs, *Missionary Movement*, 37.
26. *Southern Workman*, 9/1921, 401.
27. *Minutes of the Presbytery of Atlanta* (Griffin, Ga.: Mills, 1912), 12–15.
28. Sheppard papers, Montreat archives.
29. Synod of Virginia Records, microfilm reel VL 89.
30. Benedetto, *Presbyterian Reformers*, 215.
31. *Christian Observer*, 3/14/1900, 3.
32. Anne Vouga, "Presbyterian Missions and Louisville Blacks," *Filson Club Historical Quarterly*, 7/1984, 322–27.
33. Thompson, *Presbyterians in the South*, 3:251.
34. Lowell Harrison and James Klotter, *A New History of Kentucky* (Lexington: University Press of Kentucky, 1997), 348.
35. George Wright, *Racial Violence in Kentucky* (Baton Rouge: Louisiana State University Press, 1990), 300, 322–23.
36. Minutes of the Presbytery of Louisville, 10/22/1912, 16.
37. *Louisville Courier-Journal*, 6/22/1913, 1.

38. Minutes of the Presbytery of Louisville, 4/9/1914, 27–28.
39. Minutes of the Presbytery of Louisville, 4/13/1916, 16.
40. *Journal of Presbyterian History*, spring 1978, 57.
41. John Little, *The Presbyterian Colored Missions* (Louisville, 1914), 11–17.
42. PPC, 13.
43. George Wright, *Life behind a Veil: Blacks in Louisville Kentucky 1865–1930* (Baton Rouge: Louisiana State University Press, 1984), 145.
44. Ernest T. Thompson, *Presbyterian Missions in the Southern United States* (Richmond: Presbyterian Committee of Publication, 1934), 210, 212.
45. Lucien Rule's interview with Lucy, Sheppard's papers, Montreat archives.
46. PPC, 14.
47. Kellersberger, *Sheppard*, 27.
48. Lucien Rule's interview, Sheppard papers.
49. Kellersberger, *Sheppard*, 27–28.
50. Lucien Rule's interview, Sheppard papers.
51. William Rule, *Milestones in Mission* (Franklin, Tenn.: Providence House, 1998), 12.
52. Minutes of the Presbytery of Louisville, 4/25/1927, 10.
53. Louis Weeks, "A History of the Second Presbyterian Church" (Privately circulated, 1980), 23.
54. Minutes of the Presbytery of Louisville, 10/1/1928, 13.
55. Louis Weeks, *Kentucky Presbyterians* (Atlanta: John Knox, 1983), 139.
56. Minutes of the Presbytery of Louisville, 10/1/1928, 13.
57. Samuel Chester, "In Memoriam," Sheppard papers, Stillman College.
58. C. Newman Faulconer, *Centennial of the First Presbyterian Church* (Waynesboro, Va., 1946), 36–38.

Chapter 7: Abiding Influences

1. Thompson, *Presbyterians in the South*, 3:135.
2. W. Henry Crane, "Presbyterian Work in the Congo" (thesis, Union Theological Seminary in Virginia, 1960), 25.
3. Shaloff, *Reform*, 67, 71–72.
4. Crane, *Presbyterian Work*, 54.
5. Johannes DuPlessis, *The Evangelisation of Pagan Africa* (Capetown: Juta, 1929), 219.
6. Conway Wharton, *Leopard*, 111.
7. Washburn, *Knight*, 132–33.
8. Conway Wharton, *Leopard*, 137.
9. Washburn, *Knight*, 188, 190–91.
10. H. Richard Niebuhr, *Christ and Culture* (New York: Harper, 1951), 41, 45.
11. David Barrett, et al. *World Christian Encyclopedia* (New York: Oxford University Press, 2001), 1:212.
12. Lemarchand, *Political Awakening*, 123.
13. William Seraile, "Black American Missionaries in Africa, 1821–1925," *Social Studies*, 10/1972, 199–201.
14. Shaloff, *Reform*, 50.
15. Thompson, *Presbyterians in the South*, 3:124.
16. Morrisine Mutshi, *African Americans in Mission* (Louisville, Ky.: Worldwide Ministries, Presbyterian Church (U.S.A.), 2000), 22, 61–71.
17. Jacobs, *Missionary Movement*, 20.

18. *Presbyterian Outlook*, 8/11/1952, 6.
19. *Presbyterian News Service*, 3/15/1970.
20. Barrett, *World Christian Encyclopedia*, 1:211, 216.
21. *American Journal of Sociology*, 11/1944, 191.
22. Basil Davidson, *The African Awakening* (New York: Macmillan, 1955), 27.
23. "Kasai Konnections" newletter, 7/1999.
24. *Minutes of the General Assembly (1861)*, 55, 58.
25. Shaloff, *Reform*, 182.
26. Louis Weeks, *Be Transformed: Presbyterians and Public Issues* (Louisville, Ky.: Presbyterian Theological Seminary pamphlet, 1987).
27. Thomas Jones, ed., *Education in Africa* (New York: Phelps-Stokes, 1922), 280–81.
28. DuPlessis, *Evangelisation*, 220.
29. William Phipps, "Christianity and Nationalism in Tropical Africa," *Pan-African Journal*, winter 1972, 407–13; Lemarchand, *Political Awakening*, 122.
30. Bedinger, *Triumphs*, 48.
31. Schall, *Stony the Road*, 105–24.
32. Stanley Shaloff, "William Henry Sheppard," in Albert Berrian, ed., *Education for Life in a Multi-Cultural Society* (Hampton, Va.: Hampton Institute Press, 1968), 26–27.
33. Paul Terry, ed., *A Study of Stillman Institute* (Tuscaloosa, Ala.: Weatherford, 1946), 47.
34. *Presbyterian Survey*, 5/1972, 48.
35. Mbiti, *African Religions*, 358–59.
36. Hultgren and Zeidler, *Beautiful*, 23.
37. *Southern Workman*, 5/1915, 290.
38. *Southern Workman*, 9/1921, 388.
39. Cureau, *Journal of Negro History*, winter 1982, 342.
40. Annette Weiner and Jane Schneider, eds., *Cloth and Human Experience* (Washington, D.C.: Smithsonian Institution, 1989), 117.
41. Jeanne Zeidler and Mary Lou Hultgren, "Things African Prove to Be the Favorite Theme," in *Art/Artifact*, 126.
42. Hultgren and Zeidler, *Beautiful*, 22, 65.
43. Norman Hurst, *Ngola*, 40.
44. Hultgren and Zeidler, *Beautiful*, 56.
45. "Arts of the African Peoples," *Encyclopaedia Britannica* (Chicago, 1974), 1:274.
46. *Art/Artifact*, 99.
47. Hultgren and Zeidler, *Beautiful*, 22.
48. *Winston-Salem Journal*, 12/26/1989.
49. Hampton archives; published in *Art/Artifact*, 98.
50. *Presbyterian Outlook*, 11/22/1976, 2.
51. *Louisville Courier-Journal*, 2/29/2000, B2.
52. Wright, 279.
53. *Louisville Courier-Journal*, 5/19/1942, 1:12.
54. *Louisville Courier-Journal*, 2/29/2000, B2.
55. Fritz Malval, "William H. Sheppard Index of Correspondence" (Hampton: unpublished), 4. Courtesy of Hampton University Archives.
56. *Art/Artifact*, 102.
57. George Seaver, *Albert Schweitzer* (New York: Harper, 1955), 53–54.
58. Albert Schweitzer, *On the Edge of the Primeval Forest* (London: Black, 1928), 1–2.
59. Albert Schweitzer, *Out of My Life and Thought* (New York: Holt, 1933), 106–7.

60. A. A. Roback, ed., *The Albert Schweitzer Jubilee Book* (Cambridge: Sci-Art, 1945), 91.
61. Schweitzer, *Primeval Forest*, 120.
62. David Douglas, ed., *English Historical Documents 1783–1832* (London: Eyre, 1959), 11:740–42.
63. Jeal, *Livingstone*, 345.
64. *Indianapolis Freeman*, 2/27/1892, 7.
65. Hochschild, *Ghost*, 241.
66. Jeal, *Livingstone*, 294.
67. Ibid., 304.
68. Horace Waller, ed., *The Last Journals of David Livingstone in Central Africa* (London, 1874), 2:93.
69. Jeal, *Livingstone*, 220.
70. Luke 1:46–52.
71. David Rice, *Slavery Inconsistent with Justice and Good Policy* (Lexington, Ky., 1792), 22.
72. William Phipps, "George Bourne," *Presbyterian Outlook*, 7/13/1981, 4–6.
73. Lapsley, *Life*, 39.
74. 1 Peter 2:4.
75. Jeal, *Livingstone*, 372.
76. Ibid., 131.
77. Ibid., 146.
78. Livingstone, *Missionary Travels*, 34.
79. Schall, *Stony the Road*, 105.
80. Bradford and Blume, *Ota*, 225.
81. Rayford Logan and Michael Winston, eds., *Dictionary of American Biography* (New York: Norton, 1982).
82. Russell Adams, *Great Negroes Past and Present* (Chicago: Afro-American Publishing, 1969).
83. Marion Lucas, *A History of Blacks in Kentucky* (Frankfort: Kentucky Historical Society, 1992).
84. Dorothy Salem, ed., *African American Women* (New York: Garland, 1993).
85. Pakenham, *Scramble for Africa*, 658, 590–94.
86. Minutes of the APCM, 12/21/1903, 47; 12/23/1903, 55; 1/2/1907, 96; 12/11/1908, 29.
87. Benedetto, *Presbyterian Reformers*, 7–8, 30, 33.
88. Williams, *Evangelization of Africa*, 124, 138.
89. Ibid., 29.
90. *Richmond Times-Dispatch*, 4/27/1908, 8.

Bibliography

Adams, Russell. *Great Negroes Past and Present*. Chicago: Afro-American Publishing, 1969.

Anderson, James. *The Education of Blacks in the South 1865–1935*. Chapel Hill: University of North Carolina Press, 1988.

Art/Artifact. New York: Center for African Art, 1988.

Ascherson, Neal. *The King Incorporated*. Garden City, N.Y.: Doubleday, 1964.

Baeta, C. G., ed. *Christianity in Tropical Africa*. London: Oxford University Press, 1968.

Barrett, David. *World Christian Encyclopedia*. New York: Oxford University Press, 2001.

Bauer, Ludwig. *Leopold the Unloved*. Boston: Little, Brown, 1935.

Bedinger, Robert. *Triumphs of the Gospel in the Belgian Congo*. Richmond: Presbyterian Committee of Publication, 1920.

Benedetto, Robert, *Presbyterian Reformers in Central Africa*. Leiden: Brill, 1996.

Blyden, Edward, *Christianity, Islam and the Negro Race*. London: Whittingham, 1887.

Bradford, Phillips Verner, and Harvey Blume. *Ota*. New York: St. Martin's Press, 1992.

Bushman, Katherine. *A Register of Free Negroes for Augusta County*. Staunton, Va., 1989.

Castelein, A. *The Congo State*. London: Nutt, 1907.

Chester, Samuel H. *Behind the Scenes*. Austin, Tex.: Von Boeckmann-Jones, 1928.

Chisholm, James. *Mutoto; . . . A Brief Sketch of the Life and Labors of Bertha Stebbins Morrison . . .* Richmond: Presbyterian Committee of Publication, 1914.

Clendenen, Calence, Robert Collins, and Peter Duignan. *Americans in Africa 1865–1900*. Stanford, Calif.: Hoover Institution, 1966.

Conrad, Joseph. *Congo Diary*. New York: Doubleday, 1978.

———. *Heart of Darkness*. London: Dent, 1946 [1902].

———. *Last Essays*. London: Dent, 1926.

Crane, W. Henry. *Presbyterian Work in the Congo*. Thesis, Union Theological Seminary in Virginia, 1960.

Crawford, John. *Protestant Mission in Congo 1878–1969*. Kinshasa: Librarie Évangélique du Congo, n.d.

Dabney, Mary. *Light in Darkness*. Asheville, N.C.: Daniels, 1971.

Davidson, Basil. *The African Awakening*. New York: Macmillan, 1955.

Dictionary of American Biography. Edited by Rayford Logan and Michael Winston. New York: Norton, 1982.

Douglas, David, ed. *English Historical Documents 1783–1832*. London: Eyre, 1959.

Doyle, Arthur Conan. *The Crime of the Congo*. New York: Doubleday, 1909.

Du Bois, W. E. B. *The Souls of Black Folk*. New York: Washington Square, 1970 [1903].

DuPlessis, Johannes. *The Evangelisation of Pagan Africa*. Capetown: Juta, 1929.

Edmiston, Althea. *Maria Fearing*. Atlanta: Committee on Woman's Work, 1938.

Encyclopaedia of Missions, The. Edited by Edwin Bliss. New York: Funk & Wagnalls, 1891.

Engs, Robert. *Freedom's First Generation*. Philadelphia: University of Pennsylvania Press, 1979.

Faulconer, C. Newman. *Centennial of the First Presbyterian Church.* Waynesboro, Va., 1946.

Forbath, Peter. *The River Congo.* New York: Harper, 1977.

Fox Bourne, Henry. *Civilisation in Congoland.* London: King, 1903.

Fry, Joseph. *Henry S. Sanford.* Reno: University of Nevada Press, 1982.

———. *John Tyler Morgan and the Search for Southern Autonomy.* Knoxville: University of Tennessee Press, 1992.

Glave, Edward. *Six Years of Adventure in Congo-land.* London: Low, 1893.

Guild, June. *Black Laws of Virginia.* Richmond: Whittet, 1936.

Guinness, Fanny. *Congo Recollections.* London: Hodder & Stoughton, 1890.

Harrison, Lowell, and James Klotter. *A New History of Kentucky.* Lexington: University Press of Kentucky, 1997.

Hawke, George. *A History of Waynesboro to 1900.* Waynesboro, Va.: Historical Commission, 1997.

Hennessy, Maurice. *The Congo.* New York: Praeger, 1961.

Hilton-Simpson, M. W. *Land and Peoples of the Kasai.* London: Constable, 1911.

Hochschild, Adam. *King Leopold's Ghost.* New York: Houghton Mifflin, 1998.

Hofstadter, Richard. *Social Darwinism in American Thought.* Boston: Beacon, 1955.

Hoge, Arista, ed. *The First Presbyterian Church, Staunton, Virginia.* Staunton, Va.: Caldwell, 1908.

Hultgren, Mary, and Jeanne Zeidler. *A Taste for the Beautiful.* Hampton, Va.: Stinehour, 1993.

Hurst, Norman. *Ngola.* Cambridge, Mass.: Hurst Gallery, 1997.

Jacobs, Sylvia, ed. *Black Americans and the Missionary Movement in Africa.* Westport, Conn.: Greenwood, 1982.

Jeal, Tim. *Livingstone.* New York: Putnam, 1973.

Jean-Aubry, G. *Joseph Conrad in the Congo.* New York: Haskell, 1973.

Jessup, Philip. *Elihu Root.* New York: Dodd, 1938.

Johnston, Harry. *A History of the Colonisation of Africa.* Cambridge: Cambridge University Press, 1913.

Jones, Thomas, ed. *Education in Africa.* New York: Phelps-Stokes, 1922.

Kassai Herald. Luebo. 1902–11.

Kellersberger, Julia. *A Life for the Congo: The Story of Althea Brown Edmiston.* New York: Revell, 1947.

———. *Lucy Gantt Sheppard.* Atlanta: PCUS, Committee on Woman's Work, n.d.

Kiantandu, Mavumi-sa. "A Study of the Contribution of American Presbyterians to the Formation of the Church of Christ in Zaire." Dissertation, Union Theological Seminary in Virginia, 1978.

Klein, Herbert. *Slavery in the Americas.* Chicago: University of Chicago Press, 1967.

Lagergren, David. *Mission and State in the Congo.* Uppsala: Gleerup, 1970.

Lapsley, James, ed. *Life and Letters of Samuel Norvell Lapsley.* Richmond: Whittet & Shepperson, 1893.

Latourette, Kenneth. *A History of the Expansion of Christianity.* New York: Harper, 1943.

Legum, Colin. *Congo Disaster.* New York: Penguin, 1961.

Lemaire, Charles. *Belgique et Congo.* Gand: Vandeweghe, 1908.

Lemarchand, Rene. *Political Awakening in the Belgian Congo.* Berkeley: University of California Press, 1964.

Lindsay, Vachel. *The Congo and Other Poems.* New York: Macmillan, 1916.

Little, John. *The Presbyterian Colored Missions.* Louisville, Ky., 1914.

Livingstone, David. *Missionary Travels.* New York: Harper, 1858.

Lucas, Marion. *A History of Blacks in Kentucky.* Frankfort: Kentucky Historical Society, 1992.

Mbiti, John. *African Religions and Philosophy.* New York: Doubleday, 1970.

Merriam, Alan. *An African World: The Basongye Village of Lupupa Ngye.* Bloomington: Indiana University Press, 1974.

The Missionary. Richmond, Nashville. 1890–1910.

Morel, Edmund. *King Leopold's Rule in Africa.* London: Heinemann, 1904.

———. *Red Rubber.* New York: Nassau, 1906.

———. *E. D. Morel's History of the Congo Reform Movement,* edited by Wm. Roger Lewis and Jean Stengers. Oxford: Clarendon Press, 1968.

Mutshi, Morrisine. *African Americans in Mission.* Louisville, Ky.: Worldwide Ministries, Presbyterian Church (U.S.A.), 2000.

NAACP. *Thirty Years of Lynching in the United States, 1889–1918.* New York: National Association for the Advancement of Colored People, 1919.

Neill, Stephen T. *A History of Christian Missions.* London: Penguin, 1987.

Niebuhr, H. Richard. *Christ and Culture.* New York: Harper, 1951.

Pakenham, Thomas. *The Scramble for Africa.* New York: Random House, 1991.

Pancake, Fred. *A Historical Sketch of the First Presbyterian Church, Staunton, Virginia.* Richmond: Whittet, 1954.

Parrinder, Geoffrey. *African Traditional Religion.* London: SPCK, 1962.

Phipps, William. "Cartographic Ethnocentricity." *Social Studies,* 11/1987.

———. "Christianity and Nationalism in Tropical Africa." *Pan-African Journal,* winter 1972.

———. "George Bourne." *Presbyterian Outlook* 7/13/1981.

———. "Mark Twain, the Calvinist." *Theology Today,* 10/1994.

———. *Recovering Biblical Sensuousness.* Philadelphia: Westminster, 1975.

PPC. *See* Sheppard, William, *Presbyterian Pioneers in Congo.*

Rapport, Angelo. *Leopold the Second.* New York: Sturgis & Walton, 1910.

Reader, John. *Africa.* New York: Praeger, 1961.

Rice, David. *Slavery Inconsistent with Justice and Good Policy.* Lexington, Ky., 1792.

Roback, A. A., ed. *The Albert Schweitzer Jubilee Book.* Cambridge: Sci-Art, 1945.

Rotberg, Robert. *A Political History of Tropical Africa.* New York: Harcourt, 1965.

Rule, William. *Milestones in Mission.* Franklin, Tenn.: Providence House, 1998.

Salem, Dorothy, ed. *African American Women.* New York: Garland, 1993.

Schall, Keith, ed. *Stony the Road.* Charlottesville: University of Virginia Press, 1977.

Schweitzer, Albert. *On the Edge of the Primeval Forest.* London: Black, 1928.

———. *Out of My Life and Thought.* New York: Holt, 1933.

Seaver, George. *Albert Schweitzer.* New York: Harper, 1955.

Seraile, William. "Black American Missionaries in Africa, 1821–1925." *Social Studies* 10/1972.

Shaloff, Stanley. "William Henry Sheppard." In Albert Berrian, ed., *Education for Life in a Multi-Cultural Society.* Hampton, Va.: Hampton Institute Press, 1968.

———. *Reform in Leopold's Congo.* Richmond: John Knox, 1970.

Sheppard, Lucy. *From Talladega College to Africa.* New York: American Missionary Association, n.d.

Sheppard, William. *Presbyterian Pioneers in Congo.* Richmond: Presbyterian Committee of Publication, 1917.

Singleton-Gates, Peter, ed. *The Black Diaries.* New York: Grove, 1959.

Slade, Ruth. *English-Speaking Missions in the Congo Independent State.* Brussels: Royal Academy of Colonial Sciences, 1959.

Smith, Robert. *Zaire Perception and Perspective*. Valley Forge, Pa.: International Ministries, 1982.

Stanley, Henry. *The Congo and the Founding of Its Free State*. 2 vols. New York: Harper, 1885.

Stanley, Richard, and Alan Neame, eds. *The Exploration Diaries of H. M. Stanley*. New York: Vanguard, 1961.

Talmage, Franklin. *The Story of the Presbytery of Atlanta*. Atlanta: Foot & Davies, 1960.

Taylor, Margaret Fisk. *A Time to Dance*. Philadelphia: United Church Press, 1967.

Terry, Paul, ed. *A Study of Stillman Institute*. Tuscaloosa, Ala.: Weatherford, 1946.

Thesiger, Wilfred. *Taxation of Natives, and Other Questions, in the Congo State*. London: Harrison, 1909.

Thomas, Hugh, *The Slave Trade*. New York: Simon & Schuster, 1997.

Thompson, Ernest T. *Presbyterian Missions in the Southern United States*. Richmond: Presbyterian Committee of Publication, 1934.

———. *Presbyterians in the South*. Richmond: John Knox, 1973.

Torday, Emil. *Camping and Tramping in African Wilds*. London: Seeley, 1913.

———. *On the Trail of the Bushongo*. London: Seeley, 1925.

Twain, Mark. *King Leopold's Soliloquy*. Boston: Warren, 1905.

Union Primer. Philadelphia: Sunday School Union, 1875.

Vansina, Jan. *The Children of Woot: A History of the Kuba Peoples*. Madison: University of Wisconsin Press, 1978.

———. *Paths in the Rainforests*. Madison: University of Wisconsin Press, 1990.

Vass, Winifred, and Lachlan Vass. *The Lapsley Saga*. Franklin, Tenn: Providence House, 1997.

Verner, S. Phillips. *Pioneering in Central Africa*. Richmond: Presbyterian Committee of Publication, 1903.

———. "The Adventure of an Explorer in Africa." *Harper's Weekly*, 10/22/1904.

Vinson, Thomas. *William McCutchan Morrison*. Richmond: Presbyterian Committee of Publication, 1921.

Vouga, Anne. "Presbyterian Missions and Louisville Blacks." *Filson Club Historical Quarterly*, 7/1984.

Wack, Henry. *The Story of the Congo Free State*. New York: Sentry, 1905.

Waddell, Joseph. *Annals of Augusta County*, Virginia. Staunton, Va.: Caldwell, 1903.

Waller, Horace, ed. *The Last Journals of David Livingstone in Central Africa*. 2 vols. London, 1874.

Washburn, Hezekiah. *A Knight in the Congo*. Bassett, Va.: Bassett Printing, 1972.

Washington, Booker T. "Cruelty in the Congo Country." *The Outlook*, 10/8/1904.

———. *Up from Slavery*. Williamstown, Mass.: Corner House, 1971 [1910].

Weeks, Louis, "A History of the Second Presbyterian Church [Louisville, Kentucky]." Privately circulated, 1980.

———. *Kentucky Presbyterians*. Atlanta: John Knox, 1983.

———. *Be Transformed: Presbyterians and Public Issues*. Pamphlet. Louisville Presbyterian Theological Seminary, 1987.

Weiner, Annette, and Jane Schneider, eds. *Cloth and Human Experience*. Washington, D.C.: Smithsonian Institution, 1989.

Wellington, Henry. *The Story of the Congo Free State*. New York: Putnam, 1905.

Westermann, Diedrich. *Africa and Christianity*. London, 1937.

Wharton, Conway. *The Leopard Hunts Alone*. New York: Revell, 1927.

Wharton, Ethel. *Led in Triumph*. Nashville: PCUS Board of World Missions, 1952.

William H. Sheppard: Pioneer Missionary to the Congo. Nashville: Executive Committee of Foreign Missions, PCUS, 1942.

Williams, Walter. *Black Americans and the Evangelization of Africa 1877–1900.* Madison: University of Wisconsin Press, 1982.

Wilson, J. Leighton. *Western Africa.* New York: Harper, 1856.

Wissmann, Hermann. *My Second Journey through Equatorial Africa.* London: Chatto & Windus, 1891.

Woodward, Comer, *The Strange Career of Jim Crow.* New York: Oxford University Press, 1974.

Wright, George. *Life behind a Veil: Blacks in Louisville, Kentucky, 1865–1930.* Baton Rouge: Louisiana State University Press, 1984.

———. *Racial Violence in Kentucky.* Baton Rouge: Louisiana State University Press, 1990.

Wynes, Charles, *Race Relations in Virginia 1870–1902.* Charlottesville: University of Virginia Press, 1961.

Zeidler, Jeanne, and Mary Lou Hultgren. "Things African Prove to Be the Favorite Theme." *Art/Artifact.* New York: Center for African Art, 1988.

Index

Limited to cross-references of names and terms used more than once on different pages.

245